Readers procl

"He Never Hit Me is a valuable resource . . .   people who want to understand the impact of abuse ....d the journey towards self-discovery that can bring promise, sanity, and hope."—Raelene C.

"I read the book and I loved it! . . . a story needing to be told."
—Sandy C.

"I urge you to read this emotion-filled book and help yourself or someone you love to distance themselves from the ravages of abuse."
—Patty S.

"Great story, . . . Chart is brilliant, . . . really makes the case powerfully. Information at the end very helpful."—Dr. Linne B.

"Gripping, couldn't put it down."—Char B.

"I know five people I want to give this to right now!"—Tara L.

"Fantastic! . . . really gets to you. I couldn't put it down!"—Susan M.

"Wonderful . . . my daughter needs this book."—Catherine A.

"I wanted to tell you how much I enjoyed your book . . . the strength demonstrated was amazing!"—Cheryl L.

"As a former victim . . . I felt compelled to read this book. People always ask, "Why do you stay?" This book will help answer that. I would recommend this book to anyone who has suffered abuse or knows someone who has."—Sherry B.

He
Never
Hit
Me

A True Story

Jane D. Bryant

Bonus Section-Joel Brandley, MS, MC, LPC

Cover hand sketch by Eric Brandley
Cover flower by Melanie Silcox

Contents

To:
My parents, for love and support, here and from beyond—
My children, for making it all worth it—
My Father-in-Heaven, for lessons learned.

PREFACE

Like You Do
– written by Sandy Knox and Steve Rosen,
sung by Neil Diamond (Tennessee Moon CD),
produced by Blue Water Music. Printed by permission.

Love never doubts or suffers or cries.
Love shows no fear; love tells no lies.
And love would never leave me in the dark.
No, love never breaks my heart
Like you do. Like you do.

Love doesn't have unapproachable walls
Or a heart that beckons and then withdraws.
And love would never steal my dignity.
Love has never made a fool of me
Like you do. Like you do. Like you do.

And I have known times when love seems unsure,
But when love is unkind, it is not love anymore.

Love never threatens or frightens me.
It's not held together with apologies.
Love never screams my name,
No, and love never turns away.
Like you do. Like you do.
Like you do.

Chapter One

Flower Holes

She knelt over the moist, dark soil and carefully placed the yellow pansy back into its small hole. He had been there—in the silent, early morning hours—he had come and pulled it out and placed it on the sidewalk. Just to let her know. He could still come into the yard, still open the gate, still walk on the sidewalk. He could come within feet of her—inside the house sleeping. In spite of the protective order, he would still come. It had almost become a ritual.

She had wanted him to hit her, to strike her, to bruise her skin. No, she didn't want the pain or the humiliation, but she wanted the outside of her body to match the inside of her shredded heart. Then she would have something to show! Then everyone would know how much he really hurt her and the children, and she would have something tangible to hold on to and hold up to the world.

But he was far too cunning for that; and he knew that what he could do to her was much worse than a little roughing up. The invisible scars he inflicted reached her marrow and rooted in her soul. But she was digging up those roots, filling in the spaces with fertile, nourishing ground; and lifeblood would again flow where the dead plants had withered.

He had been the one to landscape the yard, to plant the trees. It was His Domain. And he was wonderful at it. Everything he planted grew, and the garden flourished, much the opposite of her perpetual "black thumb."

But now it was Hers. Maybe that's why she had been so intent on planting the daffodil bulbs last fall and the pansies this spring. She wanted the flowers to bloom, to splash yellow cheer across her front yard. And they did bloom, in spite of him. They were her flowers. She had done the planting. She would do the harvesting.

And she was free. He still tried to enslave her in fear, as he had done for years, but she would have no more of that. *No more*. She would keep planting flowers and keep replanting them, as long as was necessary. And she would tell her story: not a made-up story, though at times things seemed unimaginable; not an embellished story either, for things were dramatic enough without embellishment; but the truth— her truth—the story of her impossible life with him.

Chapter 2

Just a Fling

Dawn followed him down the dim hallway with a prayer in her heart. 'Please don't let him go into my room. Please don't go into my classroom.' His boots made him even taller than his six-foot-four frame, and his dark blue jeans and plaid, red-black flannel shirt complemented his jet-black hair. His mustache and beard were also very black, trimmed neatly against his tan face. His shirtsleeves were partially rolled up to reveal strong, dark forearms.

He entered the next room—Nancy's room. Dawn was so relieved. Not that she didn't want night-school students, but she knew the moment she saw him that she didn't want him for a student. An English major, Dawn wasn't very comfortable teaching basic science. Yes, she could handle the high-school students who had flunked out but not grown men (whose science know-how certainly outranked hers). Especially not intimidatingly-gorgeous grown men.

Soon Nancy, a history teacher, arrived and poked her head in Dawn's door. The two of them had arranged to teach night school on the same nights so that they could leave together and walk out into the dark, downtown parking lot in safety. Dawn was scheduled for Thursday nights but hadn't wanted to teach Tuesday, too. She thought it was too much in addition to teaching every day; but the principal had begged her, and Nancy was committed, so Dawn gave in to the Tuesday/Thursday night schedule.

"You've got a gorgeous man in your class," Dawn greeted her.

"Really?" Nancy replied. "I've been married too long. I just don't notice those things anymore."

"I think you'll notice this one," Dawn said. There was a small space where the folding doors between their rooms met, enough for Dawn to glance through as she passed by. 'What a beautiful man,' she thought. Something about him seemed so familiar. She decided that he must remind her a little bit of her brother. Still, she seemed to take every opportunity during the night to peer at him through the space in the partition.

At break Dawn walked out of her classroom and headed down the hall to the office. He was leaning up against the side of the hallway. As she approached, their eyes met. He didn't take his eyes from her, and as she looked away and passed him, she saw his head turn as he continued to stare at her. She had a strange, almost imperceptible feeling that there was something evil in his glare but shrugged it off. 'Maybe he's just flirting,' she thought, but she had the definite impression that she had certainly been looked over.

At 9:00 p.m., classes were dismissed, and Dawn waited to leave with Nancy.

"I'm going to check him out," Nancy said, as they walked together out the heavy double doors. Ever the matchmaker, she had already done some investigating. "His name's Jace Malone, he's divorced and has three children. He grew up in Snowcrest and went to Everett High. I have some friends who might know him." Dawn was intrigued when she found out he wasn't married but didn't want to get her hopes up—they had been crushed too many times before. "He has a good job," Nancy continued, "but came to night school to finally get a diploma. He's only missing one credit."

Nancy wasted no time in furthering her investigation. It wasn't long before she came to school with the news: "I don't think so," she said. "My friend Karen grew up with him, said that he and his brothers were pretty wild and were always getting into lots of trouble—something about one of them getting shot or something. She thinks he's grown up a lot since then, doesn't have so much to prove, but she knows who you are and said she'd never put the two of you together."

"That's okay," Dawn said. "I certainly don't need that." Still, in her heart, she was disappointed at the news and couldn't help glancing at him each week through the partition at school.

A few weeks later, Nancy asked Dawn to get her Tuesday night class started for her, as she was going to be a few minutes late. Dawn went into Nancy's class, trying to be personable, and gave everyone an assignment to start on. Jace Malone didn't look at her but stared straight ahead; in fact, he was so somber that she thought to herself, 'forget him,' but still couldn't help being a little disappointed. Again she dismissed the feeling and found herself looking at him through the partition.

At break she said to Nancy half-jokingly, "Maybe just a fling. Nothing serious. He's just so handsome," she moaned. "Just a fling."

At 8:30 p.m., Dawn turned on an antique projector to show a science film. As soon as the film threaded, the projector quit running; despite her best efforts, Dawn couldn't get it to work. She dismissed the class early, cleaned things up and walked into Nancy's room when she heard Nancy dismiss her class.

She was surprised to see Nancy talking to Jace, who was sitting on top of his desk and seemed anything but somber. When Dawn walked in, she explained about the projector, and Nancy took advantage of the chance meeting.

"So I think you two should get together," Nancy said. Dawn was surprised. (What about what her friend Karen had said?) "You think he's cute, don't you, Dawn?"

"He's a doll," Dawn said, still in shock and surprised at her own disclosure.

"And you think she's cute, don't you?" He nodded. "So why don't the two of you go out next week and get a lemonade after class."

"Okay," they both agreed as Jace walked out of the room, the door closing behind him.

Dawn looked at Nancy with her mouth open. "I thought you said he …"

"He seems nice, and I'm tired of your drooling," Nancy joined in. "Besides, the projector broke and it was perfect timing. Remember, it's just a fling …"

"The date was wonderful, wonderful, wonderful!," Dawn wrote in her journal as her thoughts wandered to the night before. He was sooo nice. He had been a perfect gentleman. Dawn was delighted to find that Jace was as nice on the inside as he looked on the outside. She had to admit to herself that she loved looking at him. She had dated cute guys before, but they were always so stuck on themselves, so cocky. Jace was different. He was humble in a shy sort of way, and she liked that. Besides, he was way more than cute. He could have been a model; she noticed other people looking at him, and it made her so proud to be seen with him. When he walked her back to her car in the school parking lot Tuesday evening, he told her sweetly that he was very glad that Nancy had been "forward" and that he had really had a nice time.

She echoed his feelings and thanked him for the drink.

She had driven home on cloud nine. She had never felt this way so quickly about anyone. She couldn't stop smiling and lived for the next Tuesday to come.

They met regularly on break at the water fountain, and the relationship grew. His parents lived in Snowcrest, about half-an-hour from Hilton. Dawn's mother had also grown up in Snowcrest, and her grandparents had owned a store there—"Jesse's Mercantile." Jace remembered the store, and it gave them a lot to talk about. He had asked Dawn out for the weekend, and she had given him directions to her home. Although she had gone away to college and had worked in other cities, Dawn had moved back in with her parents when she got the job in Hilton. Her father had built a beautiful home in the mountain foothills, and she loved living there.

When Jace came to her door, he told her that her house seemed very familiar to him—that he had recognized it when he drove up. "Maybe it's deja vue," Dawn replied.

"I don't know. I think I've been here before."

Dawn introduced him to her parents. Her mom and dad seemed pleased. Jace took her to The Loft, a spacious restaurant that had its beginnings as a large barn. They had a delicious and pricey steak dinner, and she learned a lot more about him. Jace worked as a mechanic in a nearby city for a very large truck dealership. He worked on diesel engines, the large semi's. He had previously lived in Wyoming and had been transferred to Hilton. It was his fifth year with the company. That had also impressed Dawn's father, who had been a flight mechanic and could fix anything. Her dad told her that the dealership was very large and successful.

Jace was just ten months older than Dawn and had been divorced for three years. He didn't give a lot of detail about the breakup but told Dawn that he had come home from work one day to find his house totally empty.

"Whoever helped her move left a six-pack of empty beer cans in the living room," he recalled bitterly.

His ex-wife had also taken the three children but brought them to him a couple of weeks later saying, "Here, I'm sick of them arguing," and left them on his doorstep. Jace gladly took the transfer to Hilton to be closer to his parents and brother and sisters.

Dawn was impressed that he had full custody of his children and was taking care of them himself. It made her respect him even more, and her heart went out to him. She felt like she had found a rare jewel in comparison to the other immature guys she had been dating. He, too, felt that he had found something special and couldn't believe Dawn hadn't been married before. "Lucky at cards, unlucky in love," she joked but admitted that she really was tired of the dating scene and just hadn't found "the one." They left the restaurant and went to a movie. When Jace drove her home afterwards, she invited him in. They sat in her family room and watched a documentary on Bengal tigers. He loved animals and told her about some of the things he had recently read. He seemed so unassuming and just plain cute as he enthusiastically told her about them.

Jace then told Dawn that he had better get home as his niece was babysitting for him, and it was getting late. She stood up to walk him to the door. As they got to the door, he leaned over and took her in his arms and kissed her, long and deep. She told him goodnight and could hardly sleep that night for all the smiling …

Spring quarter was ending, it was the last night of school, and Dawn worried that she wouldn't see Jace as often anymore. She was looking forward to her summer off from school and night school but was worried that she would have no more Tuesdays with him. Nancy was thrilled for her as she watched the two of them come together but shook her head in wonder. "There's just no way of keeping you two apart," she said. "That water fountain is a magnet!"

Jace walked Dawn to her car after class was over. Dawn was scheduled to sing at the graduation ceremony the next week. Jace persisted in finding out when it was, but she begged him not to come. If he were there, she would be scared and embarrassed. "Besides," she said, "it is so crowded and hot, and the auditorium is so small. Just enjoy your night at home." He told her he would do as she wished but that he'd like to come.

Then they kissed. He was leaning against her car, and she leaned into him, pressing her body against his. They kissed for a long time, and she didn't want the night to end. She got the feeling that he was in no hurry to leave, either. Gradually they broke apart and got into their vehicles. She secretly hoped he would come to hear her sing.

Graduation night came quickly. The students were thrilled to have made it so far, as it was an alternative high school, and many were either handicapped or older who had missed their chance earlier at a diploma. Dawn was very nervous about singing. She looked beautiful, dressed in a white blouse with tiny pearls sewn in the bodice; a black crepe skirt, trimmed with a black satin sash, emphasized her trim waist. She looked out from behind the maroon stage curtains. She could see her mom and sister sitting in the small, sunny auditorium, fanning themselves with their programs. She panned the audience for Jace. She couldn't see him. Although she was disappointed, her nervousness then left her, and she sang confidently.

After the ceremony, many staff and students complimented Dawn on her song. She hugged her departing students and told the staff goodbye for the summer. She was happy that she was able to perform well, but she felt an aching in her heart for Jace. How she wished he were there. What if she never saw him again? That night she got on her knees, and as tears ran onto her pillow, she prayed: "Please, Father, I can't go through this again. I can't love someone or have someone love me and have it not work out again. Please, if this isn't right with Jace, don't let me see him again. Please. I can't bear to be hurt anymore." She cried herself to sleep.

The next day there was no word from Jace. Dawn was afraid she wouldn't hear from him again, but Nancy called her later that night.

"I took my car out to Jace's house to get it repaired. He said he really wanted to come last night but wasn't sure what to do. He didn't want to be there if you didn't want him there." Dawn was still kicking herself for not inviting him but was glad to hear he had wanted to come. Nancy continued, "He has three cute little children. They look like they're Mexican, pretty dark. They had just been to his niece's baptism, and Jace said he thought it was really neat. He talked about the church where they went to see her get baptized and said that he goes to church sometimes and that his children go to Sunday school, but he doesn't like to go alone."

Dawn felt relieved. She knew she couldn't pursue the relationship any further if they weren't the same religion. It just was too much a part of her and meant too much to her. She became more and more hopeful.

She had just hung up from Nancy's call when Jace called. "I was wondering if you'd like to go to a movie Friday," he said.

"Sure," Dawn answered, trying not to sound too excited. "What do you want to go see?"

"It doesn't matter," he said. "I just want to be with you."

She melted.

That was the beginning of a summer full of dates. His children had gone to Wyoming for six weeks to be with their mother, so she had not yet met them; but she knew that she was falling in love with their father. She did, however, meet Jace's parents, James and Mary Malone. Jace and Dawn drove up to Snowcrest one night, and they walked in on an already-prepared fried chicken dinner.

"I told Jace to bring you up here for dinner," Mrs. Malone said, as they walked into the small, cozy kitchen. Jace hadn't mentioned to Dawn that they were eating dinner, and she didn't have the heart to tell his mom that she had already eaten. Dawn shoveled in as much as she could to be polite. "We've really been anxious to meet you."

She loved his parents. They were just plain folks, with an unassuming air about them. His dad, not nearly as tall as Jace, had pretty blue eyes behind silver-rimmed glasses and thick, grey hair. He was retired from the Security Station and loved working in his yard. He had a beautiful vegetable and flower garden. He enjoyed talking about all the things he had planted. Mary, heavier than James with dark, almost black eyes and curly ash-brown hair, seemed slightly nervous.

"When Jace told us you were a teacher, I couldn't believe it … that he was dating a teacher!" his mother exclaimed, wiping her hands on her flower-print apron. "But he told me, 'Ma, she's just like anybody else.'" Dawn was embarrassed, but Mary seemed so proud. "I'm so glad he brought you up here."

As Dawn helped Mary with the dishes, Mary confided to Dawn. "His first wife was so awful. You're so different from her. Jace is such a patient man," she beamed. "And isn't he handsome?" Dawn shook her head in agreement.

Jace's parents were familiar with Dawn's grandpa's store, and even though they didn't know him or Dawn's mother, it gave her a link to Snowcrest. The store, of course, had different owners now, and they all reminisced about the "good ol' days." Dawn felt at home sitting in their quaint living room. The carpet was a bright orange, and worn furniture was covered with a mixture of multi-colored crocheted afghans. It made her happy that Jace had told his parents about her and had wanted them to meet her. They seemed like really nice, down-to-earth people …

When July 4th came, Dawn could hardly believe that it was mid-summer. She had wanted to do something special on July 4th, but they had no plans. Jace came over to get her, and they went to the store to buy items for an impromptu picnic. Then they headed up the canyon. They drove for a long time until they found a spot that was not full of campers. It was called Lavender Flats, and it was beautiful. Dawn spread out a blanket, and they ate lunch. She wanted to spend the afternoon taking it all in, but Jace seemed preoccupied. Soon they walked back to his truck and started down the canyon.

Part way down the canyon, it was obvious that Jace's tan truck was in trouble. It was old and overheating. The climb up the canyon must have been too much for it.

"I think my transmission's going out," he said, as he put the truck in neutral. They coasted down the canyon. He waved car after car by them during the long, hot drive, as horns were continually honked at them. Dawn was impressed at his patience, even though she could tell that he was pretty hot and frustrated.

When the canyon leveled out and they could coast no more, Jace pulled over to the side of the road at the intersection. They walked to a nearby convenience store and called his sister, Susan, to see if she and her husband could tow them home.

Dawn was impressed when Jace's sister and brother-in-law drove up. Susan seemed like she was genuinely the nicest person on earth. His brother-in-law was equally as nice but a lot louder than his quiet, sweet wife. Susan had her father's blue eyes and her mother's ash-brown, curly hair and stocky build. Her husband dominated the conversation, but Jace's sister did get a few lines in.

"We're so excited to finally meet you," she said. "We've heard so much about you." Dawn was embarrassed. "Jace is really picky," Susan continued. "I've tried to line him up lots of times, but he just never liked the ones I chose. You should feel really flattered, because he won't go out with just anyone. I've tried several times." Dawn was flattered to be able to meet Jace's 'picky' standards. It was interesting to hear Susan's slant on her brother, whom she obviously adored. So she got to know his family, and he got to know hers. He met both of Dawn's sisters and her brother, all married with families. Jace had two brothers: Dave was married and lived nearby; the other, Mike, was homeless, somewhere in Georgia. Jace mentioned that Mike had had a hard time in Vietnam and had gotten into drugs. His family rarely heard from Mike. Both of Jace's sisters were married: Susan was the oldest in the family and Missy was the youngest. Both had gotten married right out of high school.

It was the most wonderful summer of Dawn's life. She spent her days resting from school and doing whatever she wanted to do. Nearly every evening was spent with Jace.

They hiked, bowled and played tennis. She loved just going to a park and sitting with him, watching the sun go down as they talked. They went for drives up the canyon and on picnics. He cooked some delicious dinners for her at his home, and she did the same for him. What Dawn found most endearing was Jace's ability to play jacks. Try as she might, and she had spent many years playing jacks with her sisters and mother as a child, she couldn't beat him at the game. She was amazed at the dexterity in his huge hands.

She invited him to a drive-in movie one night to help her celebrate paying off her car. It was a beautiful Dodge Charger that Dawn had ordered new from the factory three years earlier. They had a great time and had stayed through the playing of the first feature, Rocky II, again. Dawn had loved the movie Rocky and had even named her car, which was black and blue, "Rocky Balboa" in jest.

When the movie was over, Jace drove her home in her car. They sat out in front of her house talking. And kissing. And talking. Pretty soon, Jace started to laugh.

"Do you hear that?" he said. Dawn listened and also began laughing. It was the birds singing, bringing in the morning sun. Neither of them had realized that it was so late—or rather—so early.

"I guess I'd better get going," Dawn said, kissing him goodbye. As she walked into her house, the first shadows of light came over the top of the mountain.

Chapter 3

The Children

As he dropped her off at home after dinner, Jace asked Dawn if she were coming over the next night.

"Oh, no," Dawn said. "You get your children back tomorrow. They'll want to spend the evening with you."

"What do you bet that they'll be home five minutes and want to go to their friends to play?" Jace countered.

"Well, okay," she said. Dawn had really wanted to meet them but at the same time was nervous about it. What if they didn't like her?

When she knocked on Jace's door the next evening, a skinny, dark, friendly girl answered the door. "Hi, I'm Ida," she said perkily.

"Hi, how are you?" Dawn said, trying to match her enthusiasm. "I'm Dawn."

"I know. Dad told us all about you. He's in the bathroom giving my brothers a bath. Come on in." Dawn walked into the small, grey-paneled living room and sat on the old, ragged couch. Just then Jace came out of the bathroom carrying in his long arms a wet bundle wrapped up in a white towel.

"This is Eric," Jace said proudly as he set him down on the brown carpet and continued to dry off his hair. Eric had big brown eyes that matched a very brown face, brown hair and a wide smile. He was adorable. "Ethan is still in the tub," Jace announced as he walked out of the room. "I'll be right back."

Before Dawn had a chance to get acquainted with Eric, Jace was back with Ethan. Ethan was much quieter than Eric and Ida. His skin was very dark. He reminded Dawn of a child from India more so than a Spanish one. His eyes were even larger and darker than Eric's, and he was obviously more serious and shy than the smiling Eric.

Jace had told Dawn that his ex-wife was Mexican, but Ida expounded: "We're half-White from Dad, one-quarter Mexican and one-quarter Apache from Mom," she said proudly. Dawn liked Ida, her spontaneity and her frankness; in fact, she liked all of them. Ida was eleven years old, Ethan was seven and Eric was five. Dawn knew them from seeing their pictures on Jace's living room wall. She had never imagined herself the mother of three Mexican children, but she was getting used to the idea. Dawn's hair was very long and dark, but still she was extremely fair, much to her dismay. She had tried for years to acquire a tan but finally gave it up as hopeless. Even next to Jace, she seemed so pale, and even more so next to his children.

Jace turned on the television while the children sat on the floor. He walked over to the couch, sat down next to Dawn and started kissing her neck. At first she was very uneasy, thinking that the children were watching them, but they seemed engrossed in the movie. It wasn't long, though, before Eric climbed up on his dad's lap and snuggled against his chest. After a while, Jace put them all to bed while Dawn sat on the couch waiting. They had all told her goodnight, and she felt like they genuinely liked her or had at least accepted her.

Jace asked Dawn to come out the next night for dinner, and soon it became a pattern. They spent most of their time together at Jace's house, as it saved on babysitters. When she drove in the driveway and stepped out of her car the next night, all three children ran up to her and put their arms around her. They seemed so excited to see her. Relief swept over Dawn. She felt that she had passed whatever test they were going to give her, and she felt she could love them as she did their father. Dawn's heart also went out to the children because she felt bad about their mother. Jace could not find one redeeming quality in his ex-wife, Juanita.

"She never remembers their birthdays and always makes promises to them but never comes through," he told Dawn. "When she moved out, she took everything in the house—even my rifles—but I got those back. Then she brought the children back, but I had no beds for them, no tables or chairs, no TV. We ate on the floor for a long time with paper plates," he recalled bitterly.

Dawn couldn't imagine this. Why wouldn't Juanita want her children to have beds to sleep in and a table to eat off of? What did she need the furniture for? Apparently she had moved back in with her parents, and it was her second divorce. What Dawn couldn't imagine most of all was Juanita giving up her children. Why didn't she fight for them? It was unusual for a man to have sole custody of his children, so Dawn felt Juanita must really be an inadequate mother. Wouldn't most women fight to the death for custody—at least joint custody—of their children? Dawn couldn't imagine giving up her own children. How awful this woman must be, to not want or care about her children and to leave them on his porch. Eric was only two years old when they split up. How do you leave a darling, little two-year-old boy? Jace had told her, though, that Juanita had wanted to abort Eric. Ida also may have been a handful for her mother, because she seemed to be a handful for her father.

"I felt sorry for Dad being all alone," Ida had told Dawn, "so I told my mom I wanted to live with him." They had all walked to a park by Jace's home one night, and it seemed that all Ida and Jace did were bicker back and forth. Dawn remembered Jace's mom's comment that he was "such a patient man" with his children. Jace had confided in Dawn that Ida had been caught stealing from school, and he had been called into numerous parent-teacher conferences. Dawn thought that much of this must stem from Ida missing an involved and caring mother.

In a way, Dawn was almost glad that their mother was so inadequate. After all, she'd feel funny if Jace had any feelings for his ex. It was good that he hated her, wasn't it? Also, with her being a state away, Dawn could take care of the children and love them and wouldn't have much interference from Juanita. She felt she could be a good influence in their lives and that they would love her and she would love them.

But she was getting ahead of herself. Jace had never talked about marriage, but he hadn't let a day go by without calling her. When he looked at her, Dawn could see the affection he had for her in his eyes. Still, he had been divorced for nearly three years. Maybe he never wanted to get married again.

"Is your real name Dawn or Dawnette?" he asked her one night.

"It's really Dawnette, but I go by Dawn," she said. "Why?"

"There was a job I wanted to apply for," he explained, "but I needed to have a high school diploma. I shouldn't have dropped out my senior year, but I didn't want to live at home anymore. Anyway, when I was trying to decide whether to go back to night school or just take the high school equivalency exam, I had the feeling that I was supposed to go to night school—even though it probably would have been easier just to take the test. Then I had a dream that my best friend in high school introduced me to a Dawnette. When I saw you at night school, I wanted to meet you, but when I found out what your name was, then I really wanted to meet you."

"I really wanted to meet you, too," Dawn admitted, remembering the yearning in her heart as she had looked at him through the partition. More and more she had the feeling that this was just meant to be. Even though everyone called her Dawn (and she preferred that), from that moment on he never called her anything but Dawnette.

Chapter 4

Scars

"Are you going to spend the night tonight?" Ida asked eagerly.

"Oh, no, honey," Dawn replied, surprised at the request. But then she began to wonder how many of Jace's past dates had "spent the night." She knew that even though they belonged to the same church, Dawn's standards were different from Jace's. He had pointed out a bar to her once that he had been a regular in and had said that in his younger, "wilder" days, he had drunk enough alcohol to "float a large ship." He told Dawn that since he started dating her, he hadn't had one drink. Jace had also smoked in those younger days and then turned to chewing tobacco for a while to get off the cigarettes. Dawn had figured that out, since some of his teeth were slightly stained. She admired him for quitting; she knew it was an awfully difficult thing to do. She was also glad that he had quit long ago; she wouldn't have even looked at him if he'd had a cigarette or chewing tobacco in his mouth.

"So, do all of your dates spend the night?" Dawn asked Jace after Ida had gone to bed.

Jace looked sheepishly at Dawn and shook his head sideways. He knew that she was stalwart in keeping the standards of her religion, which included no sex before marriage. He told her, "You're the only woman I've ever respected. I've never played by someone else's rules before. In a way, I want to wait, too. I don't want to spoil anything." Dawn felt very special when he said that but knew from Ida's request that Jace had had his times with other women since the divorce. He had a beautiful, light-blue, three-piece suit that a previous girlfriend had bought him. She had also wanted to marry Jace, but he did not have mutual feelings. Still, he had never pressured Dawn to do anything she didn't want to do and had never been inappropriate. She felt that Jace was trying very hard to really change and be the kind of man Dawn would want him to be. In fact, Dawn felt pretty secure in the fact that he had already changed many of those old behaviors.

As they sat on the couch talking after the children had gone to bed, Dawn told Jace that she had had some problems with arthritis and had some surgeries, showing him the scars on her feet. "That's nothing compared to the scars under my arms," she said.

"You've got scars in your pits?" he teased her.

"Both of them," Dawn answered, "about five inches long!" She went on to explain that she had spent nearly a year having all kinds of tests trying to figure out why she had so much pain in her arms. She had been swimming two miles a day and then one day couldn't lift her arms without intense pain. After spending a horrible week in the hospital being poked and prodded, she was told that the doctors determined the nerves and blood vessels in her shoulders were being impeded by her top ribs. A heart surgeon removed the ribs from her chest cavity in two very tricky operations that left her with the underarm scars. Still, she was so grateful for the relief from the pain and had learned many lessons on endurance, suffering and patience in that trying year.

They were holding hands, and Dawn stroked Jace's left forearm with her right hand. Jace had a prominent scar coming down from his elbow, leaving some of his dark arm hairless in its place. "What happened here?" Dawn asked, stroking his arm.

"Okay … I'll tell you …" Jace sighed, as though he had just made an important decision. "I was hitchhiking to Colorado with my friend, Nick. I was only nineteen. Some lady, good-looking, picked us up. It was late, and she drove us to her house. She told us we could just sleep in her car that night. I was in the back seat; Nick was in the front. The next morning, first thing I know, her husband comes out with a rifle, opens the door and fires at me. Nick saw him coming and hollered at me, or else I would have still been asleep. I put my arms up to protect myself and the bullet went through my arm."

"Why did he do that?" Dawn asked. Jace shrugged his shoulders. Dawn recalled Nancy's words about "one of them getting shot or something."

"She called the police," he continued, "and they took me to the hospital. It hurt like hell to have the bullet taken out, especially so close to my crazy bone nerve."

So that was the gun story. Dawn felt better to know that there had been no crime involved on Jace's part. Still, it must have been a notorious story in Snowcrest if Nancy's friend Karen knew about it. She could hear the people talking about "those wild Malone boys" in that small town.

"So, did that end your hitchhiking career?" Dawn asked.

"It should have," Jace replied. "I was pretty stupid back then."

On the way home that night, Dawn cried, although she wasn't quite sure what she was crying about. The next morning, as she ate her cereal, Dawn's mother asked how things were going.

"I don't think he's religious enough for me," Dawn said hesitantly.

"Guys change," her mom said. "Look at your father. He wasn't religious at all when we got married. As long as he treats you right, that's what's important."

"But I don't think I'm pretty enough for him," Dawn replied. While Jace's features were very striking, Dawn's were very soft. Her dark-brown, long and naturally-wavy hair complemented her pale skin and milk-chocolate brown eyes.

"You make a beautiful couple," answered her mother.

"You are too pretty enough," chimed in her dad from the other room. "He's not pretty enough for you!"

"Oh, yes he is," said her mother. "There's not many around that look like he does," she shouted back to him. "Your dad's just getting used to the idea that he has three children," her mom added. "He thought he just had two …"

Jace came over to Dawn's the next night, and they watched a video together. Ida, Ethan and Eric sat on the floor in front of the TV, while Jace sat next to her on the couch.

"Oh, I hate these pants," Dawn moaned as she adjusted the pant legs of her pin-striped levis. "They're just too tight."

"No, they're not," Jace countered. "I love those pants. And I love you, too."

"I love you, too," Dawn returned. There. He said it. She said it. She had wanted to say it but hadn't dared until he did. Now that they had said it, things seemed different, more intense. And what they had said once, they now said often.

Dawn's sister, Pat, had also come over to visit that night with her new baby. Dawn's mother held her as Dawn and Jace looked over her shoulder.

"Isn't she cute?" her mother said to Jace.

Jace nodded. "I'd have ten of them if I could afford them," he said. That made Dawn love him even more as she, too, loved children.

As she later kissed him goodnight, she opened her eyes and was surprised to see him looking at her. "What are you looking at?" she asked.

"I'm just watching you," he said, his green eyes looking sleepy underneath the long, dark lashes. "You're so pretty. I love you—very, very much."

Often when he would leave her at night, he would kiss her on the top step of the front porch. Then he would interlock his fingers in hers and back slowly down the steps as he gradually let go of her hand. She loved how he did that. She yearned to go with him and didn't want him to leave …

Jace had asked her to go camping with his whole family. Dawn was so excited. She had made several treats in preparation to take with them and had packed her things as neatly and compactly as she could. She loved the mountains and loved to camp. It was something her family never did, so she was thrilled to be included.

She loved being in the mountains. After arriving, Jace unpacked the truck and set up a tent that was large enough for both of them and all of the children. His mom and dad, two sisters and his brother had already set up their families' tents at nearby stations in the same campsite. It was so beautiful. Ida, Ethan and Eric were off immediately playing with their cousins in the streams that flowed through the camp.

She enjoyed getting to know his sisters and his sister-in-law, Anne. Anne and Dave had a large family and seemed very happy together. Dave was a big guy, very robust, with a curly brown beard. He seemed big and gruff on the outside, but everyone professed him to be a pussycat on the inside. Anne was a perfect match for Dave, in both size and temperament. Susan's family was large, also. Both Susan and her brother, Dave, had married their high-school sweethearts. Dawn wasn't sure if Dave had even finished high school, as Anne told her that Dave had moved in with her family when he was only sixteen. Jace's younger sister, Missy, had also married young and had three children. She didn't seem to be as happy in her marriage, though, as Dave and Susan were in theirs.

"Is Juanita really as horrible as everyone says?" Dawn asked Susan that evening.

"She is," Susan shook her head definitely. "She had a terrible temper and was loud and hard to live with. We didn't like to be around her. Jace has every reason to be bitter. You're quiet, just the opposite of her." As they talked, the wind was blowing slightly, just enough to spread the pollen from the pines. Soon, some of it had gotten into Dawn's eyes, and tears streamed down her face as she walked to the table for a Kleenex.

Jace walked over to her, put his large hands on her face and gently pulled up on her eyelid, trying to look for foreign objects. "I'm sorry," he told her tenderly, as he pulled her close and hugged her. "I know it really hurts to get things in your eyes."

"I guess I'd better take out the contacts," Dawn replied. She was glad she had brought her glasses, as she was nearly blind without them, but was embarrassed to wear them. When the sun began to go down, Dawn headed for the water faucet with a flashlight. She wanted to brush her teeth before it got too dark. Jace was busy arranging the sleeping bags in the tent and getting his children ready for bed. He had their bags in a row next to his right, with Dawn's bag on his left. Dawn stood by the campfire as Jace put them all to bed. They had played hard all day and were very tired. As the night air got colder, Dawn decided that a warm sleeping bag sounded better than the dwindling campfire. She walked to the tent and climbed into her bag while Jace stayed out and talked to his dad for a while.

When Jace came into the tent, he scooted into the bag next to hers. "I used to think it was my mom that was crazy, but now I think it's my dad," he whispered to her.

"What do you mean?" she asked.

"I don't know. All he does is complain about Ma. She gets really nervous and drives him crazy. They just don't get along very well."

"That's too bad," she said. "I can't imagine my dad complaining about my mom to anyone. They really love each other." She thought how hard it would be to hear one of her parents criticize the other.

"Not my parents," he said. "They drive each other nuts."

Dawn leaned over on his bag, felt his soft, trim beard and began kissing him. He kissed her back, long and hard. The night air was cool, and the pines smelled wonderful. She loved being with him and being next to him.

Soon he said, "We've either got to stop, or you've got to change your mind." She knew what he meant.

"I'll stop," she said abruptly, even though that's not what her heart was saying. Dawn wanted so much to be with him, to be a part of him, and for a moment questioned her own resolve. Still, her beliefs were a very strong part of her. "Goodnight, I love you," she finally whispered.

"I love you, too," he said.

Chapter 5

Back to School

It was hard for Dawn to get back into the routine of work. Jace had told Dawn that it had been the best summer of his whole life. She felt the same way. There hadn't been a day that they had not either been together or had talked. Even when she had been serious with other guys, they had not called her *every* day. Dawn had had a couple of guys ask her out during the summer, but she had turned them down. She was smitten, but she wasn't the only one.

Jace called her the night before school was to start. He had one more class to complete at night, and she, of course, was teaching at night; but wasn't ready for teaching all day again. "You'll go to school tomorrow, and some guy will go after you," he said.

"Yeah, right," Dawn replied. "Some high school kid." Several older people came at night to complete their degrees, sometimes even during the day. But most of the day students were younger. And no one like Jace. Dawn had never expected to meet anyone at work.

"I had a nightmare about you last night," he told her. "I woke up, and I was crying."

"Why?"

"I dreamed that you weren't who you said you were … that you were fooling around. I dreamed you were in bed with some guy and that you sat up and pointed at me and started laughing, saying, 'I fooled you!'"

"Jace, I've never been with any guy that way. You know I'd never do that to you, ever." She felt bad that he had had such an awful dream, especially about her.

The first day of school went smoothly. It was good to see Nancy again. They had talked very little over the summer. "You're not engaged, yet?" Nancy inquired. "I thought for sure …"

As Dawn told her all of the wonderful things Jace said to her and did for her, Nancy felt it wouldn't be long. "I had a sore throat one night and couldn't see him," Dawn told her. "He sent a dozen red carnations that night. He's always telling me how pretty I am, but he's the one who's pretty."

"Well, when he does propose, you'd better call me," Nancy said.

"I'll do better than that," Dawn said. "I'll invite you over for some of my famous spaghetti, and we'll celebrate."

Jace took her out to dinner that night, to the same place where they had had their first lemonade together. Only this time, instead of facing each other at a table, they were sitting next to each other in a dark, corner booth. Jace planned on driving to Wyoming the next night to go to court. Juanita was suing him for custody of the children. "You're ten times the woman that she is," Jace had told her. Dawn had talked him into taking her car to Wyoming. He had protested, but it was a lot more reliable than his beaten-down truck. He had driven her car to the restaurant and was planning on taking it after taking her home.

When the waitress brought the check, Dawn told him, "You spend too much money on me." Jace shook his head. "Yes, you do," Dawn persisted.

"I should put a ring on your finger," he said. "Then you wouldn't cost me so much."

Dawn's heart leapt inside of her. "Yes, you should," she agreed, as Jace placed cash in the black tray with the receipt. The waitress came over and picked up his cash. There was an awkward silence.

"Let's go," he said.

The drive to her house was quiet. She thought Jace must be worried about court, and she wasn't quite sure what to say after what he had said in the restaurant. He pulled into her driveway and turned off the motor of the car.

"I want to know," he said awkwardly, not looking at her. "If I put a ring on your finger, will you wear it?"

"Oh, yes," she said, as she threw her arms around his neck. "Yes, yes, yes! I want to be the best for you. Forever!"

Chapter 6

Spaghetti

"So, I was wondering," Dawn said to Nancy nonchalantly as she walked into her room the next morning, "if you could come over sometime for spaghetti."

Tears streamed down Nancy's face as they embraced. Dawn had never seen Nancy cry before; nor had she seen her so speechless.

Jace returned to Hilton the next night. His court case had been dismissed, and Jace retained custody. Dawn was so happy for him. As she sat next to him on the couch, he pulled a thin, gold band out of his pocket and placed it on her finger. "You get the real one in a couple of weeks. It's still being sized." She was a little disappointed that he hadn't asked her to pick out her own ring but was curious to see what he had picked out. She had never really wanted a diamond but had wanted a pearl or an opal, her birthstone; but she had never told him that and didn't want to hurt his feelings, so said nothing. She loved the gold band. It was simple and beautiful. He had told her he had never given Juanita a ring and that they had just gone down to the courthouse in levis to be married, as Juanita was pregnant with Ida. Dawn felt special.

They planned to be married the fourth of October, exactly six months to the day that they had met. They hoped that the weather would stay warm, so they could be married in her parent's beautiful, but simple back yard.

"Everyone's going to wonder why I'm not getting married in the temple," Dawn told him. She had planned her whole life on going to the temple of her faith to be married, as she looked on marriage as an eternal commitment.

"Let's get married first, and then we can go together to church. Later we can go to the temple," he said. "There isn't anywhere I wouldn't go with you, and I don't think there's anything I wouldn't do for you."

She could feel the love he had in his heart for her as she looked into his eyes.

She felt she was the luckiest woman in the world, to be able to marry someone so sweet and so handsome. He was so strong and so smart (he had gotten straight A's at night school, and Nancy had told her he was bright). He could fix anything, grow anything and was such a good father. She didn't want him to go to the temple for her—she wanted him to go because of his own beliefs. It was just too serious a commitment. She knew he hadn't attended church regularly for a long time, but he had indicated that it was something he wanted to do.

A few weeks later, Nancy and her husband, Ron, came over for spaghetti. Ron brought with him a list of questions he had written that he thought should be asked before two people got married. Ron read the list, and when he finished Jace said teasingly, "Any one of those could make for an argument."

"He's so easy to get along with," Dawn replied, a little surprised at Jace's comment. "Whenever we go do something, he just wants to do what I want. I don't understand why he's divorced."

"You have to do that, if you want to stay married," Jace said.

As they made plans for the wedding, Jace went along with everything Dawn wanted. Maybe it was because he knew deep down of her wishes to go to the temple. Maybe it was because it was his second marriage. He went with her to pick out a dish pattern and to register for gifts. She picked out a beautiful soft-green lily pad design for her stoneware. Jace said he really liked the design. She chose yellow and white for her colors, and he said that yellow was also his favorite color. She sat at his dinner table   addressing invitations, with Ida looking on.

"You have beautiful handwriting," he told her. "And such soft, beautiful hands," he added as he took them in his and kissed them. Dawn had a long list to send out to her family and friends and was very busy addressing the invitations. Jace's mom had given her a list to send to their family members, but it was very small. Jace invited no friends. Dawn respected that he wanted to keep things private from the mechanics he worked with but thought he would invite a couple of the friends he talked about. She actually had never met any of Jace's friends. She figured he was just a family man, and that was okay with her, especially considering his past reputation for being "wild."

"I'm afraid you're going to have a shy groom," he told her. "I'm not much of a people person."

"That's okay," she told him. "You'll be with me, and I'm quiet, too." Even though she was reserved, Dawn was very much a "people person" and had many friends.

"You're such a neat person," he told her. "You're so perfect — we'll probably all drive you nuts."

"I'm far from perfect," she replied, shaking her head sideways.

"I never thought anyone like you would even date me, let alone marry me," he said as he took her in his arms. Dawn didn't understand his humility. All of her friends were drooling over him. He must have women after him all the time.

Dawn had four wedding showers—one from her night school students, one from her close friends, one from her extended family and one from the neighbors. No matter what shower she was at, everyone seemed to gush over how handsome the groom was. Dawn, who had waited so long for her "handsome prince," was especially proud. She had been afraid at times that she would never marry. To marry someone like Jace was more than she could ever have hoped for.

Jace had very few belongings, and they were both delighted with all of the shower gifts. Dawn felt financially prepared for marriage. Her car was paid for, she had no debts, and she had accumulated necessities while previously living away from home. "We're going to have to buy something big after we're married," Jace told her. "Together we'll be making good money, and we'll have too many taxes."

Jace's family didn't offer to do a wedding breakfast, and Dawn didn't push things since it was Jace's second marriage. She was a little disappointed that they didn't offer but was glad that Jace took care of the tuxes and the flowers.

Jace told Dawn that he had been wearing his seatbelt driving to and from work the past week, something he seldom did. "I really want to get married," he said intently.

Dawn's mom and dad worked hard on their back yard, making it extra nice for the wedding. Dawn had wanted the children to be involved as much as possible: Ida was to be her maid of honor, Ethan would be the best man and Eric would be the ring bearer. Dawn made Ida a pretty yellow dress, and Jace rented yellow tuxes for the boys. Everything was ready.

Chapter 7

Wedding Day

The sounds of her mom and sister in the kitchen woke Dawn. It was her wedding day! She wanted the day to be perfect and had tried to get a good night's sleep in preparation. Dawn's mother and sisters had made several pumpkin cakes to serve at the wedding, along with nut cups and apple cider. Dawn and Jace had gathered fall leaves to put on the tables for decorations. The phone rang, and it was Jace.

"I'm just calling to make sure that you still want to do this," he said.

"Of course, I do," Dawn replied. She could hear her sister, Pat, in the kitchen. "He's so romantic!" Dawn repeated what Pat said to Jace.

"No, I'm not," he said somberly. He then told Dawn that Juanita had called the night before and wished him well. "She said, 'I hope you'll be happy.' Then she talked to Ida for a while. Probably brain-washing her."

Dawn's father and uncle were in the back yard setting up chairs. They came into the house and told Dawn that she'd better prepare for rain. They had made plans to go to the church in case of rain, but Dawn had really wanted an outdoor wedding. She asked her uncle if he would say a prayer. They knelt down, and he offered a beautiful prayer in her behalf.

A breeze blew firmly all morning, as though a storm were on its way, but it was still a warm breeze; and the sun continued to peek through the clouds. It had been an unusually warm fall, and Dawn hoped it would continue for just one more day. She took a shower, dried her hair and put it up in electric curlers. Soon Jace came with the children, and he took the boys to a room downstairs to get them all ready. Dawn helped Ida get dressed and fixed her hair. Ida was her usually chatty self, but Dawn found herself being a little irritated by it. She had too much to think about and wasn't in the mood to share her pre-wedding jitters with Ida.

Outside the guests were arriving, and even though it was still breezy, it was warm. Dawn had arranged for the soundtrack to one of her favorite movies, "Somewhere in Time," to be played, and at a certain point in the music they were to go out the back door. Jace stood outside with Ethan, his best (little) man; Eric and Ida proceeded out the door and down the steps in front of Dawn and her father. The boys looked darling in their tuxes, and her father looked very attractive in his suit. Jace was especially handsome in his dark tux and grey-striped ascot.

Dawn stepped out into the sunshine. It was the happiest day of her life, and she smiled without ceasing. She loved all the people in her backyard and was so happy that this day had come. As she walked down the aisle, she had pictured in her mind that Jace would be at the front gazing at her in her beautiful dress; but he didn't. He didn't turn around. Ethan turned and looked back once, but followed his dad's cue and also faced forward. Dawn was disappointed. Why didn't he look at her? She told herself that it was because he was just shy with all of the people there, but that was a moment she had looked so forward to that she had to just let the disappointment of it go. It was her wedding day. Nothing would spoil her day.

There were no props to stand by, as they had a beautiful natural backdrop of oak, dark green foliage and red berries arching in front of them. The yard was beautiful, and the breeze was blowing ever so slightly. The gentle, soothing breeze brought great peace to Dawn's heart as she listened to the words of the bishop. She was so happy that she wasn't sure she could contain it all. To have Jace and three beautiful children all at once was the realization of her dreams. She had yearned for a family of her own and had prayed earnestly for that but hadn't expected an instant one. As the ceremony concluded, Jace took her in his arms and kissed her so hard that she was a little embarrassed.

As they greeted guests and began posing for pictures, her family took down the chairs and set up tables in their place, moving the chairs around them. So far the weather was cooperating.

Nancy came over and hugged Dawn. "It was perfect," she beamed. "It was cloudy as we sat waiting for the ceremony to start, but as soon as you walked out the back door, the sun came out from behind the clouds. Isn't there something about 'lucky is the bride when the sun shines on her face'—something like that?" She turned to Jace: "You take good care of her," she ordered.

"Oh, I will," he smiled. Jace's sister, Susan, who was keeping the children while they went on their honeymoon, came over to them and said that they were going to leave and take the children.

"Can't they stay a little longer?" Dawn pleaded. She had wanted the guests to meet her new family.

"Okay," Susan said, somewhat surprised. "We'll come back a little later and get them."

Jace's dad wasn't feeling well, and he and his wife, Mary, came to say their goodbyes. "I'm sorry we can't stay longer," James said. "I'm just not feeling well. We've waited for this day for a long time."

"We've been praying for this," Mary added sweetly.

Dawn felt bad that they had to go, but James didn't look well at all.

Guests came steadily, and Dawn continued with introductions, as nearly all of the guests were from her friendships and family. Her former bishop came up to them and looked Jace steadily in the eyes. "I love this woman," he said to Jace. The 'you'd better be good to her' was in his eyes but unspoken.

"I do, too," Jace replied affectionately.

Dawn was so busy greeting people that she hadn't noticed the weather getting increasingly foreboding. With only half an hour left, they found themselves in a downpour. The remaining guests huddled under the patio roof as her family hurriedly took down the tables and whisked the decorations inside. Dawn had always loved rain, though, and it didn't dampen her spirits.

Susan returned to pick up the children. "Can I have a hug good-bye?" Dawn said to them as they began to walk away. She hugged Ida and stooped down to hug Eric and Ethan. As Ethan threw his arms around her, she lost her balance in her high heels and fell backwards into a puddle. Ethan started to cry.

"Oh, it's okay, honey," she said, as she pulled him to her again. "Don't worry about it." He calmed down, and as they left, Dawn and Jace hurried into the house. As Dawn changed her clothes, she wondered if the mud would ever come out of her beautiful, white dress. She was arranging her suitcase when Jace came in.

"You don't act like you're married, yet."

"What do you mean?" She was confused by his comment.

"Nothing," he said, as he changed the subject, but his comment had caught her as off-balance as Ethan had. She hugged her family good-bye as they ran out to her appropriately-decorated car. Jace started the car, and they drove off in a torrent of rain.

Chapter 8

Honeymoon

The drive in the storm up the dark and foreboding canyon was more than nerve-wracking. It was raining so hard that Jace had difficulty seeing the wet and narrow winding road. Dawn was relieved when they reached the lodge in the mountains. It was beautiful, surrounded by towering cliffs. Jace grabbed both his luggage and hers as they ran into the lobby. He was so strong. She felt so protected and taken care of.

She had hoped he would lift her romantically over the threshold, but maybe that was a tradition he wasn't aware of. In some ways he seemed more naïve than she. He had given her the wedding band to wear during their engagement. He didn't put the diamond on her finger until the ceremony. Not wanting to hurt his feelings, Dawn didn't have the heart to tell him he was doing things backwards. The naivete and sometimes-shyness of this tall, handsome man was part of her attraction to him.

"I've had to keep my hands off of you for so long that I'm not sure where to start," he said to her, closing the door behind him.

"Well, I'm certainly not going to slap your hands," she teased, but he didn't laugh. He turned on the TV, and they sat on the bed. He began kissing her as his hands went down to the buttons on her blouse. As he pulled the blouse off of her shoulders, she hoped that he wasn't disappointed with her body. He had told her so often how pretty she was, but she hadn't heard that once today—on her wedding day. Maybe he didn't like her dress, she wondered. Maybe he was just nervous, but this was the area where he was the expert and she the novice. He stopped for a moment as he decided to turn off the TV and the lights. She was glad that he turned off the lights—she was a little embarrassed at her nakedness. As he stood at the end of the bed and began to remove his pants, she moved over to the side of the bed to remove her pants. The room was dark, and her eyes were adjusting to what light there was.

"Come down here and do that," he said to her gruffly.

"It's okay," she said shyly. "I can do it right here," as she already had removed her pants and dropped them by the side of the bed. But she could tell it had made him angry. Dawn could feel the tenseness in the room and didn't understand why he would be angry with her. It was the first time she had heard that tone of voice from him, and it confused her. She couldn't understand why such an innocent gesture made him angry. It had been a hard drive, though, and a long day. Maybe he was just tired. She regretted that she hadn't obeyed his command right off. She climbed on the bed, and as he approached her she reached for him and began kissing him. She could feel him soften and relax.

"You need to tell me what you like," he said gently.

"I like you," she whispered …

They slept in late the next morning and when Jace pulled back the heavy curtains, they were surprised to see at least a foot of snow. How fortunate they had been to have had a garden wedding just the day before!

They dressed to go down to breakfast. As Dawn was getting ready, he said, "You still don't feel married, do you?" When she asked him what he meant, he again shrugged her off. As she sat across from him at breakfast and waited for their order to come, Dawn looked into Jace's pretty green eyes.

"I feel so different," she said.

"What do you mean?"

"I don't know. I just feel so different—like I've been awakened somehow. I loved having sex with you."

"I know," he replied. "I think I've created a monster."

Again, his comment unnerved her. "Didn't you like it?" she said, not understanding what he meant.

"Oh, yeah," he nodded.

The waitress came with their order. Dawn was disappointed that Jace didn't seem to want more lovemaking after breakfast. They spent the afternoon seeing the sights of the lodge. After a late dinner, they showered together at Jace's suggestion, and he made love to her again. She was becoming more and more comfortable with her body but let him do all of the initiating, as she felt so inexperienced and insecure in comparison to his years of marriage and other "stay-over" girlfriends.

This was something she had never done, even though she had had many boyfriends. She did not want him to consider her a "monster," though, so she held back, as the comment still disturbed her. She didn't know then that it would disturb her for years to come.

Jace and Dawn returned from their weekend lodge honeymoon Sunday afternoon. They went to Dawn's parents and opened their wedding gifts and then picked up the children at Susan's. They had already moved Dawn's furniture into Jace's small home. "It must be true love," her mother had said, when she had seen Jace's tiny, old, rickety home.

Dawn had set out some memorabilia that meant the most to her on her dresser. She had had them on her dresser at home, among other things: a wood carving of her name that a friend had given her; a picture framed by her brother; a swimming trophy; clay figurines from some friends.

"It looks like Dawnette's room," Jace said, when he walked into their bedroom. "Not ours." Jace had nothing of his own out—the grey-paneled room was bare of anything, even pictures. Dawn took everything off her dresser and placed them in her cedar chest, closing the lid. "That's better," Jace said approvingly.

That evening, Jace told the children to get ready for bed. "Come on," he said as he came into Dawn in the bedroom. "You might as well do this with me, now." He led her to their beds as he tucked them in and kissed them goodnight. Dawn leaned over them and gave them each a kiss, also. Later as they lay together in bed that evening, Jace turned to Dawn. "It's nice to have you here," he said sweetly. "It's nice to be here," she said, as he began kissing her.

Chapter 9

Home

The sound of Jace's alarm buzzing startled Dawn out of a sound sleep. She turned over to go back to sleep, but the alarm soon sounded again and a large light beamed on from the ceiling and startled her once more. Jace had to leave for work an hour before Dawn needed to get up. She had assumed that he would let her sleep as he quietly got ready and kissed her goodbye. Apparently his assumptions were the opposite. She was extremely tired after the eventful weekend and not ready to go back to work. She stumbled out of bed and headed for the bathroom.

"So where's breakfast?" he asked, as he pulled on his uniform pants.

She stopped and looked at him with half-open eyes. "I didn't think you ate breakfast," she said.

"I don't," he teased. "I'll just grab some coffee at work. If you don't want me to drink coffee, though," he said, "I'll stop."

"That's totally up to you," Dawn replied, a non-coffee drinker herself. "I really don't care for the smell and don't know how to make it," she said, closing the bathroom door. She returned and lay on the bed as he finished getting ready. It was a shock to her that he had awakened her, and she realized that she had spent her life aware of her father getting up quietly in the dark, fixing his own breakfast, and leaving without waking her mother. Her father had always treated her mother like a queen. Her mother had wanted to stay home and raise her family, and her dad supported her in this. She had never worked and had always been there for all of her children. Somehow Dawn felt that it would be the same for her.

Jace leaned over and kissed her goodbye. "Have a good day," she said as he headed out the door.

Dawn got down on her knees to say her morning prayers. She

realized that the honeymoon was really something in the past, and she sobbed into the bedspread. The planning, the excitement, and the wedding were over. She was overwhelmed with thoughts of waking up the children, getting them ready, feeding them, taking them to the babysitter before school started and then getting to work herself and having to teach all day. Then when school was over, she would have to pick them up from the babysitter, take them home and get dinner ready before Jace got home from work. He had an hour's drive both ways to get to and from work. Her comfortable, single life was over—overnight. How had that happened? Now she was a wife—and a stepmother—all at once. Somehow it had just not all sunk in until that moment; she had been so enamored with Jace and the romance of it all. And it sunk in hard, as she wept through her prayers …

"Did Dad ever want you to get up and fix his breakfast?" Dawn asked her mother later that day.

"No, he never asked that of me," her mother said. "He had to get up so early. Does Jace want you to fix his breakfast?"

"No," Dawn said. "He says he doesn't eat breakfast." Still, Dawn felt herself feeling guilty for not doing so.

"Well, I should hope not," her mom said. "You've got enough to do taking care of those children. Remember, you can train him or he can train you …"

When Jace got home that evening, Dawn asked him what time he would like to eat dinner.

"Soon after I get home would be good," he said.

So Dawn fixed his dinners and adjusted to married and family life. She tried to be the best wife and mother she could be and be everything he wanted to make him happy.

"I'm afraid I'm not a morning person," she explained to him and hoped that he would let her sleep. But the alarm buzzed loudly every morning, and Jace hit the snooze alarm three times each day before he finally got up. When he did get up, on beamed the ceiling light, and Dawn would find herself covering her head with the bedspread.

"Hey, lazy bones, why don't you get up?" he would kid her, but she relished that last hour of sleep. She just wasn't used to getting up at 5:00 a.m.

She was looking forward to sleeping in their first weekend Saturday morning but was awakened by Eric standing by the side of their bed. "Daddy, I don't feel good." The next thing she knew, Jace was in the bathroom with Eric as he vomited into the toilet. Jace was so caring and loving with him. She watched him place his large hand on Eric's forehead and support his back as his stomach wretched.

"You can come get in bed with us," he told him. It was only a couple of hours later when Ethan started in. Dawn was glad it was a Saturday and that they could be home. Jace gave Ethan the same gentle care that he had given Eric. His boys adored him, and Dawn could see why.

It wasn't surprising when Saturday night, Ida started feeling ill. "I don't feel good, Dad," she moaned when he told her to do the dishes.

"Oh, you're okay," he said. "Get the dishes done." Soon Ida found herself vomiting into the sink.

"What the hell are you doing?" Jace yelled at her. "Get to the damn toilet!"

"Daddy, I don't feel good," she pleaded. Dawn felt bad for her and went with her into the bathroom. "Why doesn't he treat me like the boys?" she cried to Dawn.

Dawn didn't have an answer for her and was wondering the same thing herself. There must be some history between them that she didn't know about; but didn't feel comfortable getting into the middle of it. "He loves you, honey," she tried to comfort her.

After a Saturday full of sick children, Dawn was relieved that she and Jace felt okay on Sunday. She was especially glad to feel well since it was her birthday. They had made plans to go to her parents for dinner, but Dawn went alone while Jace stayed home with the children.

"You doll," he looked her over as she kissed him goodbye. He had given her a beautiful card and flowers, but she wished he could come with her. Dawn didn't want to expose her parents to the flu, though, and had an enjoyable evening alone with her family …

It was the beginning of November, a beautiful, fall Saturday. Jace and the children were outside raking up leaves and piling them in garbage cans. Dawn was inside, tidying the house and feeling more melancholy than she had in a long time. Soon she was dissolved into tears, tears that seemed uncontrollable. What frustrated her most was that she couldn't find any real reason for her sad, sad mood. Normally she had a really good disposition.

Jace came inside for a glass of water and found her in tears.

"I don't even know what I'm crying about," Dawn told him in frustration.

"I do," he said confidently. "You're pregnant."

"What?" she gasped. They had only been married a few weeks. It couldn't be possible.

"I'll bet you anything," he said.

Just the thought of the possibility gave Dawn much to think about, and her tears subsided. Where would they put a baby? There was hardly room for Dawn in their tiny home. Eric and Ethan slept in bunk beds in the back entryway—they didn't even have a bedroom to call their own.

Later in the week, an appointment with the doctor confirmed Jace's diagnosis. Dawn was at school when the doctor's office called her with the news. Dawn wanted to race in and tell Nancy but thought that Jace should be the first to know. She couldn't wait with her news and called Jace at work.

"You were right," she said. "We're going to have a baby," she announced to him over the phone.

"That was easy," Jace answered.

"It certainly was," she replied. Sometimes the biggest changes in life seemed to happen so easily. Dawn was so happy, and she was happy that it wasn't hard for her to get pregnant. She had so much wanted a family, and that answer to her prayer was being multiplied. She would add mother to her title of wife and stepmother—a title she wanted most of all. How different her life was from a few months ago!

Dawn often walked in the gym at school during her lunch hour for exercise. As she walked around with her eyes on the yellow, wood-plank floor, her thoughts turned to the baby and where she would put her. (At least she hoped it would be a she.) There just wasn't room. Suddenly, it was as if a light bulb went off in her head. Her sister, Paula, was selling a second home she and her husband owned in nearby Wheatfield. It would be perfect. It wasn't too large; they should be able to afford it. Best of all, it had an acre of land to go with it and was zoned for animals. Jace loved animals and gardening. He would love having a large yard. Why hadn't she thought of it before?

When she told Jace about it that night, and the strong feelings she had as she was walking, she was glad that he was receptive to the idea. They drove out one night to take a look at the house. Paula had been renting it out, and since her husband was a real estate agent, he was taking care of the sale. Because the renters were committed for six more months, it wasn't yet on the market. Dawn loved the location. It was on a quiet, dead-end street in the country. A split-level, it was considerably larger than their present tiny home. Coincidentally, it was less than a mile from where Jace's sister, Susan, brother Dave, and their families lived. Jace told Paula that they would put down earnest money on the house and to tell her husband to make the arrangements. Paula reduced the selling price since they were selling it to family. Everything fell into place. Paula's husband would put Jace's home on the market. Dawn knew that for some reason she was supposed to live in Wheatfield.

That night Dawn dreamed that there was a little boy with big brown eyes and brown, curly hair out on the front porch. She sat up straight in bed. "I've got to go let him in," she said to Jace.

"What?" he answered sleepily.

"He'll be cold. I need to go let him in."

"You're dreaming," he said. "Go back to sleep."

Dawn then realized that she had indeed been dreaming. And she realized that the baby girl she had hoped for would be a baby boy.

Chapter 10

Doughnuts

Dawn was especially tired when she got home from school that evening but had managed to make a casserole for dinner. She had always liked to cook but wasn't used to having to prepare dinner every night. It was beginning to seem more and more like a chore. As they sat at dinner that night, Ethan refused to eat.

"You like all the ingredients," Dawn coaxed him. "It's just all mixed together in a casserole."

"It looks yucky," he said stubbornly. Again, Dawn pictured in her mind what her father had done. "You eat or you starve," he would have told them in defense of their mother's cooking. Dawn didn't remember anyone in her family protesting her mother's cooking. If it were something that they really disliked, they just ate more of something else on the table. She couldn't believe what Jace did next.

"You don't have to eat it," he said. Jace stood up, went to the refrigerator and pulled out a package of doughnuts. Ethan's face lit up with a smile as Jace handed him a doughnut. Dawn looked at him in disbelief.

"How can you do that?" she said. "After the dinner I cooked, and you give him a doughnut instead?!" She stormed into the bedroom.

Jace stayed in the front room for much of the night with the children. Dawn got ready for bed and climbed wearily into the covers. "I don't know if I can do this," she said to him, when he came into the bedroom. She was looking for some evidence of support from him. He didn't answer her but turned away from her and went to sleep. Dawn cried in frustration.

The next morning before Jace left for work, he said to her sternly, "If you can't do this, then tell your sister we don't want the house. I'm not going to be left with a big house payment on my own again."

"I would never leave you!" Dawn exclaimed with tears running down her cheeks. "I love you!" She couldn't believe they were having this conversation, but that was what Jace needed to hear. He softened immediately and kissed her. She threw her arms around him and sobbed ...

Dawn repeated her story to Nancy later that day. When she told him what Jace had said about the house, she looked worried and said, "That doesn't sound like him."

"I know," Dawn agreed.

Later that evening, Jace helped Dawn do the dishes. She was relieved that there had been no fights over dinner. Picky Ethan had liked what she made for dinner that night. "It's my fault that he's picky," Jace explained to her. "When we were on our own, I just pretty much fixed them what they asked for."

"Well, they can't eat doughnuts every night for dinner," Dawn said. "That's not good for them either."

"I know," Jace agreed.

Changing the subject, Dawn asked Jace something else she had been wondering about. "How come you never tell me I'm pretty anymore?"

"Do you have to hear it everyday?" he said.

"No," she said, "but it would be nice to hear once in a while." While they were dating, he complimented her several times every day. Now he never even told her he loved her, unless she told him first. "I just don't want us to take each other for granted," she said. Other than her birthday, the compliments had nearly stopped. They seemed to stop on their wedding day. He did make love to her nearly every night, and she looked forward to it, although it seemed to taper off more and more as time went on. She guessed that was just normal. It couldn't be intense forever.

"It won't happen if we don't let it," he answered. "By the way," it was his turn to change the subject, "we might need to write a letter about the bankruptcy before we get a loan on the house."

Dawn was terribly confused. "What bankruptcy?" She didn't know what Jace was talking about.

"I told you," he said. "Don't you remember? I told you that I had to take out bankruptcy after the divorce. I had to buy new furniture for the house 'cause Juanita took it all. Then I had to pay for day care all day for the children and pay for the lawyer and the house payment—I couldn't do it all."

Dawn was sure he hadn't told her. She would have remembered something like that. She didn't know she was entering into a marriage based on a bankruptcy. Maybe he had thought that he had told her.

"Well, I have good credit," she said. "Paula's husband will help us to get the house. Hopefully we shouldn't have any problems."

That night when she went to bed, she found a note on her pillow from Ida:

> Dear Dawnette,
> I love you a lot and ever cence you came along everything has changed and been realy good and I'm realy very happy that you came to live with us and it is very nice to have you as a stepmother my dad sure has good taste in ladys!
> Dawnette, I love you a lot. I love as if you were my real Mother and I hope that you love me to.
>> Senciraly,
>> Ida Malone

Dawn felt so good to get the note, but it also worried her. How bad had things been for Ida before they were married? Jace seemed like such a good father. Dawn didn't really know Ida well enough yet to know what to believe and what not to believe. Jace had told her of problems with her stealing and lying, but Ida seemed sincere in the things she told Dawn. Dawn was finding out more and more each day how difficult being a stepmother could be.

Chapter 11

Socks

Dawn was startled out of a comfortable morning sleep as the covers were ripped off of her. She looked up to see Jace ranting, his face scarlet and the veins exposed in his large, thick neck. "Where are my damn socks? Can't you manage to get the laundry done? Maybe if you got up in the morning, things would get done!"

"I … I did do the laundry," she stammered, not quite awake and not quite sure what was happening. Who was this man screaming at her? "They must be in the dryer," she remembered.

"Well, next time, get them in my drawer!" he yelled as he slammed the dryer door and walked out the front door.

Dawn felt terrible as she went through the school day. She could hardly keep her mind on her work, as her thoughts kept returning to the morning. She rehearsed what she would say to Jace when he walked through the door that night but was surprised by his pleasant demeanor when he came in.

"How was your day?" he asked as he took her in his arms and kissed her. Before she could answer, he started talking about a customer at work as though nothing had happened that morning.

'I must be overreacting,' Dawn thought, as she vowed to herself to always have the laundry done and put away from now on.

Chapter 12

Business Trip

Jace was scheduled to fly to North Carolina with his co-worker, Rick, for training on large engine repairs. Dawn dreaded him being gone but was determined for things to go well while he was.

"I'm not gonna eat this," Ethan had declared one night at dinner.

"Then I'm afraid you'll just have to go to bed hungry," Dawn replied. She certainly wasn't fixing something else and wasn't going to give him doughnuts.

Ethan realized that Dawn wasn't budging. He played with a few mouthfuls of food and had soon eaten more than he had planned on. After dinner, Dawn made some large labels to put on the outside of the boys' dresser drawers.

"If you put your pants in this drawer, and your shirts in this drawer, and your underwear and socks in this drawer," she instructed as she stuck on the appropriate labels, "you'll always be able to find your clothes, and they won't get so wrinkled." She then did the same project with Ida but made smaller labels that she could keep on the inside of her drawers. Jace had put Ida's mattress on the floor in desperation, so that she couldn't throw any of her clothes underneath. Ida seemed receptive to the label idea, and Dawn patted herself on the back for putting some organization into their lives. The next morning, she made sure that they had made their beds before leaving for school.

Jace called the next evening, and Dawn proudly told him how the children were making their beds, putting their clothes away and eating her dinners. She thought Jace would be so pleased, but she just met with silence on the other end. 'Maybe he doesn't want to say anything in front of Rick,' she thought.

She also had some other news for Jace. While she had called the roll at school that afternoon in her last class of the day, she had been hit in the head with a wallet full of change. A student, who had just been released from a correctional facility and was spending his first day in Dawn's class, had thrown the wallet. Dawn didn't know the boy at all but was still devastated and had a large goose egg on the side of her head. She decided to press charges, but the boy had already run from his new group home. She was told he had a history of assaulting other teachers. She thought that when she told Jace he would be furious, or at least concerned for her safety, but he didn't seem to care about the incident at all. Had she told her father, he would have been outraged. Why wasn't Jace?

"We've rented some movies, and then we're going to bed," Jace told her. But when he told her the names of the movies, they sounded pretty raunchy. "Rick needs to see some sex, he hasn't had any lately," Jace teased him. She could hear Rick in the background protesting Jace's accusation.

"I miss you," Dawn said.

"I miss you, too," Jace replied. "I'll see you Friday…"

Friday soon came, and Dawn wasn't sure what time Jace would be home; when she hadn't heard from him by ten, she put the children to bed and got into bed herself. She slept restlessly in anticipation of Jace climbing into bed with her. She couldn't wait to have his arms around her again. She was awakened to pounding on the front door.

Jace was still pounding by the time she got up and got to the door.

"What took you so long?" he said impatiently.

"I thought you had your keys," she said sleepily. She glanced at the clock. It was 2:00 a.m.

"I do, but I've also got these damn suitcases!"

Dawn stood in front of the heater in the kitchen, trying to get warm as Jace unpacked. She often stood there. It was an old, gray, metal heater that didn't heat the entire house very well. Cold-blooded by nature, much of her time was spent standing in front of it in an effort to warm herself.

Jace came over to her and placed his cold hands under her nightgown. Dawn pushed his hands away. "I'm already cold!" she protested, as he chuckled. Somehow this wasn't the homecoming she had envisioned. As she warmed herself further by the heater, Jace got ready for bed. When she climbed back into bed, Dawn pressed herself next to him. "I missed you so much," she said.

"Me, too," he said, as he began to kiss her.

Chapter 13

First Christmas

Dawn's night school students during winter quarter had been especially fun. An older group of ladies, they had come prepared Thursday night with presents in hand for a surprise baby shower. Dawn was relieved that it was her last night of night school. It had been nice to come with Jace, but he was through with his classes and had earned the credit he needed. She planned on spending her nights at home now with him and the children.

She thanked all of her students for their gifts as she hugged them goodbye. She was relieved it was over. She had enjoyed them immensely, but the "morning" sickness that lasted all day and into the evening had worn her down. She was still waiting for it to subside, but it hadn't happened yet. She kept soda crackers at her bedside to consume before she lifted her head off the pillow in the morning. It seemed to help a little, but she was still miserable much of the time.

Dawn was also relieved that the children were visiting their mother this Christmas. She really needed time to be alone with Jace. That was probably the most difficult thing in her new marriage for her—wanting the romance of being a newlywed but having an instant, constant family at the same time. She also had a hard time relinquishing her privacy—she hadn't realized how much she valued her time alone until she never had any.

The day before Christmas Eve, the children were excited for their mother to come. Dawn had seen pictures of her but had never met her. When Juanita got to their home, it was late, and she didn't get out of the car. The children ran out in excitement to the car with their bags. Juanita's boyfriend, Darren, put their bags in the trunk, got the children in the car, and drove off. Dawn went up to Jace, who was standing looking out the kitchen window, and put her arms around his neck.

"Alone at last," she whispered but could tell that Jace didn't appreciate the comment.

They went out to a nice restaurant that evening, but Dawn couldn't enjoy it—she was still having a hard time with her all-day nausea. She would be so glad for it to end. Her friends had told her that it would only last three months. She didn't have long to go.

Christmas morning was especially quiet without the children. Dawn had spent all the money she had on a beautiful pocket watch for Jace. She couldn't wait to give it to him. He seemed pleased when he opened it and then handed her a box to open. "Knives!" she said, as she opened a box containing four sharp kitchen knives in a wooden block.

"We don't have any good sharp ones in the house," he said. "I figured you could use them."

She was a little disappointed. She was hoping for something a touch more romantic, but it certainly was a practical gift. She knew there was little money. She hadn't realized that Jace had borrowed money from his dad for their honeymoon. She had worked on paying him off after their return. Jace had also signed up for payments to get Dawn's diamond. Since she was helping to pay off their honeymoon and her diamond, she figured that the knives, being paid for, were a good gift. What was romance, anyway?

Chapter 14

Baby

Dawn was looking forward to their first summer together. Dating last summer had been so wonderful, and she was happy now to be able to stay at home and be a fulltime mother. She was relieved that Jace hadn't wanted her to work once the baby came. She had said her good-byes at school (except for Nancy—that friendship would continue). Now she was at home building her "nest." As they did last summer, the children had gone to visit their mother for six weeks. Dawn loved them but again was looking forward to having some time to herself and having time alone with Jace.

She couldn't wait for the baby to come. She hadn't gained a lot of weight. She spent the first half of her pregnancy throwing up so much that the doctor had ordered her to gain some weight. "See all those fat women out in the waiting room?" he had said to her. "I don't tell anyone to gain weight. Gain some weight." Jace had teased her about getting fat since the beginning of her pregnancy. Their sex life had certainly suffered, since she started putting on a few pounds. There were days that she just ached for him to touch her. Jace hated fat women. Dawn was starting to look pregnant now and only had a month to go. She was nervous about the delivery. How would it feel to actually have the baby?

Mistakenly, Dawn had thought that when the children left, they could enjoy the romance and closer relationship of the summer before. But there was a resentment in Jace that Dawn just couldn't break through. He always seemed angry about something. Maybe it was because the children were with his ex, whom he despised. Maybe he resented Dawn staying at home while he worked. She didn't know what it was, and Jace didn't acknowledge it, so she was left to her own suppositions. She looked so forward to him coming home at night, after being alone all day, but when he came home he seemed distant and preoccupied.

July came quickly and it was time for the children to come back. Jace's divorce decree stated that he was to meet halfway between the two homes to drop off and pick up the children, but Juanita called to say that she wouldn't bring them back. "If you want them, come and get them," she said. 'How awful she is,' Dawn thought.

Dawn suggested that they borrow her parents' motor home, drive to Wyoming to pick up the children and then stay overnight at a campsite with a pool. "It would be great for the children. Let's take your parents with us and make it a vacation." Jace seemed to like the idea, Dawn's parents were more than willing to let them borrow their motor home, and Jace's parents enjoyed the drive. When they pulled up to the tiny home where Juanita lived with her parents, Jace took his pistol out of the glovebox and put it in his pocket before exiting the vehicle.

Juanita's father was the first one out of the house, followed by Ethan and Eric. "You buy that with the child support she sends you?" he yelled at Jace bitterly.

"Absolutely," Jace replied, ushering the boys into the motor home.

Juanita came storming out of the house after them and put her ruddy, worn face into the motor home door. She was short, chubby and not-at-all attractive. Dawn wondered what it was that Jace had seen in her. "Ethan! You didn't tell me goodbye! Get over here and give me a kiss!" Ethan, embarrassed, obeyed.

Ida was last out of the house, reluctantly plodding into the motor home. "You're just putting nails in your coffin," Juanita continued, pointing her finger at Jace. "She doesn't want to go with you!"

"It's terrible that he cares about her!" Dawn said out the window as they pulled away and understood why Jace had a gun in his pocket. Ida was sullen and moody the first part of the trip and stayed in the back of the motor home, talking to her grandmother. When she finally came up front to Dawn, Dawn blurted out, "What have you done to your hair?" Ida had dyed it a horrible red, which Dawn thought looked terrible.

"It's only temporary," Ida explained, hugging Dawn. "Just a rinse." Dawn was relieved. When they got to the RV park, the children ran for the pool. After they had been swimming, Ida seemed back to her old cheerful self; and they had a pleasant evening and ride back home the next day.

On the last day of the month, Dawn felt restless and decided to make an apple pie. She had never made one before, but it sounded good to her. While the pie baked, she stayed up late, trying to get some bills paid and paperwork done. She finished around midnight and was ready for a good night's sleep; however, as she climbed into bed, she felt a contraction. Soon another came. Sleep was out of the question, as she began to time how far apart they were.

She watched the clock off and on for the next few hours, not knowing if she should be alarmed or not. At 4:00 a.m. she woke Jace and told him that she thought it was time. Jace took a "before" picture of her as she stood in profile in the living room. Dawn would later marvel at the picture; she looked so small. They woke the children and drove them to her sister, Paula's, home. They would stay there until the baby was born.

At the hospital, Dawn changed into a gown and sat on the bed as the nurses hooked her up to monitors. The contractions were steady now, and Dawn was surprised at how much they hurt. Jace sat in a recliner chair opposite her and dozed off. It didn't seem fair to Dawn, who had not slept at all and who was getting increasingly nervous with each increasingly painful and longer contraction. Jace stirred long enough to call into work: "Hey, my old lady's goin' to calf today," he said lazily. "I won't be in."

'Spoken like a true farmer,' Dawn thought.

Hours later, an anesthesiologist came in to administer an epidural but was late in getting there. Dawn was in intense pain and felt like she was being ripped apart. He mentioned that he needed to hurry, and the doctor concurred. The baby was in distress; after each contraction, its heart rate was very slow in returning to normal. Apparently, he had had a bowel movement in the womb, which had put him in distress. Dawn screamed in pain and was sure that she was being split open. She was praying that the epidural would soon take effect. The doctor said he would have to suction the baby out quickly.

Jace was now dressed in a gown and mask. Dawn's parents entered the room.

"I could hear you yelling all the way down the hallway," her mother said. "I told your Dad, 'that has to be Dawn'."

Dawn was embarrassed that she could be heard in the halls. She was normally a very quiet person, but she thought she was going to die. She had never experienced such intense pain.

"A doctor told me once to imagine stretching my lower lip over my head," Jace joked, "if I wanted to know what it felt like to have a baby." Dawn didn't appreciate the comment at the moment.

The pain was beginning to subside, and the doctor told Dawn to push. She tried with all of her might, but because of the epidural, she couldn't tell if she were pushing or not. That disappointed her, but she was glad to have some relief from the intense pain. It wasn't the cramping that had put her over the edge but a burning pain that seemed to sear her in half.

One more push, and the baby's head emerged. "You've got a big baby here," said the doctor.

"I bet he's at least ten pounds," said one of the nurses. Dawn was astounded. She didn't feel that she had gotten that big. Another push.

"It's a boy," Jace announced calmly, seeming very pleased. The doctor clamped the cord and had Jace cut it; the nurses whisked the baby away. The baby began to cry. The sound was absolute heaven to Dawn, and she began to cry.

The nurses cleaned up the baby and weighed him. "He's not even seven pounds!" the doctor informed her. "I could have sworn he was bigger," he said.

"Me, too," she heard others agree. "It's because his head's so big."

"I do wear the largest hat size there is," Jace offered.

"Now's a great time to tell me," Dawn countered, exhausted.

"He's a very healthy baby," one of the nurses said, as she laid him on Dawn's chest.

"Hello," she said to the baby quietly, as she counted his tiny fingers and toes. It was all she could do to comprehend what had just happened. It had taken so long for him to get there, and now here he was. As she gazed at him, she knew her life would never be the same.

Her mother was soon holding the baby, and Dawn began to shiver. It was a side effect of the epidural. Dawn had no feeling at all now below her waist, as the injection had finally kicked in.

"You need to go get more silk," said the doctor to one of the nurses, and she headed out the door. "Not only did your vagina tear," he explained to Dawn, "but your vaginal wall has separated." He continued to sew her up. "You're going to be the owner of the first bionic vagina!" he joked. Dawn was just grateful to feel no pain.

Later, as she rested in her room, in came her sisters and the children. They were excited to see the baby, and Dawn was glad to see them. She was surprised when she first got up to use the restroom how sore she was. It was all she could do to walk; but having her baby boy next to her somehow made it all worthwhile.

Chapter 15

Motherhood

"I think she should be able to name the baby," Jace had told Dawn's mother, "since it's her first child." But every name she considered, Jace had negated. He had finally agreed to Joseph; but when he heard her tell her friends over the phone, he denied that he had agreed to it.

"I never agreed to that name!" he countered her.

"I thought you said …"

"I said I knew a guy named Joe in high school, and I couldn't stand him!"

"That's what you said about the name Jeffrey!"

"Yeah, I can't stand that name either!"

That afternoon, a neighbor lady that Dawn had come to adore, came over to see the baby. She was older, her husband had retired, and she often tended the children after school. "I really want to name him Joseph and call him Joey," Dawn said, "but Jace doesn't like that name."

"Oh, I love that name!" she said.

"So do I," Dawn said, miserable that Jace didn't agree. He didn't seem to agree to any name she chose. "My first choice was Jeffrey, but Jace won't agree to that name at all, so I was counting on naming him Joe. I always loved Little Joe on the show Bonanza when I was young. Nothing else seems to fit."

"Go with your heart, dear," she advised.

So Dawn went with her heart, and Jace finally consented to Joseph, since he had told their families that he was letting her choose. She was relieved, but it was only the beginning of the arguments.

They had put Joey in a bassinet in their bedroom; there simply wasn't room anywhere else in the house. Every time he cried, Dawn ran to pick him up and comfort him.

"You're going to spoil him rotten," Jace would say in exasperation. But from what Dawn had read, an infant couldn't really be spoiled. Jace wanted her to stay in the living room with him and watch TV and let Joey cry in the bassinet alone. Dawn tried to appease him but yearned to be with the baby. One night, she couldn't stand it any more and went into her bedroom to pick him up. She held him to her chest, but he wouldn't be comforted and continued to cry. She thought a change of scenery might help, so she brought Joey out into the living room. He continued crying, however, and Jace wanted no part of it.

"If you can't leave him alone, don't be bringing him in here!"

"But the baby book says that …"

"I don't care what some damn book says! Don't you think I know anything? I've raised three kids. You're just spoiling him rotten!"

Dawn took Joey back in the dark bedroom and walked with him around the small room, rocking him in her arms. She couldn't bear to put him down, no matter what Jace said. "Don't cry, honey, don't cry," she whispered, as the tears rolled down her cheeks …

Dawn loved staying at home with the baby, but it was a huge adjustment for her. Her efforts at breastfeeding, which she wanted so much to do, only met with frustration. Joey cried so much that she felt she couldn't satisfy him. She was also worried about one of the children walking in on her. She wasn't comfortable at all with them watching her breastfeed and never felt truly at ease. Then there was Jace. Apparently his first wife had milk and then more milk, and he never missed an opportunity to tell Dawn she was doing things wrong. In fact, nearly everything she did with Joey was wrong—from burping him, to changing his diapers, to putting him to sleep—according to Jace, she did everything wrong.

On a sunny Saturday, Dawn and Ida had gone to a mother/daughter activity and luncheon at their church. They played a game similar to "The Newlywed Game" to test how well the mothers and daughters knew each other. Dawn thought it ironic when she and Ida won the prize—they had known each other little more than a year—but they had had an enjoyable time. As Ida told her father that evening that they had won the game, he seemed more irritated than pleased as Dawn walked in holding Joey. "You and Dawn should play the game," Ida offered, but Jace only scoffed. "You sure don't treat her very well, Dad," Ida said.

Dawn was surprised; not at what Ida was saying but that she had said it out loud. It validated what Dawn felt in her heart. If Ida had noticed, maybe he really didn't treat her well. Dawn had been thinking that she was doing things terribly wrong and was trying to adjust to wife-and-mother-hood. Maybe he really just didn't treat her well, and why didn't he? She tried so hard to be and do everything to make him happy.

Dawn's parents had given her a rocking chair for her birthday. Dawn loved it and loved sitting in it and rocking Joey to sleep, but even that was wrong. Jace looked on it as another way to "spoil" Joey and seemed to resent any time at all that Dawn spent with him. Was he jealous of his own son? 'No,' Dawn told herself. 'He has three other children.'

Even though Jace worked all day and she was able to be home, Dawn was tired beyond any tiredness she had ever known. Because Jace had to get up early and go to work, it was Dawn's duty to get up each night with Joey. What she would have given for a full night's sleep! And she was trying to build up her milk so much that she would get up every few hours in order to feed him. One morning, she went into the bathroom to put her contacts in. As she opened the case, she noticed that it was dirty and needed washing. Not realizing that she hadn't put her contacts in yet, she rinsed out the case and, in the process, rinsed her contacts down the sink. Dawn cried in desperation, as she was nearly blind without them. She didn't relish wearing her old glasses in the meantime. She vowed to herself to get more sleep but didn't know when she would do it. When the baby napped, it was her time to clean the house, do the laundry, and get dinner fixed. Her exhaustion certainly wasn't helping her milk supply, either.

But, oh, how she loved Joey! She had never known such joy before. As she cared for this tiny being who had been the source of months of vomiting and then heartburn and then the literal searing at his birth—this being who demanded her presence at every turn and kept her from getting precious, needed sleep—she realized that she had never known such love in all her life. She thought she loved her stepchildren; but when Joey was born, she knew that whatever affection she felt for them was a pittance in comparison. She didn't love them at all! The thought made her feel very guilty; but how could she? How could she ever feel for them what she felt for this baby who was such a part of her?

Chapter 16

Bones

Dawn's brother-in-law had found a buyer for their home, the renters were out of his home, and the time had come to move. Dawn was so excited to have more space. The children would actually have rooms. There was a spacious family room in the basement, and there was an even more spacious yard, as it was located on an acre of land. She knew Jace would love working outside and making it his own. Still, she had reservations. Jace was so constantly critical of her that at times she wondered if their marriage would survive and if she should commit to buying a home.

The closing costs and down payment required to purchase the home turned out to be more than they had planned for. When Dawn quit teaching, she had taken out her retirement money—retirement seemed way too far away to not use the money now. It took the entire retirement she had accumulated—$5,000—to put down on the mortgage in order to obtain their home. The sale of Jace's tiny home (which would later prove to be full of termites) didn't net them a lot of money but did help a little.

They had plans to start the move on an early Saturday morning and hoped to be able to sleep there that night. The Thursday night before the weekend, they had a surprise visit from Jace's parents. As they came in and sat in their tiny living room, Jace's mom and dad both started to cry.

"They found Mike's body under a tree in Georgia," Mary stammered through her tears. "We hoped it wasn't him, but they matched his dental records. His body had been there a month—there's nothing left of him!" She began to sob.

"There was a gun …" James spoke up but had a hard time composing himself. "They say it was self-inflicted."

Dawn felt bad that she would never meet Jace's younger brother.

And she felt so bad for his parents. How hard it must be to deal with their son's death but even harder when they hadn't seen him for so long and then have to deal with his suicide. After they left, Dawn wanted to be there for Jace, but he didn't seem to want any comfort. Dawn wished he would cry and let go of some of the grief, but she never saw him cry.

The move went along as planned on Saturday. All went well, and with both sides of the family helping, they were able to finish in a day. She was so tired by nightfall, all she wanted to do was to fall into bed. The boys were afraid of sleeping in their new rooms, however, and slept in the family room on the floor. Jace wanted Dawn to join them, but she wanted to be upstairs in her own bed next to Joey, who would still stay in their room for a while. She could tell Jace was perturbed with her, but she was just too beat from packing and unpacking everything to spend the night on the floor. The arthritis she continually battled would not make for a pleasant night's sleep on the floor. Jace slept by the boys in the basement, and she and Jace spent the first night in their new home sleeping apart.

Sunday was busy, as they used the time to unpack more boxes. Jace had arranged to have Monday off for a graveside service that was scheduled for his brother Mike. The cemetery where he would be buried was next to the shore of the reservoir in Snowcrest. Dawn had swum in it many times; it was one of her favorite places.

It was snowing heavily the morning of the service and was very cold. The reservoir seemed so different now, covered in snow with bleakness everywhere. Dawn took her place in one of the cold, folding chairs placed at the gravesite. They had left the children with her mother. Soon the hearse arrived, and Jace and the other pallbearers appeared on the gray horizon, carrying the coffin up the hill. Jace seemed calm and composed— almost too composed. Dawn could hardly bear to look at his dad; he was so broken up, and the tears flowed. She felt so bad for him.

After putting the coffin in its place, Jace came over and stood next to Dawn's chair. Dawn took his large hand in hers as a prayer was said. The snow was coming down heavily now, and the wind was blowing. An image that would ever haunt her was that of the coffin, rocking back and forth in the wind.

She would later hear Jace tell his cousin how easy it had been to carry the coffin. "There wasn't anything in there but bones," he said.

Chapter 17

Ghosts

James called the next morning while Jace was at work, just needing someone to talk to. Dawn tried to comfort him as best she could but was feeling very inadequate.

"I knew she beat him," he said. "I would come home from work, and Mike would be lying on the couch, so sad. I'd ask him, 'What's wrong son?' but he wouldn't say anything. I knew she was beating him." She could hear the grief in his voice turn to anger. Dawn didn't know what to say. Mary beat Mike. She was trying to register the thought. Had she also beaten Jace?

"I'm so sorry," was all she could think to say. She loved James; he was very sweet to her, but there was seldom a time she was around him that he wasn't irritated with his wife. And he had no misgivings about sharing that irritation in front of her. Mary would laugh it off nervously, but it had to hurt. And Dawn was beginning to see a pattern. Maybe Jace inherited his dad's tendency to criticize his wife. At least Jace never criticized Dawn in front of anyone else (except the children). Still, it was hard to listen to. Then again, if Mary had abused her children …

"He called me from Georgia," James continued, "and wanted money. I told him no, but I shouldn't have. I should have sent him something … I should have …" James broke up again in grief and told Dawn he would talk to her later.

Dawn tried to piece things together. Jace was always hesitant to leave the children with Mary; in fact, if James wasn't there, he didn't. Dawn's mom watched them much more than Mary did. Was it because Mary also abused Jace when he was young? Jace was so large now, that was hard to imagine. Did their constant bickering drive all of their children out of the house? Dawn couldn't imagine her father talking about her mother the way James talked about Mary. Both Susan and Missy married right out of high school; Mike joined the service the minute he was eighteen; Jace and Dave left home long before they turned eighteen. Something was very wrong somewhere.

Chapter 18

Working Nights

Jace's shift had been changed to afternoons, and Dawn tried to adjust to the new schedule. She got up in the morning and quietly got the children off to school. Jace got up in the afternoon, had something to eat, and then went off to work. She spent a lot less time with him, but the nights were certainly much more peaceful. There were no conflicts over dinner, as Jace wasn't there to give into the children, and they went to bed early on school nights.

What bothered Dawn was that when Jace came home, he didn't come to bed. They never had sex any more. He seldom touched her at all. When he got home in the middle of the night, Jace went downstairs and watched videos. "They're just videos that the guys at work gave me," he explained. "I'm not ready to go to sleep when I get home—I need to unwind."

One morning while Jace slept, Dawn picked up a video off the floor and pushed it into the VCR. A close up of an enlarged penis filled the screen. Dawn was sickened and immediately turned off the TV.

Jace's midnight movies became the routine, as Dawn slept alone upstairs. 'Maybe he just doesn't find me attractive anymore since I've had the baby,' she thought. She had lost most of the weight from the baby and really hadn't gained a lot to begin with.

"I think we should go see a counselor," Dawn approached Jace one morning.

"Go ahead," was Jace's answer.

"Won't you go with me?" she pleaded.

"Hell, no! If you think you need a counselor, go ahead and see one."

So she did. She made an appointment with a man that her bishop recommended to her. She sat nervously in front of him, as this was something she had never had the need of before.

"Well, I don't think you have any symptoms of depression," the counselor summed up after asking her about her sleeping and eating habits. "I know the pornography is distressing to you, but there is nothing I can do for you unless you can get your husband to come in here."

"I don't think I can," she said meekly.

"Well, see what you can do," he encouraged her. "Tell him that I don't take sides, that I will be absolutely impartial—just do what you can to encourage him."

Dawn told him that she would, and she tried but got absolutely nowhere. So went her first encounter with counseling.

That evening, Ida left a note on Jace's pillow. Dawn read it after climbing in on her side of the bed. Ida wrote:

> Dear Dad,
>
> I don't mean to make matters worse, but it started out small with you & mom (I don't mean to bring in the past.) & then got worse & you guys got divorsed! Don't let that happen with you & Dawn please. (Its possible!) I don't want to make you feel bad or for you to be mad. OK? Dawn does a lot for you & us & we just make her feel unappriciated because we never tell her thank you, or make a complement. I'm going to try & make her feel more appriciated & I would like it if you would try to also. (please.) Show her that you love her because I know that she feels like you hate her & she probably just wants to get up & leave! But she loves you to much. She did not put any of these words into my mouth either! I just want it to work out for you guys & believe me I really do care about what happens to you guys & your marrage.
>
> Ida
>
> P.S. I hate listening to you guys fight & I know you hate to fight so just try not to carry any of your arguments to far on. Love you.

Dawn replaced the note and turned off the light. It seemed she had an advocate in Ida.

Chapter 19

Hawaii

The more Jace told Dawn about work, the more she wondered why he still had a job. He often told her that he had mouthed off to the boss or lost his temper at work. Jace sounded like he was anything but congenial to work with, although he did have some friends there who felt the same way Jace did and had the same difficulties with the supervisor. Dawn wasn't sure what to think. One thing she did know was that Jace was an excellent mechanic and very fast. Because of that, she figured he got away with a lot of things that he might not have otherwise.

Jace had told Dawn about an incentive they were incorporating at work, giving away a trip to Hawaii. Each mechanic was able to enter a ticket into the drawing for completing a job in minimum hours. Jace had told Dawn that he had many more tickets in the box than anyone else, and Dawn had been praying that Jace would win the trip. It would be the honeymoon trip that they never really had. In fact, Dawn had a feeling that she would be going to Hawaii. On the day of the drawing, Jace came home coolly and nonchalantly pulled the plane tickets out of his uniform pocket.

Dawn jumped for joy. They would have ten days in Hawaii, all expenses paid! Neither she nor Jace had ever been there. She immediately called her mother and asked her if she would keep the baby. Jace asked his mom and dad if they would stay with the other children. Jace agreed that it would be easier on both moms if they split up the children. Dawn couldn't imagine leaving Joey with anyone but her mother. He was still so little. Dawn's mother was more than willing to tend him. "I'm so glad you can go on this trip," she had said to Dawn. "I think it's just what the two of you need—to get away for a while." Even though Dawn hadn't told her mom much about the difficulties she had had with Jace, her mother must have sensed it.

Dawn had been so excited to go. She loved flying, swimming, and the ocean. She had certified as a scuba diver a few years before. Dawn had been diving in Acapulco and Jamaica but had never been as far as Hawaii. Jace, however, was the opposite. He hated flying and wasn't at all fond of the water. Not once during their entire Hawaii trip did he wear a swimsuit or even short pants. He sat on the beach in his levis and flannel shirt while Dawn went on a guided underwater tour with a paid guide and another tourist. They did enjoy seeing the sights of the island together, however.

Dawn's uncle and aunt lived on a nearby island. Dawn longed to charter an intra-island flight and go see them. She would have loved to see them and knew that they would show them the sights of the island. But when she mentioned it to Jace, he balked at the idea. Dawn didn't bring it up again.

Halfway through the trip, Jace called home to see how the children were doing. Mary answered the phone, and all seemed well. She mentioned that Dawn's mom had come over with Joey so the children could all be together for a while. When Jace got off the phone, he was angry. "Ma doesn't think you trust her with the baby," he said. "You could tell she feels bad that she doesn't have the baby."

"But you agreed that it would be best to split them up," Dawn countered, wondering where this sudden anger was coming from. They were on vacation. Was he going to yell at her in Hawaii, too? Here they were arguing about Joey again. "I asked you the night that you came home with the tickets if it were okay if my mom kept Joey," she continued. "You said it was fine with you!"

"Well, it's not fine with me now," he said somberly.

Dawn had never mentioned James' call about Mary to Jace, but from things Jace had said about his mother and from the things that James insinuated, she would never have left Joey with Mary. She wouldn't have left her little six-month-old baby with anyone but her mother for ten days. She couldn't have gone on the trip otherwise. She went into the bathroom and cried in disappointment. She had wanted to come to Hawaii for ten days of romantic bliss, but Jace had hardly even touched her and here they were in another argument. Why couldn't they get along? Why did Jace go back on nearly everything he agreed to so easily? Dawn always seemed to be off balance.

The plane ride back home seemed so much longer than the ride over. Perhaps it was because Dawn was so anxious to hold her baby again. Although Jace easily dozed off in the airplane seat next to her, she had never been able to sleep sitting up. She tried to rest her head on her arms on the tray in front of her but still couldn't sleep. In desperation she leaned her head on Jace's shoulder. He jerked his shoulder away. "I'm not your couch," he said grumpily. She couldn't imagine him acting this way when they were dating. He had been so sweet, so loving. It was all he could do to keep his hands off of her then. Why had marriage changed things so much? Things seemed to change the moment she said, 'I do.'

When they got home, Dawn wanted nothing but sleep. Her mom said she would bring out Joey that night—until then, Dawn just needed some precious, deep sleep. She had just settled under the covers when Jace came in holding a wooden car. "There's a pinewood derby tonight for cub scouts," he said. "You need to run to the store to get some paint for Ethan."

"Jace, I can't," Dawn protested. "Please. Let me sleep. I didn't sleep at all on the plane. Can't you please take the boys with you and go get some paint?"

Jace walked out of the room angrily as Dawn buried her head under the covers. A fitting conclusion to their blissful Hawaii vacation, she thought.

Chapter 20

Chain Link

Spring had come, and Dawn was under the sink cleaning out the kitchen cupboard. She wanted to put new contact paper down in each of the old, dark wooden cupboards to freshen them up. With her head buried in the cupboard, Jace came into the kitchen to tell her he was running some errands.

"Why are you wasting your time with that?" he asked her. "It will just get dirty again. You know you can't keep up with the housework."

Dawn looked up at him from under the sink, questioning her own move into this house with this continually critical man. "Why can't you just be nice to me?" she pleaded, with tears in her eyes. It must have struck a chord with him somewhere, for when he returned, he was holding a beautiful Easter lily.

"Thank you," Dawn said, standing on her tiptoes to kiss him. He could be so sweet. Jace had taken over the outside, designing fencing to fit the yard and pasture. Dawn was so glad he enjoyed doing yard work—it had just never been her thing, and she had her hands full with the house. Dawn had suggested that a fence would be nice in front to keep Joey from running out into the street when he got a little older.

Jace worked so hard, nights and weekends. Dawn looked out the bedroom window that afternoon and watched him as he cemented in some of the fence posts. Feelings welled up for him in her heart. She knew she loved him. He was so strong. And so handsome. She loved looking at him and admired him for all of the know-how he had around the house. It seemed there was nothing that he didn't know how to fix or build. She was proud to be married to someone who was so able to do so many things. And it was seldom that someone didn't comment to her about what a nice-looking man she was married to. Even their dentist had told Dawn's mom what a handsome son-in-law she had. "And he's such a nice guy, too," her mother had said back.

Pretty bad when even other men noticed his good looks. Jace had told her about a guy at work who was shocked that Jace had been divorced. "Who would leave a good lookin' guy like you?" he had said. The first day they had attended their new church, the Sunday school teacher had commented on Jace's neatly-trimmed black beard. "I wish I could grow a beard like that," he had said to the class.

"Smile, he's giving you a compliment," Dawn whispered to Jace who stared somberly ahead but broke into a grin at Dawn's suggestion.

Joey interrupted her thoughts as Dawn heard him crying in his crib.

"Hi, big boy," she greeted him as she lifted him from the mattress. She held him close to her, inhaling his beautiful baby scent with all that she could gather in. She rubbed her nose in his feather-soft blonde hair. How she loved her beautiful boy! "How about a walk while Daddy works on the fence?"

Dawn put booties on Joey's feet and a light sweater around him. Once outside, she placed him in the baby buggy and breezed by Jace on her way out the driveway.

"We'll be back in a bit," she said cheerfully.

"What the hell are you doing?" he yelled at her. Dawn stopped in her tracks.

"I'm just taking Joey for a walk," she returned, confused at his irritation.

"Then why am I putting up a stinking fence, if you're going to take him out in the road?"

"He's in a buggy, for heaven's sake! Does that mean I can't take him for a walk?" She was livid.

"Then there's no use putting this up!" he yelled.

Dawn kept walking, much faster than she had planned. 'He's crazy,' she thought. 'I've married a crazy man.' Was she to stay in her house, behind the chain-link fence forever? Couldn't his children come and go as they pleased? Did they have to stay in the yard? He was so irrational. What could he be thinking? Couldn't she even take her baby on a walk down her own quiet, dead-end street?

The more she thought, the more she felt imprisoned in something crazy that she must escape. Jace made more demands on her at dinner that night, telling her there wasn't enough "color" in the meal. They had to have a full-course meal, and it had to look good, too. One night a fork had gone flying across the room. "Don't give me that fork anymore!" he had screamed at her. She wasn't sure what was wrong with the fork—they had several forks made from different patterns. She gave it to him again by mistake, a few nights later. He never noticed. She decided it wasn't the fork. That evening he told her that he was through working in the yard as long as she continued to take Joey out on the road in the stroller.

Dawn slept little that night and made plans to escape the next morning after Jace left for work. 'I can't live with someone who's insane,' she thought. 'He's insane.' When she called her dad after a sleepless night, she was in tears and asked if he could come out and help her load up her things.

"Is he brow-beating you?" he asked her. Dawn wasn't really familiar with the term but indeed felt beaten down. Still, Jace had never touched her, so she told her dad no. "Well, if he is," he continued, "I'll come out and clean his clock!" She appreciated his support but didn't want any more conflict.

"No, Dad," she said, "we just have trouble agreeing on things. We just can't get along." Dawn's mom and dad had visitors from out of town staying with them, so Dawn made plans to stay with Paula. She had a nice, large home with plenty of room for her and Joey to stay in. Dawn left Jace a note, telling him she would be at her sister's and needed time to think things through. She left some small presents she scrounged up from some of her own belongings for the children— some perfume for Ida, one of her prize kites for Ethan, and a stuffed animal for Eric. She wrote to Ida:

> Ida,
> I'm so sorry this had to happen, but there's nothing more I can do. I've tried everything I can think of, but nothing is right anymore. I'm sorry for all the fighting you had to listen to—and for times when I got angry. Maybe one day you'll understand. No matter what has happened or what your dad says, I love you all very much. I even love your dad, but we just can't get along. Hope you can use this perfume.
> Love, Dawn

Dawn called Susan, who said she would come over and be there when the children got home from school. Dawn wasn't prepared, however, for the feelings she had as she drove away. She felt like her heart was ripping in two. Indeed it was. She loved this man. She had given him all she had—including herself. She had waited and prayed for years to have a family of her own. Now she had one, and she was tearing it apart; but she couldn't live with the constant criticism and demands and control. She couldn't make him happy. Maybe she was doing him a favor by leaving.

When she got to Paula's, she put Joey down for a nap and called Susan. She poured out her heart to her, telling her how much she loved her brother but couldn't take any more arguing. Growing up, there was rarely an argument in her parents' home. Her father never said a bad thing about her mother, and they would have been in a world of hurt had they said something derogatory about their mother. Yet, all James and Mary did were argue—in front of everyone. Dawn knew she didn't want a marriage like that. Susan acted as go-between between Jace and Dawn. Susan told him, "You had reasons for ending your marriage with Juanita, but what's your excuse with Dawn?" Dawn appreciated her support and spent most of the evening talking to her while Paula looked after Joey.

When she woke up the next morning, she dressed and walked downstairs and fixed herself a bowl of cereal. As she sat there in the kitchen, she couldn't remember a time when she felt more depressed. She felt so alone and hurt so bad. The hurt was nearly unbearable; she had put so much of herself into her marriage. Things just couldn't end this way. Tears rolled down her cheeks and into her Cheerios.

Chapter 21

Walls

Somehow, between the tears and the anguish and Susan, Dawn was returning home. Jace had agreed to go to counseling if she would come back home. She felt like she hadn't been married long enough to really give things a chance. She must be doing something wrong. She would try harder.

Susan's husband helped Dawn load up her things, and she went back. As she tried to rearrange things in the living room, Jace ranted about the mess. "Well, I can see I made the right decision," Dawn said sarcastically.

Jace stopped. Maybe that was the key, she thought. Use humor. That evening was another note on her pillow from Ida:

> Dear Dawnette,
> I thought that I would & should write you a little note about how I feel. So here goes. I have been a little bratt quite often. I haven't given you any appologies because at first, I didn't mean them. But now I am sorry because I know you have been through Beep & back with my dad & I haven't made anything easyer. I will miss you lots if I get to live with my mom. Really, you are pretty much the only one I miss, besides Joey. If you ever have to leave, I wouldn't come back, because the same exact thing will happen. I know I should have probably warned you about how he is, but I didn't think things would be bad like this. If I ever had another choice for a step-mom, beleive it or not, I would pick you! I am proud to have you as my step-mom. You are pretty! I love you.
> > Love you always,
> > Ida
> P.S. This is more like a short letter.

Dawn had an appointment the next day with her gynecologist. Jace had agreed to see the counselor that her doctor recommended so that he would be "impartial." He didn't want to go to anyone that Dawn or her family happened to know or to anyone their bishop might recommend. When Dawn asked the doctor for a recommendation for a marriage counselor, he gave her only one name: Dr. Samuel.

As they sat in front of him, Dawn unloaded with everything she saw in their marriage as trouble. She told him, "Please tell me what I'm doing wrong and I'll change it. I don't want my marriage to fail." Jace sat quietly, for the most part, but didn't fail to tell the doctor all of the things he could find wrong with Dawn.

"Jace, tell me about your marriage with Juanita," Dr. Samuel looked at him through his thick, oval glasses.

"Not much to tell," Jace answered.

"Why did your marriage end?" Dr. Samuel queried.

"We just grew apart," Jace said evasively.

Dr. Samuel looked him squarely in the eyes. "I'm going to tell you what I think, Jace, and you tell me if I'm right or wrong."

"Okay," Jace answered.

"I think, Jace, that when your ex-wife left you, she not only tore your heart out, she ripped it up and smashed it into little pieces."

"That's exactly what she did," Jace said, without hesitation. "I swore I'd never let another woman do that to me again." A light bulb went off in Dawn's head.

"Well, this is how I see it," Dr. Samuel continued. "You've built a big wall around you, and unless you make a window for this woman and let her in, you're not going to have a marriage."

'So that's it,' Dawn thought. He was pushing her away from him, consciously or unconsciously, with the constant criticism so she couldn't get too close to him and hurt him like Juanita did. When Dawn became his wife, she was in the same position that Juanita had been in, to hurt him.

"I'd like to have a session with you alone," Dr. Samuel said, "to talk about your previous relationship with Juanita."

"About what?" Jace asked. Dawn could feel his defenses going up.

"I'd need to ask you some questions about your first marriage."

"What kind of questions?" Jace became more and more defensive as Dr. Samuel attempted to set up an appointment with Jace. He finally got Jace to say that he would see him the following week.

As Jace drove them home, Dawn's thoughts turned to the session they had just had with Dr. Samuel. Maybe that's why this all started the moment they got married. Up until their marriage, she wasn't a viable threat to him. Once she was his wife, she had more power to hurt him, and he'd already been hurt so badly already. Her heart went out to him. 'I must make him feel so secure,' she thought to herself, 'that he can see I'll never be a threat to him, that I will never hurt him.' She vowed to herself to love him even more diligently, to ignore his hurtful comments and criticism as just a defense mechanism, and to do all she could to make him feel secure in his marriage to her.

When next week came and it was time for his appointment, Jace refused to go. Dawn had hoped that he would go but wasn't surprised at his refusal. Dawn went instead. "I'm willing to work on or change anything I'm doing wrong," she told Dr. Samuel.

"You're not the problem, Dawn. You married into a train wreck of a family, and they're blaming you. When I confronted Jace about his ex-wife," Dr. Samuel explained to her, "we connected for a very brief moment. I could see it in his eyes, and I could also see that it scared him." Dawn knew he was right. "I'm sorry to say, however, that there's little I can do, if anything, if he won't come in." Dawn knew he was right about that, too. "See what you can do to encourage him," he told her as he shook her hand goodbye. As she walked out the door, Dawn knew that Jace would never return.

Chapter 22

No Marks

The move out and then back in and then the counselor visit had been all the upheaval Dawn could take for a while. She decided that she would stay with Jace and do all she could to make him feel secure in their marriage and make him happy. Even Susan had told her, "Don't even think of divorce as an option." So she put it out of her mind. She concentrated on the joy Joey brought her and devoted herself to being wife and mother.

Joey had grown into a darling toddler, and it wasn't long before Dawn was pregnant again. She was overjoyed and thought that this might help bring the two of them together. But Dawn hadn't counted on another wildcard: Ida.

Ida became more and more rebellious as time went on. Her relationship with her father was wanting, and she longed to go live with her own mother. "I've got enough to put Dad away," she told Dawn one day. Dawn asked her what she meant. "One night before you guys started dating, he'd been drinking a lot." Dawn acknowledged to herself that that was likely true—Jace himself told her he used to drink a great deal, but she hadn't known him to drink as long as she had known him. "Well, one night when he put me to bed, he French-kissed me."

Dawn didn't know what to say. She excused Jace's actions, telling herself that if he were drunk, he didn't know what he was doing. She had never known him to be sexually inappropriate with Ida at all during their marriage. She decided to dismiss it as another one of Ida's stories. Still, in the back of her mind it bothered her. She had caught Ida many times lying and developed less and less trust for her. But there must be some reason for her acting out. She was wearing lots of makeup and dressing more promiscuously.

One day Dawn was looking for the scissors and remembered that

Ida had been using them. She went into Ida's room but couldn't see them on her dresser. She opened the top drawer, and lying on top of the scissors was a folded piece of paper. Dawn opened it to see a pencil drawing of a penis, labeled underneath in Ida's handwriting, "Kevin's size." Dawn felt that Ida had put it there for her to find—but when she showed it to Jace, he just yelled at her for snooping in Ida's things. A report that Ida was passing out condoms on the bus further concerned her, but Jace didn't seem to want to deal with any of it.

When Ida told Dawn that she wanted to have a baby, she really became worried. 'Does she think she wants this because I'm pregnant?' Dawn wondered. Ida had seemed so happy when Dawn told her she was pregnant again, but maybe deep down she was jealous. Dawn wasn't sure what was really happening with Ida, but she decided to commit herself to Jace and disregard Ida's accusations.

Ida dropped another bomb unintentionally one day when she mentioned the incident when her father got shot. "You know," Ida had said, "when he went to bed with that lady." Dawn didn't know she knew about it. Why did she know those details? She later confronted Jace.

"You never told me you slept with her," she said to him.

"Sure I did," Jace said nonchalantly. "You just weren't listening."

'No wonder it was all the gossip in Snowcrest,' Dawn thought, knowing full well that he had left that detail out of his story. His comments often made her question the validity of her own reality.

A week later, Ida spent the night at her friend Ashley's, who lived at the end of their road. The next morning Dawn called to tell Ida it was time to come home.

"She's washing her hair," Ashley said, "and can't talk right now."

"I'll wait," Dawn replied, becoming suspicious. She could hear Ashley talking to someone in the background.

A few moments passed, and Ashley got back on the phone. "She's not here," Ashley admitted. Dawn queried her some more. "She went with some boys last night. She hasn't come back yet." Ashley further admitted that she didn't know who the boys were. Dawn dreaded calling Jace at work. She knew how he liked to shoot the messenger. Dawn was grateful when Ida soon returned.

Things got worse when some of Dawn's friends had asked Ida to babysit for them. When they brought her back that night, they had some disturbing things to report. "When we got home, Ida had put the baby to bed," she said, "and the baby was fine. But there was a boy there. He took off running when we pulled up. Ida said he was a friend of hers."

When Dawn questioned Ida, she said it was a boy who just happened to be walking by their apartment. Ida didn't know him, she claimed. He just came in, and they talked for a while.

A few weeks later, Ashley's father called, waking them out of a sound sleep. Jace talked to him momentarily and then started pulling on his pants. "Where are you going?" Dawn said sleepily.

"I'm going with Ashley's dad to look for Ida," he said, irritated. "Apparently he went to pick them up from skating, and they're nowhere to be found. I think it's time I gave her a whipping."

"Yeah," Dawn agreed sleepily.

Jace and Ashley's dad later found the girls in the mall parking lot. When Jace brought Ida home, Dawn heard Jace downstairs yelling at her. "Do you hate me?" he screamed at her. "Do you want to hurt me? Do you want to worry me to death?" he yelled.

Dawn could hear Ida crying. 'He's not actually beating her, is he?' she thought. No. She had never seen Jace hit any of the children. 'But maybe she does need a spanking,' she thought. She had been lying so much lately. The yelling subsided, and Jace came to bed. He was so angry that Dawn didn't dare say anything to him.

The next morning Ida went next door to see her friend, Julie. When she didn't come home, Dawn became concerned and called Jace at work. "I'll take care of it when I get home," he said. "She probably just needs some space."

Dawn saw Julie's mother in her backyard and went out to talk to her over the fence. "I've called Social Services," she told Dawn angrily before Dawn could say anything. "I don't know what's going on in your house, but apparently your husband's been beating Ida, and you've been letting him do it! She's staying with us. And, by the way, she thinks she's pregnant."

"What?" Dawn said, incredulously. She couldn't believe what she was hearing, but soon after Jace got home from work, Social Services, Ida, and a sheriff were at her door.

"We'd like to see the rest of the house," they said. Dawn took them into the kitchen, and they seemed to be satisfied. 'So if my house were dirty,' Dawn thought, 'would that mean I was a child abuser?' She had never gone through anything even close to this before. She was incredulous.

They asked Jace several questions. Dawn couldn't believe how cool and calm he was—he was so smooth—too smooth. Dawn, on the other hand, was livid. She was angry at Ida—how could she say such things?—and angry with her neighbors for believing her. As she looked at Ida, Ida looked at Dawn with such hatred in her dark eyes that Dawn felt it was another person. Where had cute, perky Ida gone? Who was this dark, sullen, moody girl in front of her?

Jace admitted to the sheriff that he had spanked her—with a belt— and told the sheriff what she had been doing to provoke him to do so. Ida had shown them marks on her buttocks. Dawn wondered if Jace had made her take her pants down when he spanked her. "Ida," Jace looked her directly in the eyes, "have I ever in your entire life spanked you before?"

"No," she admitted.

"Have I ever done anything to hurt you?" he asked her earnestly. Dawn was impressed with how he was handling everything.

"No," she said.

"Are you pregnant?" Dawn asked her anxiously, trying to hide the anger that she felt at that moment.

"I don't know," she said belligerently. "The night I went to babysit, I had sex with the guy that was there."

"Did you even know him?" Dawn said, becoming more agitated.

"No, I didn't know him!" Ida retorted angrily. She looked at Dawn with hatred. Dawn didn't know what to think or believe anymore.

"Well, I can see that there's some feelings here, especially with your wife," the social worker said. "I think it would be best if Ida spent the night at a group home we have for troubled children. If all goes well, you can pick her up tomorrow. That will give everyone a chance to calm down."

Dawn knew the comments were directed at her. She was resentful that Jace could be so unnervingly calm through all of this. The woman left with Ida after she went downstairs and got a change of clothes. On his way out the door, the sheriff said flippantly to Jace, "Next time you spank her, just make sure you don't leave any marks."

Chapter 23

Daughter

Ida came home the next night with Jace and seemed calmer. Dawn had calmed down but was unsure of who this girl that she was living with really was. She vowed not to let Ida upset her for the sake of the baby. She did no confronting and tried to let Ida have the space she needed. Dawn just wanted a calm, peaceful household. Jace had told Ida that she was grounded for two weeks and would go nowhere. Dawn was hoping that in those two weeks she would settle down. She was grateful when Ida told her that she had started her period. Dawn still didn't know what to think about the boy who was with Ida while she was babysitting.

Apparently Ida convinced her mother to sue for custody. Dawn had no idea what she was telling her mother but was sure it wasn't the truth. They received documents from Juanita's lawyer ordering psychological evaluations on Jace, Juanita and their children to determine the best placement for them.

Ida did seem to calm down and spent a lot of time in her bedroom. A week later on a sunny Saturday afternoon, Ida took a shower, did her hair, and put on lots of makeup.

"Why all the makeup if you're grounded?" Dawn asked her.

"No reason," Ida said. "I just felt like it. I'm tired of being grungy."

But Dawn realized the reason for all the makeup when Ethan came running into their bedroom Sunday morning.

"Ida's gone!" he exclaimed. "She went out through the basement window—it's wide open."

Jace and Dawn spent the day trying to find her. They called all of her friends that they could think of, but no one seemed to know or admit to where she was. She must have been angry with Ashley. She and her family had been out of town Saturday night and came back to a home that had been trashed. Ida had written graffiti all over Ashley's bedroom with many choice words and her signature. Ashley's parents were thinking of pressing charges.

Jace traced Ida to a home full of children who had "crashed" there. It looked like there had been quite a party there the night before, but they refused to let Jace in; he had the feeling that Ida was there, but no one was being cooperative. It wasn't long before they heard from Juanita, saying that Ida had made it to her home in Wyoming. Somehow Ida had orchestrated the whole thing. Jace was furious and intent on bringing her back home.

Ashley's bedroom wasn't the only one to be trashed. Dawn went downstairs and found Ida's room also had been trashed. Ethan, in tears, easily admitted to what he had done. He was angry for what Ida had done.

"I hate her," he said, resentful at her acting out, causing problems, and running away.

A few days later, Dawn woke up to a gush of water in her bed. She woke up Jace. "My water broke!" she exclaimed. She was surprised, as her water hadn't broken with Joey. She wasn't sure what to do, though, as she had no labor pains. She called the hospital and was told that she would need to come in and be "started" to avoid infection.

Dawn didn't like the hard contractions that came with being started. Labor was certainly shorter that way, though. Jace was even less attentive with this baby than the first. As Dawn winced through contraction after contraction, Jace made phone call after phone call to authorities in Wyoming trying to get Ida back. He was angry that Ida was with Juanita when he was the one who had custody.

Although Dawn had ached for a baby girl and deep down felt that it was a girl growing inside of her, Jace had wanted it to be a surprise. Ultrasounds weren't available when his three children were born, and that's how he liked it. So again, the baby's gender wasn't certain until the final push. Dawn was ecstatic to learn that her baby was indeed a girl—and what a beautiful girl she was. She looked so different from Joey. When the nurses brought her to Dawn, she couldn't believe how much hair she had—a bushel of very black hair.

"That must have tickled," one of the nurses said, jokingly. 'Not hardly,' Dawn thought. But she was so beautiful. Dawn could tell from her first glances at her that she would take after her father. Her skin was noticeably darker than Dawn's, and that gorgeous black hair! And no blue eyes for this baby. Her dark eyes matched her dark hair. She was definitely her father's daughter.

Naming Joey had been such an argument but not so with this baby girl. She was such a beauty that both Dawn and Jace wanted to name her after one of the most beautiful women in the world. Her dark eyes, brows and hair reminded them of Elizabeth Taylor in her younger days. Neither of them was fond of the name Elizabeth but both liked the name Taylor for a girl. And so she became Taylor Malone. Dawn was amazed at how easily they agreed. But that was the only thing that came easily.

It was Dawn's first Sunday morning after coming home from the hospital. Taylor was in the bassinet in their bedroom as Joey once was. They had tried putting her in Joey's room, but the first time she cried she scared him. He couldn't tolerate her crying; so she would stay in their bedroom until she slept through the night. As the morning sun crept through their bedroom window, Dawn took the opportunity to talk to Jace when he stirred awake.

"I couldn't go back to sleep this morning," she told him, "after I fed Taylor. I've been thinking a lot about Ida, Jace, and I … I think you need to let her go." She didn't look at him but stared toward the bedroom window as she spoke.

"What?" he said incredulously. "Let Juanita have her?"

"Well, think about it," Dawn said. "All Ida's wanted to do the past while is be with her mother. If you make her come back here, all she'll do is resent you—and all of us. But if you let her stay, I think that pretty soon she'll miss us and want to come back. You're here, her brothers are here, and now she has a baby sister. She won't want to stay up there with Juanita and Darren for long."

"I don't know," Jace said. "All I know is that I'm sick of this shit." Dawn could feel the anger welling up inside of him.

"I just think you need to let her go," Dawn concluded. "At least for now. If you don't, I think you'll lose her altogether."

So Jace let her go. At least physically he let her go. But he held Dawn as ransom. And Taylor. His resentment—that Juanita seemed to win this round—was focused on his current family, not his past one.

Again Dawn had trouble breastfeeding, and again it was most likely due to stress. Dawn was more determined than ever this time to be successful, and Jace was ever more cruel in his treatment of Dawn.

"Oh," he said, as he came into their bedroom one night as Dawn was feeding Taylor, "you're doing your impersonation."

"What impersonation?" Dawn asked him innocently.

"Your human-pacifier impersonation," he said sarcastically.

Dawn was devastated. She was trying so hard, but she felt like such a failure. She loved the times where she could sit and hold her babies close and nourish them. But they got very little nourishment. At the next baby visit, the doctor told her she would have to supplement. "She weighs less than five pounds," she said. "You're going to have to supplement."

Dawn came home in tears, after stopping at the store to buy formula. 'Oh, well,' she thought. 'Jace will be happy.' She wondered why he gave her such a hard time about nursing. Juanita had nursed their children. Was he jealous of her babies? Why did he have to be so cruel?

Dawn was not the only one he pushed away. Jace seemed to have made a vow the day Taylor was born: if he couldn't have Ida, he would not have Taylor. Taylor didn't seem to exist in his eyes. She was so beautiful and such a good baby, but Jace hadn't bonded with her at all. He seldom picked her up, if ever. Dawn wondered if it were because he resented Dawn for having so much joy in her little daughter while his oldest daughter was away from him. Still, Taylor was as much his as Ida was. Why punish Taylor? Or was punishing Taylor his way of punishing Dawn?

Punishment was the name of the game, though. It didn't seem to matter what Dawn did or what she tried, she was criticized for it. At the same time, another dynamic began to take place: Ethan and Eric were elevated above the rest of them. Dawn was left with the care of them much of the time, but Jace took more and more authority away from her by negating her views and any attempts at discipline. The more he elevated Ethan and Eric, the more he denigrated Joey—and Taylor didn't exist at all. Dawn thought that maybe things would improve when Ethan and Eric went for their summer visit, but still Dawn felt isolated after they left. She waited for Jace to come home, but when he did come home, all she felt was his anger and resentment. So she lived somewhere between deep loneliness and the wrath of her husband.

One morning Dawn saw a program on Oprah about "misogynists." She had never heard the term, but it certainly seemed to describe Jace. Men who hate women. He might not hate all women, but he certainly seemed to dislike his wife. Dawn purchased and read the book and even pointed out some of the things to Jace, hoping to break through, but got nowhere. Dawn tried reasoning and got nowhere. She tried pleading and got nowhere. She didn't know where to turn. Counseling had met a dead end. Each day seemed to be a dead end, just like the street they lived on.

Dawn sat down and read through the journal she had been keeping. She needed perspective. Phrases from it caught her attention. They all added up to a dead end.

"Jace became angry today that I took Joey to the doctor. The doctor said he had a bad sore throat. Jace was angry that it cost $20 …"

"I stayed in bed today with the flu. Jace complained that I didn't get up to fix him and the children lunch. When I asked him to hold Taylor and give her a drink, because I was vomiting, he told me he had work to do. He took out the garbage for Ethan and did Eric's dishes …"

"Mom came out today and helped me vacuum. When I told her not to move the furniture, that it would make Jace angry, she looked at me with a worried look …"

"Jace got mad at me on the way to dinner to meet Mom and Dad because we had to hurry to get there. Then he was mad because I didn't tell him that we were going for birthday cake afterward. I assumed he knew, as I had a present for Dad …"

"Jace got mad when the car was empty and we needed money for gas. He put in $5. He wanted me to drive but criticized me the whole time …"

"Jace yelled at me tonight because we ran out of bananas …"

"Jace got mad at me tonight because I walked in front of him while he was playing pacman …"

"I invited some friends over for dinner. Jace said okay at first, but when it was time for them to come, he raged at me until I was in tears. He called them 'a-holes' and said he didn't want them in our house. When they got here, dinner was very late and I was a mess, but I tried to keep up a good front. I guess I'll never have friends over again …"

And it went on and on and on …

Dawn had gotten a part-time tutoring job for some wealthy people in town. She tutored at their private school while her mom watched the children. Dawn enjoyed it, was paid very well, got to see her mom, and it gave her a break from home. But home was a heartache. No matter how hard she tried, she couldn't penetrate Jace's tough, tough exterior. He wouldn't let her in. She didn't think he would ever let her in. She could stand the iciness and isolation no longer and made plans to move, this time permanently, feeling she had no other choice.

Coincidentally, an old friend of hers and his family were moving to California, and they were putting their house up for sale. Dawn talked to them about the possibility of renting it until it sold. As no one had purchased it by the time they left for California, Dawn made plans to move. Everything was arranged for a Friday morning, after Jace left for work. Since all the children were with their mother, Dawn was glad that at least she wouldn't have to tell them goodbye.

Friday morning, Dawn was restless and got up when Jace did. As he started for the door, she touched his arm. He stopped momentarily, and Dawn stood on her tiptoes and kissed him goodbye. She knew in her heart that she still loved him, but she also knew that it hurt too much to stay with him. She couldn't bear things the way they were. She went downstairs and typed him a note on the computer. She told him that she hated to leave the way Juanita did—for him to come home and find her gone—and that she was sorry, but she couldn't do it any other way. (She didn't want Jace to know where she was going—she was very unsure of his anger—and had plans to start her life anew.) She poured out her heart to Jace, telling him that she didn't want their marriage to end and that she still had feelings for him, but she couldn't live the way she had been living.

Dawn had confided in her sister-in-law, Anne, about her plans. Anne stopped by, walking in on a mess of boxes half-packed. Anne couldn't contain her tears as she hugged Dawn goodbye.

After the difficult kiss that morning with Jace, knowing it was goodbye, Dawn was able to keep her emotions in check—until she started packing some of the Christmas decorations. She came across Christmas stockings she had embroidered—matching ones saying "mommy" and "daddy"—and broke down. She left the "daddy" stocking there and again had the horrible feeling that she was tearing out half her heart.

The feelings stayed as she pulled away, a passenger in her dad's truck. They took her belongings to what would be her new home. Her parents and sister helped her set up the beds and crib, so Dawn could sleep there that night, but most of the unpacking was still left to do. As Dawn settled in, she called Jace's mom and dad to tell them of her decision. She didn't tell them where she was but told them that she had moved so that they could be there for Jace that night. She wanted him to have some support. She knew it would be a shock to him to come home that night and was feeling guilty, in spite of her continual pleadings to him. She took care of her babies, got them in bed, and then fell into her own bed exhausted and still in tears.

When she awoke the next day, she was surprised at how noisy the neighborhood was. Although she wasn't right in the city, there certainly was a lot more traffic than in small Wheatfield. It was usually the crowing of one of their roosters that woke her up, but here it was noisy cars that resided much closer to her than any did on her acre lot in Wheatfield. It was a beautiful house, and she loved how it was decorated, but she still missed her humble home in Wheatfield. She missed the large yard, the garden, even all of the animals that Jace had brought in. But she went about making the home temporarily her own and unpacked her boxes.

Chapter 24

Sick

Dawn had been away from Jace for nearly a week. She had spent much of her spare time writing Jace a very long letter, still trying to plead, reason, get somewhere with him. She had told her employers about her move, and they were more than supportive. They offered to increase her employment to full time and increase her salary so that she could have insurance if a divorce went through. It was such a blessing to Dawn to have such supportive and understanding employers. They were really more than employers—they were her friends.

Wednesday morning, Dawn dropped her children off at her mother's and went to the school to tutor the oldest daughter, Ellen. As she sat across from her, Dawn began to feel very ill. She told her that she was sorry but was feeling very bad all of a sudden, left and went back to her mother's. She was glad she left, because she soon began to vomit, and continued to vomit and have diarrhea the rest of the day and the next. Her parents took care of her, and Dawn tried to drink Gatorade but couldn't keep it down for long—and the vomiting and diarrhea continued. The following morning, her father insisted on taking her to the doctor.

"It's just the flu," Dawn protested, as she really didn't feel like going anywhere. "I'm not throwing up as much."

"You've got nothing left to throw up!" he replied. "You'd better get dressed. It's been forty-eight hours now, and you're not any better."

Dawn followed her father into the Insta-Care facility. As he registered her, Dawn sat down in a chair and put her head in her hands. She was so weak, it was hard for her to sit and hold up her head.

The nurse soon came and ushered her to an exam room, and Dawn lay down on the paper-covered, upholstered mauve table. The nurse took her blood pressure and then quickly left the room. The doctor came in immediately and listened to her heart. Soon her dad was in the room, and the doctor was asking him questions about how long she had been ill.

The doctor came over to Dawn and looking down at her said, "I'm calling the hospital right now to have you pre-admitted, so that your father can take you over there and you can go right in. I'd call an ambulance, but I think it might be faster for your dad to take you. You're extremely dehydrated, and your blood pressure is dangerously low." Dawn had remembered hearing "sixty over forty" but wasn't sure. Her head was clouded, and she felt so very weak. She couldn't believe she was going to the hospital from having the flu a couple of days.

Her dad quickly drove to the nearby hospital. The Insta-Care doctor had certainly prepared them, as they were met with a stretcher, and Dawn was wheeled into a room where she was poked and prodded.

"How long has it been since you've had anything to drink?" one nurse questioned as she tried to get a needle in her arm.

"I've been drinking Gatorade," was Dawn's reply. Apparently not enough, though, as more than once a nurse tried unsuccessfully to get a needle into her veins.

"You're very dehydrated," another nurse said, finally successful in getting an IV in her arm after bruising the other one in a couple of places. They took a sample of her blood off to the lab, as a bottle dripped nourishing water into her veins.

Soon a nurse came back and said to Dawn, "It's a good thing we got you in here fast. Your potassium was so low, your heart could have stopped beating at any time." Although she didn't realize it at the time, her father had saved her life.

Dawn was too weak to have it all register, but she was still having a hard time believing she was so sick from two days of the flu.

The doctors came in and asked her question after question. Dawn answered yes to one: "Had she been camping lately?"

When she replied yes and that she had swum in the mountain lake, the doctors suggested that she might have "giardia." After other tests came back negative, they started her on a medicine to treat the giardia. Dawn hated it. It left her with a horrible taste in her mouth and nauseated. She thought it ironic that they were treating her nausea with a drug that made her nauseous. She had nothing to eat but jello water and broth to the point that it sickened her. The diarrhea continued, embarrassingly so.

Two mornings later, Dawn awoke early to find she had soiled her bed again. She seemed to have no control over the continual diarrhea.

"I think it's useless to give you pajama bottoms," the nurse told her as she changed her sheets again. Dawn apologized, feeling bad for the trouble she was causing the nurses and frustrated at her lack of control. She had never known anything like this. She felt so weak. As the nurse walked out of the room, Dawn's phone rang, startling her. It was 5:30 a.m.

"You bitch." Dawn recognized Jace's voice. Dawn had told Mary that she was in the hospital, hoping she would tell Jace and that he would be concerned about her. "You f-ing whore. I'm gonna get the kids. What makes you think your a-hole parents can f-ing have them?" Dawn wondered if he had been drinking, but that didn't seem likely so early in the morning. She knew he would be leaving for work soon. "I want your damn ring, too—it's not yours anymore. And if you think that you're covered by insurance, whore, you're crazy. I'm canceling it today, bitch. F- you." The phone went dead.

Dawn lay in the stark, sterile, dark room with thoughts churning through her mind. She pictured a showdown between Jace and her father in her parents' front yard. She thought of a hospital bill growing each day with no coverage. She worried about her children being taken. What had she done? Tears rolled down her cheeks. Certainly if the hospital personnel knew about the threatening call she had just received, they would stop it. But she had told them nothing about her separation. She was having a hard time dealing with the fact herself. Was the stress of the separation the real cause of her illness?

She watched the clock, worrying, thinking, crying. When it was finally 8:00 a.m., she phoned her lawyer. He allayed her fears.

"Any judge is going to look very poorly on someone who cancels his wife's insurance when she's in the hospital. In fact, I'm not sure he can take you off the policy right now. He has no right to go into your parents' yard. Tell your parents that if he shows up to keep the children in the house and call the police. And the ring isn't his, either—it's yours."

Later that afternoon, Dawn was pleasantly surprised when Dr. Samuel came into her room. The psychiatric facility he worked in adjoined the hospital, and he explained that he saw her name on the admission record and had stopped by to see how she was doing. When she told him about the phone call she had received that morning, he asked her, true to counseling mode, what she thought about the call.

"I think it means that he's really hurting," she replied. "That he loves me."

Dr. Samuel nodded. "I imagine he is really hurting," he replied. "Usually, though, when a loved one is in the hospital, that is a time when amends are made and feelings become tender. If he doesn't treat you well when you're in the hospital …"

Dawn made the connection, but didn't want to deal with that thought. She chose, instead, to dwell on the fact that Dr. Samuel seemed to agree when she said that Jace really loved her. If he didn't care about her, he wouldn't have been so angry, would he?

Five days later, Dawn found herself still in the hospital. The diarrhea was beginning to subside, but the medicine still made her nauseous. Still, she felt a little stronger each day. That afternoon, one of her neighbors from Wheatfield came to see her. As she was sitting talking to Dawn, she noticed Jace coming down the hall. "Your husband's here, dear," she told Dawn. Dawn's heart leapt in her chest. "I'll talk to you later," she said as she bid Dawn goodbye. Jace waited in the hall until she left.

As he came in the room, Dawn teared up.

"I came to bring you this," he said as he handed Dawn his ring.

"I can't keep that here," Dawn said. "You keep it. I gave it to you." She put it back in his hand.

Jace looked at her, his face full of pain.

"Can't we work things out?" Dawn pleaded with him.

"I don't know. I don't know about anything anymore." Dawn could hear the anger in his voice. "I've got to go," he said nervously. "Hope you feel better," he said, as he walked out of the room.

"I love you, Jace," she said after him.

A few minutes later, the evening nurse came in the room. "Was that your husband standing out in the hallway?" Dawn shook her head. "He's so good looking! Wow, what a handsome man you're married to. There's not many like him around."

"Thanks," Dawn said weakly, thinking to herself that somehow she just couldn't let him go.

Chapter 25

Reconciliation

A few days later, Dawn was able to go home to her parents. When she left, she was told that "your output is still more than your input," but she was on the road to recovery. Still, she had lost a lot of weight—it was the first time in her life that she weighed less than what it said on her driver's license—but she was grateful to get home and start eating a little solid food—anything but jello and broth! A couple of weeks passed, she got stronger and stronger and moved back to her new temporary home.

One morning her mother called to tell her that Ida had phoned. "I gave her your phone number there," she said. "I'm sorry if you didn't want me to, but she seemed really anxious to talk to you."

It wasn't long before Ida phoned. "We figured out you weren't there anymore," she said. "Dad sounds drunk on the phone, and we could never hear anything in the background. The boys aren't coming back," she continued. "Mom's going to keep them here. They're afraid of Dad. He threatened her, and he always brings a gun when he comes. We were supposed to meet him, but Mom didn't go. She's going to court to ask for custody. Don't go back to him, Dawnette. He'll just hurt you and your children."

As usual, Dawn didn't know whether to believe Ida or not. She seemed so sincere. Still, Dawn had no reason at all to trust Ida. Not long after Ida moved back in with Juanita, they had received a bill from a psychiatric hospital in Wyoming. When Jace requested a report from the hospital, the admission records said that Ida had accused a boy there of rape. The police investigation turned up no evidence, and it was determined that Ida had been lying.

Jace called Dawn, and when she told him about the phone call, he became increasingly angry. "I didn't threaten to shoot anyone," he said angrily, but she knew that he carried a gun. "I went to Wyoming and waited and waited. She never showed up, so I called and told her that she'd never do that again. Then I came home and called my lawyer. I have to wait till we go to court—they might as well be out of the country as in the next state," he said with frustration.

So whom to believe? Dawn recalled the psychological evaluation they received on Ida stating she was a "pathological liar, conduct-disordered, oppositional, defiant, disobedient, impulsive, provocative, difficult to control, narcissistic, egocentric, self-centered, selfish and demanding" and decided she couldn't trust this mixed-up girl who had called her on the phone.

She began talking more and more to Jace over the phone. His story about Juanita seemed genuine. He was very upset that he couldn't get the boys back. He had made no more threats to Dawn or their children and had not cancelled her on the insurance. Dawn had seen that threat as an attempt to keep her from leaving permanently. She wrote to herself the things that troubled her most about the relationship. Much of it—the controlling, the criticism, the anger—she really didn't understand. She knew they wouldn't make it without a counselor. She suggested to Jace's parents that maybe having a contract would help. They suggested it to Jace, and he seemed agreeable. She wrote up a contract and read it to Jace over the phone. He gave his input, changed some of the terms, and Dawn felt they were on solid ground. Dawn wanted to live apart while they went to counseling. She didn't want to have to move again; but Jace refused to go to any counseling at all unless they were back together. "I'm not going to date you," he said.

So Dawn conceded. Jace agreed to a relationship with Taylor—that he would quit ignoring her and help in the care giving. Dawn agreed to work more hours, which she had already worked out with her employer. Apparently Jace had big money concerns since taking out bankruptcy once before. The biggest concession of all was that Jace agreed to go to counseling for an entire year, to work with the counselor and do everything the counselor suggested for improvement. Dawn felt secure that he would keep the contract. She knew that it had been hard on him not having her or his children there with him that summer.

To be sure of things, Dawn called Dr. Samuel and told him about the contract, seeing if he approved of her moving back in. "It seems to be a step in the right direction," he said. He gave Dawn names of people who would be good to see, as Jace refused to see Dr. Samuel. Dawn read a list of names that their insurance would cover to Jace, not telling him that Dr. Samuel had recommended them, and they chose a man named Dr. Thomas.

When the weekend came, Jace and his brother, Dave, moved Dawn and all of her belongings back home. Dawn's parents didn't agree at all with her decision to move back but, other than refusing to do any physical moving themselves, supported her as much as they could. It was different than her first move back—Jace wasn't angry and screaming at her but was kind and helpful. He also picked up Taylor and held her close—something Dawn hadn't seen him do in months. Joey seemed glad to be back home, and Jace was also cute with him. That night, Dawn was exhausted from the move, and her head was pounding. Jace wanted to be intimate, which was something else Dawn had not seen from him in a long time. Jace understood her exhaustion, however, and they postponed that reunion one more night.

When they met with Dr. Thomas, Dawn was pleased. A tall, soft-spoken younger man, he was easy to talk to. Dawn expounded on all the things she saw as problems, as Dr. Thomas took many notes. "Boy, let me roll up my sleeves," he said, when Dawn told him all that had gone on. Jace said very little but seemed to like him. It was a relief to Dawn to pour out her heart to someone, telling him all the things she had been experiencing. She put great faith in their sessions that all would be healed.

Chapter 26

Court

"Maybe I should just go up there, shoot them all, and then shoot myself," Jace said to Dawn, frustrated at his inability to get his boys back home.

"It'll all work out," Dawn tried to console him. "Doing that wouldn't solve anything." She had never heard him make statements like that before, and it worried her. They had an appointment at court the next week. Jace's lawyer threatened to "throw the book" at Juanita, charging her with contempt of court for refusing to bring the boys back, among other things.

This time Dawn would be going to court also in support of Jace. She had never been in a courtroom before, and the morning of court dressed in a classic, white jumpsuit that she loved. She had told her employers that she would be coming in later that morning to tutor. She dropped Joey and the baby off at her mother's and met Jace in the parking lot.

Dawn took Jace's hand, and as they walked into the foyer of the courthouse, Jace's lawyer took him aside to talk to him. Sitting in some chairs by the elevator were Ida, the boys, and their grandmother. Ida immediately stood up and came over and hugged Dawn. Dawn hugged her back, surprised at the show of affection for her and seeming lack of affection for her father. Jace motioned for Dawn to join him in the next room, and Dawn followed him. They sat in some padded chairs directly opposite Juanita, which made Dawn nervous; but Jace was his cool, composed self. He almost seemed to enjoy sitting opposite her. No words were spoken as they waited for the hearing to begin. Jace explained to Dawn that his lawyer didn't feel she was needed in the hearing. Her presence outside the room was enough to show that he was still married and their home intact.

In the psychological evaluations, the psychologist ruled in favor of the boys staying with Jace. In reference to testing on Jace and Juanita, the report stated that "both mother and father are troubled individuals who struggle with chronic difficulties in relating intimately to other adults. Both also have a strong tendency to project total blame on the other, and both convey this contempt to the children. However, Eric and Ethan see their current home environment as nurturing. Eric does feel a very strong attachment to his stepmother, feels support from her and caring and concern from both parents. He feels comfortable in his current living situation and demonstrates no desire to change at this time."

Dawn waited outside the room as the hearing took place. When it was over and Jace came out, he seemed relieved. "They found her in contempt of court," he explained hastily to Dawn as he headed out the doorway toward the elevators. He told the boys to get their belongings and come with him. Immediately Ida became hysterical and held onto the boys. Their mother came around the corner, barking orders at the boys, telling them that they had to go with their father but that somehow she would get them back. Dawn and Jace stood there watching the scene. Dawn became incensed at her dramatics. All she knew of her was the seeming lack of interest in her children, dropping them off on Jace's doorstep, sending gifts late for birthdays, calling infrequently. She felt Juanita made up the whole story of Jace's threats and just wanted the boys there now for Ida's benefit. Dawn looked at Jace and said, "What a bunch of crazy people."

Ida's grandmother unfortunately heard Dawn's comment and began directing profanities at her. Juanita joined in. "You," she said pointing her finger at Dawn, "you ought to be put in a padded room! You told Ethan he would miss his animals if he didn't come back. Well, what about me? What about me?"

"And what kind of mother are you?" Dawn countered, "telling your children that their father's going to come shoot them with a gun?" The next thing she knew, Dawn was reeling from a hard slap on her jaw and realized she had been struck by Ida. Jace stepped in front of her, and a security guard quickly ushered Juanita, Ida and her grandmother onto the elevator.

"Why didn't you protect me?" Dawn looked at Jace in tears, holding the side of her face.

"I didn't even see her until I heard the hit!"

Dawn called her employers to say she wouldn't make it and went instead to the emergency room to have her face x-rayed. She was already bruising, and her jaw ached. She wanted to make sure no bones were broken.

When she got home, the boys had made a mess of the kitchen. When she asked them to please clean it up, they ignored her. Dawn went upstairs to Jace in their bedroom.

"You need to tell them," she said, still upset from the events of the morning.

"Tell them what?"

"Remember the contract … that you'll support me with the children?"

Jace called the boys upstairs. As they stood in the doorway of their room, he said, "While you're here, Dawn is your stepmom, you understand?" They nodded. "And you're to do everything she tells you. If she tells you to clean your room, you do it, okay?" They nodded. "Now go clean up the kitchen."

That was the most support she had ever seen from Jace in front of the boys. Unfortunately, it was also the most support she would ever see. To hear him say that, though, was gratifying to her. Jace's lawyer called that afternoon to see how Dawn was doing. He said he had written a letter to Juanita's attorney telling him to have Juanita keep Ida home from now on and that she was guilty of assault. Dawn half wanted to press charges but didn't want anymore to do with Jace's daughter, agreeing whole-heartedly with the evaluation on her. She lay down to rest, trying to forget the events of the morning and chiding herself for even opening her mouth at the courthouse. Such was her reward for sticking up for Jace.

That evening she went into Ethan and Eric's bedroom with Jace to kiss the boys goodnight. Ethan looked at his father and said, "Do I have to kiss her goodnight, Dad? It's the worst part of the day."

Dawn never went into their room at bedtime again.

Chapter 27

Stairs

Dr. Thomas listened with interest as Dawn told him what had gone on at court the previous week. He told Jace that he would like to meet with him individually for a while. Jace was resistant at first but knew the bounds of the contract and so complied reluctantly. Dawn wondered about things, though, as Jace was very quiet after the sessions and implied that Dr. Thomas had said some unkind things about her. Dawn tried to let it go and keep her trust in the therapist, hoping to be able to talk to him alone at some point. She felt like things were better, now that she had someone to report to. She felt like Jace had been trying.

A few weeks later, Dawn woke up feeling especially melancholy, and tears flowed and flowed. In checking the calendar, she realized that she hadn't had her period last month and was late this month. Tracing the days to the night after her return back home, Dawn realized that she must be pregnant. Jace came into the room and saw that she had been crying.

"What's wrong now?" he asked her.

"I think I'm pregnant."

"You sure?"

"No, but I haven't had a period, and all I want to do is cry. That's usually a pretty good sign." Dawn tried to read Jace's reaction but couldn't tell if he were happy or not about the situation. Dawn wasn't sure what to think—at the time she was too emotional to trust what her real feelings were herself. She had always wanted lots of children and thought Jace had also; but after giving birth to Taylor, he had wanted her to get her tubes tied. She refused. Things were so hard with him, though; she just didn't know if she would make it.

More weeks passed, and a visit to the doctor confirmed Dawn's suspicions. Morning sickness set in, as usual, and Dawn did her best to make it through the months of vomiting with as little suffering as she could. She always looked forward to that magic fourth month when it subsided. Nancy called one Saturday morning and asked Dawn to meet her for lunch. They tried to keep in touch on each of their birthdays, and Dawn's birthday had been a few weeks earlier.

Dawn went downstairs to talk to Jace. He was sitting on the couch watching TV. "I thought I would stop at the store on the way home and get some milk," she said to him. "The kids are out of milk for their cereal. Nancy's paying for lunch," she continued, "but I'll need a few dollars for groceries."

"I don't have any money," he replied, irritated.

"We've got to have milk, Jace. The children have to eat. Please, can't you spare a couple of dollars? I've used all I have to pay the bills."

"I told you I don't have any money!" he yelled at her.

It made Dawn angry that he would yell at her. She felt the emotion rise within her. She knew he had money—all she needed was a couple of dollars and felt like she was begging.

"I'm not going to live like this," she said, walking out of the basement and upstairs to her bedroom.

She stood in front of her mirror and began putting on her mascara. She suddenly saw Jace in the mirror behind her as he entered their bedroom, and before she could finish he grabbed her by the upper arms. The mascara tube dropped to the floor.

"You want out?" he raged at her. "You can have out!" he yelled as he dragged her out of the room to the top of the stairs in the hallway. Dawn couldn't speak. He had such a firm grip on her arms that she couldn't break free. He totally overpowered her. As they reached the top of the stairs, her thought was that he was going to kill her. She knew that he was going to throw her down the stairs, and she thought that she would die. As she felt him begin to hurl her body forward, she screamed with all of her might.

It startled him. He stopped. It was as though he came out of a trance, and he set her free. She stumbled back to the bedroom. Jace walked down the hallway stairs into the living room. She was shaking too much to put on any more makeup, and the tears were washing it all away as it was. She was grateful that the children were outside and had not heard the commotion. She grabbed her purse and jacket and started for the door.

"I'm going to lunch," she said as she walked out the door. "I'll be back later."

Chapter 28

Marks

When Dawn walked in the restaurant, she tried but couldn't hide her emotions from Nancy. Nancy knew immediately that something was wrong.

"Come into the bathroom with me," Dawn beckoned to her. Nancy followed her in, and Dawn removed her jacket, unbuttoned the top of her blouse and pulled it down so the back of her arms were bare. "Do you see any marks?"

"I see two, very distinct handprints," Nancy said, dismayed. "One on each arm. Both of your arms are very bruised," she continued. "Did Jace do this to you? What happened?"

Dawn told her the events of the morning as they left the restroom and returned to their table. "I don't know what to do," she said, dissolving into tears. "I thought things would be better going to a counselor."

"The marks on your arms—I once worked in a hospital—those marks look just like we would see on abused children when a parent would grab them and shake them," Nancy told her. "I think you ought to call your counselor."

"On a Saturday? I hate to bother him on a Saturday," Dawn protested.

"That's what he gets paid for," she said firmly.

While they waited for their order, Dawn used the phone in the restaurant lobby and called Dr. Thomas. He didn't sound very thrilled to be called at home but advised Dawn, "You need to do whatever you feel you need to do to be safe. If you don't think you're safe going back, you need to leave. It's really up to you, but you need to keep yourself safe in the meantime."

Dawn returned to the table and told Nancy what Dr. Thomas had said. "I'll do whatever I can to help you," Nancy offered. "I can't help you if you go back, but I'll do whatever you want me to do to help you now."

"I really appreciate that," Dawn told her, hesitating. "I … I just think I need to give us a chance to work this out in counseling. I don't think he'll hurt me any more, and I really think Dr. Thomas can help us work this out." She didn't know whom she was trying to convince more—Nancy or herself—but knew that Nancy wasn't convinced. It hadn't even been six months since she moved back in, and she couldn't handle the thought of moving out again. She had been so happy to be back. And now with the baby coming—how could she support herself and take care of a baby and two toddlers? The thought was just too overwhelming. She would go back and try.

When she walked in the door at home, things were different. She could feel it. Their relationship would never be the same, now that he had bruised her. She felt his marks were burned into her flesh. Was she one of those abused women, now, who went around hiding the bruises on their faces and their black eyes and making excuses for their batterers? She didn't want to be one of those women. Denial was more comfortable. She wasn't one of those women. He didn't beat her. He had only grabbed her. That didn't make him a batterer.

Jace took Dawn and all the children out for a hamburger that night, stopped at the store for groceries, and suggested they go see the movie, "The Bear." Dawn complied, wondering about the money he suddenly had to spend but too exhausted to care. Hopefully, a movie would take her mind off of things. As she sat next to Jace in the dark theatre holding Taylor on her lap, next to the baby in her womb, tears ran and ran down her cheeks.

Chapter 29

Therapy

Dawn recounted the events of the weekend before to Dr. Thomas with Jace at her side. She was anxious to hear what he would counsel them to do. The building was noticeably empty. It was early evening, and most of the staff had gone home when Dr. Thomas called them into his office. The last of the day's sun streamed into the west window.

Dr. Thomas seemed somewhat nervous after hearing Dawn recount the same story she had told him over the phone. He addressed his remarks, which seemed planned, to both of them as he said:

"There's a story about a woman who goes into counseling to get help. She tells the counselor all of the horrible things her husband does—his drinking, losing jobs, no money, coming home late, abusing her and her children, etc. The counselor listens to her story and then replies to her that he knows what her problem is—her husband is an alcoholic."

"Dawn," he continued, "I'm afraid that the therapy Jace and I have been doing is only making him more and more angry, to the point that I fear for your safety. Jace is not an alcoholic, but Jace is who he is. I don't see him changing. He cannot see that he is doing anything wrong. He can't see that he is doing anything to hurt you, even though what happened last weekend was certainly inappropriate on Jace's part." Jace shook his head in agreement. "It's really just up to you, Dawn, to decide how long you can put up with it. (Her mother often said the same thing: "How long are you going to put up with it, Dawn? How long?") I'm sorry," said Dr. Thomas, "but I see no hope here."

'No!' Dawn thought in panic. 'How could this happen? I've moved back! We have to be able to work things out! I'm going to have a baby! I can't do that alone!' She couldn't hold back the tears and began to sob. She felt her whole world was falling apart. "But Jace promised to come for a year!" she exclaimed.

"I don't think the amount of time will change anything," he said sympathetically. "You could try and see someone else. Maybe they would have different results, but I don't think so. I really can't take your money anymore."

As they walked out the door, Jace seemed relieved that he wouldn't be coming back. Dr. Thomas put his hand gently on Dawn's shoulder as he told them goodbye. Jace said nothing on the way home. Dawn sobbed, feeling like all the air had been knocked out of her, as they drove toward the setting sun.

Chapter 30

Reconciled

There was no way she was going to go through her pregnancy and have a baby as a single woman. She decided that right off. Dr. Thomas was wrong. He had to be. She would prove him wrong. She put her energy into her children, her pregnancy, and into making Jace happy. She would fix things. She would make them right.

Things had been going well, and they planned to go to a movie that weekend. She was excited to be with Jace and to be seen with him. She always noticed people staring at him. He was a head-turner, that was for sure. If she had a nickel for every person, female *and* male, who told her how good looking her husband was, she would certainly have more spending money. Even she loved looking at him and never tired nor got used to his good looks, but she often wished that there were more beauty and serenity to the soul inside him that seemed so tortured.

The movie lobby was especially crowded that night. They leaned on the brick pillar next to the red-velvet rope that held back the crowd, while the first feature finished playing. Dawn held Jace's hand in hers as she surveyed the crowd.

Jace looked down at her. "Wouldn't it be fun to take a machine gun and blow everyone's head off?"

Dawn couldn't answer him and just shook her head. His comment came from nowhere and certainly unnerved her. 'What have I done?' she thought. 'Who is this person I am married to? Oh, what have I done?' She had a hard time keeping her mind on the movie that night.

As they drove home, Dawn mentioned how much her hormones affected her while she was pregnant. "I can smell into the next county," she joked. "My sense of smell is so much greater, it's hard to believe."

"I know about hormones," he said.

"Yeah, right. Like you've ever been pregnant."

"No, but a doctor put me on hormones once. You know … tes … whatever."

"Testosterone?" Jace nodded in agreement. "What were you on testosterone for?" she asked in amazement. This huge, muscular, hairy, masculine man—why on earth would a doctor give him testosterone?

Jace immediately clammed at her questions and changed the subject. She knew she would never get an answer from him. He delighted in keeping things from her.

She attributed his violent statements about shooting to an aftereffect of the therapy. Dr. Thomas was right about that. Jace was becoming more violent. It was good, then, that therapy was terminated. But what was the answer? She knew Jace was still upset about Ida and extremely angry about Juanita's attempts to get custody of the boys.

A few weeks later, as Dawn prepared dinner, Jace stood at the sink cutting up an apple. As he turned on the disposal and shoved the peelings down the sink, he said, "I could cut her up and put her down the disposal. Nobody would ever find her."

"No you couldn't!" Dawn replied.

"I saw a place by the underpass today as I was driving to work," he continued. "I thought it was a perfect place for a body. No one would ever see her."

"You've got to get over your hatred of her," Dawn said, becoming increasingly agitated at his statements.

"Or I could put her in a dead cow and haul it out to Summit Mountain. No one would ever find her."

"You wouldn't do that, would you?"

Jace angrily retorted, "Nothing would give me more pleasure than slitting her throat and pissing in it while I watched her bleed to death."

Chills went down Dawn's spine. The mental image of it was horrifying. She later confided to Anne about Jace's statements, and Anne asked her husband, Dave, if he thought Jace would really kill Juanita.

"If he could get away with it without being caught," his brother said, "he'd do it in a minute."

Dawn reconciled herself at that point to staying with Jace forever. At least if she were married to him, he probably wouldn't kill her. But to be his second ex-wife … that would most certainly be lethal.

Chapter 31

Infection

She had called her lawyer. She couldn't believe she had made an appointment, but she began to believe that she couldn't stand it any longer. Maybe it was hormones, but she couldn't live feeling so isolated and so belittled. He continually belittled her. She no longer had her tutoring job, as her prized pupil had graduated, and money arguments became more and more frequent. Jace seemed to delight in denying her basic necessities, while spending more and more on cattle and other animals to fill their pasture. She had moved out once. She could do it again, she resolved. This time, though, she would move farther away, and there would be no contact.

An irritating part of this pregnancy was a swishing sound that she constantly heard in her ears. She made an appointment with an ear, nose and throat doctor one Friday to see if he could help alleviate her symptoms. After a thorough examination, he told her that it was just a part of her pregnancy. What she was hearing was the blood flowing through her veins because of the increased blood supply and extra vessels that came with pregnancy. Dawn went home determined to live with this new complication—as if she had any choice.

But as the weekend ended and Monday morning came, a new complication set in. Dawn woke up to a room that was spinning around her. She tried to sit up and immediately vomited into the garbage can next to her bed. As she crawled to the bathroom, groping the walls for support, she continued to vomit. After using the bathroom, she made it back to bed and lay as still as she could on her back. Any movement brought more vomiting. She had never known such dizziness.

Jace got up for work, irritated at the interruption.

"Please stay home today," she begged him. "I can't take care of the children. I can't move—I'm so dizzy."

"You've just got the flu," Jace said, dismissing her pleadings.

"It's not the flu—I'm so dizzy."

"Well, I can't miss work."

"Don't you have sick leave?" she asked, knowing that he did but also knowing what his answer would be.

"You'll be fine," he said, as he walked out the door. "Call your mother."

Dawn's mother and father had gone to Reno to see Dawn's sister, Paula, who had recently moved there. Jace knew that. Dawn called her other sister, Pat, for help.

"I'll be out as soon as I can," Pat told her.

Dawn remembered that she had an appointment with her lawyer that morning. She called and cancelled the appointment, telling herself that it just wasn't meant to be; but was even angrier at Jace for leaving his pregnant, sick wife home alone. Where was the man who had been so concerned about the speck in her eye when they were dating? There was just no way that he could love her. What was she doing staying with him? There was no way that she could keep this appointment, though. Maybe God was trying to tell her something.

Immediately after calling her lawyer, she called her doctor and told him what she was experiencing. When she moved the phone to her left ear, she realized that she could barely hear, and thought it might be the phone. "If I even move my head a little bit, I vomit," she told the doctor, moving the receiver back to her other ear.

"You've likely got an inner ear infection," he told her. "You're just going to have to lie flat and be as still as you can. I'll call in a prescription for you that will help stop the vomiting and won't hurt the baby. In a few weeks, when the dizziness subsides a little, we'll need to do a scan to rule out a tumor; but we'll have to do it without the dye until after you have the baby."

'In a few weeks!' Dawn thought. 'How long will I be like this?' She called her sister back and asked her to stop at the pharmacy and bring the prescription with her. Again, she had trouble hearing with the receiver on her left ear. She reached for her watch on the end table by her bed and held it to her ear. She was disturbed to realize that she couldn't hear it tick. She held it to her right ear and heard the tick. 'And now I'm going deaf besides,' she thought.

She was so grateful when her sister came and was in tears by then. She knew it couldn't be good for the baby for her to keep vomiting and was so grateful for the medicine. She still had four months to go and had just gotten over the morning sickness phase. Now she was vomiting again.

She couldn't do anything but lie there. She couldn't read, she couldn't watch TV, she couldn't move. Trips to the bathroom were agony. All she could do was crawl, and the motion caused her to vomit automatically. She had never known anything like this and knew it wasn't "just the flu." She was grateful when the medicine took effect. Her sister left just before Jace came home. Pat was irritated with him for not staying home with Dawn. "I'll be back out tomorrow," she said. "Hope you feel better."

When Jace came home, Dawn told him what the doctor had said. "You've just got the flu," he said, irritated that he would have to fix his own dinner and take care of the children.

Dawn had to crawl to the bathroom because of the dizziness but was relieved that she wasn't vomiting. Other than that, she didn't leave her bed.

Days turned into weeks, as the dizziness continued. Dawn hadn't ventured beyond the bathroom, and the stairs into the living room were out of the question. Her neighbor came over to get Dawn's and the children's breakfast each morning, and her sister or niece came later and took care of the children. Joey helped with Taylor in the meantime. Dawn depended on him more and more. Jace continued to treat her as though she were faking the whole thing. He did come home early one day to drive her to her doctor's appointment. Dawn sat down and scooted herself down the stairs. Jace helped her to the car, as she was unable to stand.

The doctor had arranged for Dawn to come in for a scan. She told him that she was still extremely dizzy, so he arranged for the hospital staff to meet their car with a stretcher to wheel her into the examination room. A couple of weeks later, she saw the doctor in his office. She was able to walk on her own by then but was still unsteady. He told her he wanted her to put one foot directly in front of the other and walk on the line he had taped on his floor. She couldn't do it and fell over. In testing her hearing, he told her that she had lost a substantial part of her hearing in her left ear and that it likely was permanent.

"Are you planning on nursing your baby?" he asked her.

"I wanted to… but I don't seem to have much luck doing so," she said hesitantly.

"The minute you're done nursing, I want you back for another CAT scan. We need to make sure of some things with dye. This one showed some irregularities, but we're not sure without the dye."

'Great,' Dawn thought. 'Just what I need—a brain tumor.'

Chapter 32

Baby Boy

Dawn woke up to contractions and knew what was happening. Thankfully, her water hadn't broken this time. She didn't want to be started again. The doctor was going to do a tubal ligation after the pregnancy. She didn't want to have it done, but Jace had talked her into it. This man who had told her he wanted ten children had not wanted any more after Taylor was born. She told Jace to take care of things himself, if he didn't want any more children, but he refused. "If we ever get divorced," he had said, "I might marry someone who wants children."

Still, she felt like she was doing the right thing: this pregnancy had been so hard, she couldn't go through another one like this; she was getting older and didn't want to have children when she was in her forties; her marriage was so shaky that she probably shouldn't be bringing any more children into it; and, she reasoned, maybe the chance of her getting pregnant was the reason Jace never touched her. She hoped that if she got her tubes tied that their sex life would improve and maybe then he would be more affectionate with her. She longed for affection. She longed for him to touch her, to kiss her, to hold her. He never held her. He never really touched her at all and only kissed her when she kissed him first. It unnerved her and made her feel ugly. She felt like she just wasn't attractive enough for her obviously-gorgeous husband.

Dawn recalled going to a Christmas dinner party with Jace a few years earlier, sponsored by the company he worked for and held at a hotel. She was thrilled to be able to fit into a beautiful black dress she had worn on a special date to a dance just out of high school. She remembered going into the restroom during the party, where a full-length mirror covered the entire wall. Dawn stood in front of the mirror. She was very slender, and her hair was longer than it had ever been, dark, thick and curled. She looked better than she ever had in her life; yet she felt empty inside, longing for some acknowledgement from her husband.

James had once told Jace, "You'd better watch out for her—she's a looker." Her brother's friend, not knowing she was married, had recently wanted to date her when he saw her.

Still, despite what the mirror said, Jace's imposed isolation could only make her feel ugly and unworthy, the "monster" that he said she was. 'What's wrong with me?' she almost said out loud as she gazed into the huge mirror. 'Why doesn't he want me?'

Earlier that summer the newspaper had sponsored a contest for the "best beard." The winner would be featured in the paper. Dawn felt that Jace would win the contest if she entered him—and so she did. She sent in one of their engagement pictures—one of the only pictures she had of Jace in a suit. It wasn't long before the newspaper notified him that he had won, even though more than 60 men had entered the contest. The win validated what Dawn already knew—she was married to an extremely handsome man.

The baby came quickly. In fact, the doctor barely made it in time for the delivery. They had quickly given Dawn an epidural before the delivery so that she could be numb for the ligation. But when the doctor began the surgery, Dawn cried out in pain. One of the nurses put a mask over her mouth. She knew nothing more until she woke up in her room. She tried to talk but couldn't. Apparently, she had clenched her jaw so tightly during the surgery that she now had a difficult time even opening her mouth. She felt horrible. She looked over to see Jace sitting there.

"The doctor had trouble finding one of your tubes," he said. "It was buried or something. They had to put you out."

Dawn could tell by the way her jaw felt that the surgery wasn't an easy one. What was worse, she didn't even feel like seeing the baby. She was angry with Jace. This surgery wasn't her idea. Why didn't he have surgery? It just wasn't fair. Soon her mom came in, and the tears rolled down her cheeks. She could hardly speak; it hurt so much to even open her mouth. Her sisters and their children were planning on coming over to see her, but her mother told her that she would tell them to come the next day when she was feeling better.

"He's a beautiful, big boy," her mom told her. Dawn had agreed to let Jace name him David, after his brother, whom Dawn was also fond of.

As evening came, she began to feel better, and the nurses brought in her baby. He was the biggest one yet, and he was beautiful. Dawn brought him to her face and drew in his wonderful smell. Somehow, again, he seemed to make everything worth it. Dawn would later realize, when Davey became a toddler, that this brown-eyed, dark-haired baby was the little boy out on the porch in her dream before Joey was born. She knew that now her family was complete.

Chapter 33

New Job

When Jace came to pick Dawn up at the hospital, she hoped that they would have a quiet night together at home. But the moment they got home, Jace left to haul hay. Dawn wasn't feeling well and hoped that he would help take care of her and the baby, but he was too busy stocking up on hay. He had purchased so many cows, it seemed that there was not enough money for anything else.

Dawn nursed the baby for only a short time before supplementing. Her ENT doctor ordered a scan soon after her delivery. Dawn was relieved when the test came back normal. She was also relieved to find that much, but not all, of her hearing returned in her left ear.

As it got deeper and deeper into fall, Dawn worried more and more about money. There was nothing extra for Christmas. She saw an ad one morning for a sportswriter—a stringer—in the paper to cover women's sports. It was something Dawn had done just out of college, and she already knew some of the reporters at the paper. Because of that, when she called they offered her the job over the phone. She excitedly told Jace, who was glad for the extra money. But when he found out that she would be working many nights and weekends and he would have to watch the children, he balked.

"I'm not babysitting while you work," he said. "Find something during the day when I'm gone too."

"But I've already committed myself," she said. "And it's something I can do and like to do. It's just during the basketball games over the winter. It's just temporary and will give us money for Christmas."

"Whatever," he said obviously irritated. "But I'm not watching the kids."

So began her night shift. Every time she went, though, she had to take all three of the children to her parents. It was hard on the children, it was hard on her, and she knew that it was hard on her parents. Often she didn't finish until midnight, but she enjoyed the work. On one particular night, however, her family couldn't babysit. Jace had told her he would watch them just one night, but as she prepared to leave he began raging. She couldn't stay and argue anymore and walked out the door, hoping that he wouldn't take things out on the children. Hadn't she watched his children when he worked nights?

"Don't expect any diapers changed," he yelled at her as she got into the car.

She had trouble concentrating on the basketball game. At halftime she called home to check on things, but Jace was still angry and oppositional. Dawn called to see if her parents were home. They had just returned, and Dawn poured out her heart to her father.

"I'll go out there right now and get the children, if you want me to," he offered.

"No, it would probably just make things worse. Thanks for listening, Dad." She hung up in tears.

When she got to the newspaper office to type in the night's story, one of the other sportswriters, whom she had known before she was married and often worked the same nights, sat opposite her.

"How's it going?" he asked.

Dawn had a difficult time hiding her frustration. "Oh, things could be better," she said, trying not to sound too upset, but not doing a good job.

"What's wrong?"

"Oh … my husband … marriage just isn't all it's supposed to be, sometimes."

"Well, I know a cure for that," he said.

"Yeah," she said tiredly. "I could use a cure."

"Name the time and the place," he said. "I'll leave right now if you're serious."

Dawn was surprised. She hadn't meant to lead him on. She was just so tired of Jace's continual demands and tantrums. "No," she stammered, "I couldn't … thanks for the offer, though." No matter how she felt about Jace, she wasn't into adultery. Suddenly she was feeling very uncomfortable being alone so late in the office with this man and finished up her story as quickly as she could. She vowed to herself that she would never tell Jace. She wanted to finish up the season. They needed the money so badly …

The newspaper offered to continue Dawn's job through the spring and summer months. As much as she wanted to take the offer, she had to turn them down. She was flattered, "but my priority has to be my children and husband, and he wants me home at night and on weekends."

She also hated to turn down the offer because money was so tight. She could go back to teaching but didn't want to leave her children all day either. She decided to make it a matter of prayer and fasting on Sunday.

When she returned from church on Sunday, Dawn opened the want ads of the paper. She was surprised to see a new job listed that seemed made for her: It was teaching adolescents in a hospital setting; a Special Education Degree and experience in teaching was required; best of all, it was part-time. Dawn called the number excitedly and arranged for an interview. When she was told, however, that her interview would be with a Dr. Samuel, she thought, 'Oh, well, there goes that job.' She thought it best that she didn't tell Jace with whom she had an interview.

As she left the morning of the interview, Jace commented, "How come you never dress like that for me?" She was pleased that he would notice and thought that it was the closest he had come to complimenting her in years.

When Dr. Samuel came into the foyer of the hospital, he greeted Dawn with a smile. "Nice to see you again. How are things going?"

"Okay," Dawn answered. "I'm a little embarrassed about this interview, though. I think you know things about me that my mother doesn't even know," she joked.

He put her fears to rest. "Dawn, anything I know about you is to your credit, not otherwise. In fact, when I saw your resume, I thought, 'At least we have one applicant who is qualified.'"

"Thank you," Dawn replied, relieved. The interview included two other administrators, and Dawn felt that it went well. 'If I'm meant to have this job,' she thought, 'I'll get it.' And she did. She was so excited. What was wonderful about it, also, were the hours. Joey was starting first grade. She would be there to get him off in the morning, have time to take Taylor and the baby to her mother's, and be home in time for the babies to nap before Joey got home. It was perfect.

Chapter 34

Ride

The pamphlet had come in the mail and when Dawn saw it, it intrigued her. The more she thought about it, the more she thought she had to do it. The Multiple Sclerosis Society was sponsoring a 75-mile bike ride for charity. Before Dawn married Jace, she used to ride her bike to work. She rode several miles each day, and the ride home each night to her parents' was nearly all uphill. She was in excellent physical condition then and was dating Jace at the time.

The bike ride was in June. It was now April. She would have two months to get in shape, and it would take her mind off of her worries at home. It would also help her feel better physically and emotionally. She needed Jace's support, though. He would need to drive her to Laketown to make the ride. He would also need to watch the children for a while each night while she rode.

To her surprise, he agreed to it, albeit reluctantly. She began training. When she couldn't leave the children, she rode the stationary bicycle in the basement. She worked up to riding 35 miles, but it was all on flat ground. The pamphlet advertised that the ride was customized to all types of riders, with rest stops all along the way. Dawn did very little practicing on hills. She did a couple of practice rides up to her parents' home on the weekends, but most of her training was done on the flat grounds of Wheatfield.

The day came for the ride, and Dawn was nervous. Jace drove her to the starting point, and Dawn was amazed at the number of people riding. She had over $500 pledged for the ride, which made it all worth it to her; but she was doing it for other reasons, too. She told Jace goodbye; he wished her luck and told her he would meet her at the finish line.

The beginning of the ride was very easy. There were a few small hills, here and there, but for the most part the ride was downhill. The scenery was beautiful—they would circle around a reservoir—and the weather was pleasantly warm. The morning went very quickly, and soon Dawn stopped at a park where lunch was provided. Even though she was tired, lunch refreshed her, and she still had enough energy to keep on going.

Several riders were way beyond Dawn's level. She thought they rode past her on the way back while she was riding up. They were very fast. Dawn, on the other hand, was very slow by comparison. It had not yet been a year since she had given birth to Davey. As the incline gradually increased, she wished she had practiced more on hills instead of in flat Wheatfield where she lived.

It wasn't long before she was in the middle of the canyon, and it was all uphill. She couldn't believe how difficult it was. Several riders had gotten off their bikes to walk. Dawn refused. She would not get off the bike. She had to complete the ride. She wondered if the planners of the ride were joking in planning the ride. The downhill part should have been at the end—not the uphill part.

The afternoon sun became warmer and warmer. Dawn had applied sunscreen at lunch to protect her pale skin. She didn't need to be burned along with being sore. As she came around each bend in the canyon, she thought it would be the end of the climb; but it only continued and continued. Dawn thought it would never end. Sag wagons came by and picked up some of the riders who could go no further. Dawn would not join them. She would not get off of her bike.

Finally she came to a rest stop. She was so relieved to get there. She sat down to peel a banana, but her hands were shaking so bad that it was all she could do to pull the peel. She was beyond exhaustion; dust and sweat had clouded her contacts long ago and things were a blur. But she wouldn't stop. She couldn't stop. She had to show Jace that she could do this. Maybe then he would respect her, like he did when they were dating. The pledges were a motivation—she wanted to earn money to help those with M.S. Before Dawn had her ribs removed and had been hospitalized for tests, she had been told by a mistaken intern that she most likely had multiple sclerosis—which was causing all of her pain. She came home from the hospital depressed and dejected, thinking that she had the disease. This ride was a way to give back to those people who were actually ravaged with the disease. Pride was also a motivation, as many family and friends knew she was doing the ride, as well as her children. She wanted to do it for them and for herself; she wanted to show herself that she still had it within her to conquer challenges. But her prime motivation was Jace. She never wanted to hear him say that she couldn't do it.

Ten miles remained after the rest stop. Thankfully, they were relatively flat, but dusty, miles. Because of her blurred vision, Dawn took a wrong turn and missed the finish line. She wondered if anyone were even at the finish line. Realizing she missed it, she headed toward the hotel parking lot. She found their car and parked her bike next to it. As she got off the bike, it was all she could do to walk, as her legs were shaking so badly. She couldn't see Jace anywhere. He had probably given up and gone to their room, she reasoned. She went to the hotel desk and found that he had not checked in. As she walked out of the lobby, she saw Jace coming in.

"Where have you been?" he questioned her. "Riders have been coming in for hours."

"I know," she stammered, nearly collapsing into his arms, "but I made it!" She was so glad to see him. She was so happy she was still married and had someone to come back to …

It took Dawn several days to recover from the ride, but she felt proud of herself for finishing it, even though she was slow. She collected her pledges and turned in the money, which was very gratifying to her. Her real reward, however, came the day after the ride when she overheard Jace on the phone with his father.

"I never could have made it on hills like that," he told his dad. If her 6-4, 220-pound husband couldn't have done that, maybe she was doing all right.

Dawn would ride in other rides for charity, but never again would she do more than a forty-mile ride. And she would certainly check out the hills beforehand.

As summer came to an end, Jace's garden needed to be harvested. Dawn was more than busy as she canned beans, pickled cucumbers, froze corn on the cob and bottled tomatoes. Dawn had never liked spicy food, but Jace loved it; so she asked Susan for her salsa recipe. It would please Jace if he had salsa to eat. Susan told her that the recipe was much better if the peppers were roasted. After roasting, the peppers would need to be peeled. "Make sure you use rubber gloves," Susan cautioned.

Dawn worked all day on the salsa. She peeled and smashed tomatoes and peeled and chopped onions. Peeling the roasted peppers was difficult, especially with the clumsy rubber gloves. The gloves were too large and cumbersome and not especially made well. Dawn chided herself for trying to save money and buying the cheapest she could find. The strong pepper juice permeated the gloves; soon her hands felt like they were on fire. She ran them under cold water but to no avail. Each time she took her hands out from under the water, pain won out, and she resubmerged her hands. She was having an extremely hard time even finishing the salsa, getting it into jars and boiling them. After finding no relief from the pain, she called the "ask-a-nurse" emergency number that was on the refrigerator magnet.

"It's going to hurt for a while," the male nurse on the other end of the line told her. Dawn was surprised when he told her to put her hands in warm, soapy water. "Just do a big batch of dishes."

Dawn was relieved that the warm water felt more soothing than the cold. She brought a chair over to the sink; she was too tired to stand anymore. Jace came in from outside, and she told him of her predicament. As usual, he had very little sympathy for her and went downstairs to watch TV.

It was midnight when he came upstairs to the kitchen, disgusted that she still had her hands in the water. "Where's my chocolate cake?!" he bellowed at her.

She was angry that he had the gall to want a chocolate cake. She had spent all day on salsa for him—she didn't even like salsa—and was miserable because of it; but it still wasn't enough to make him happy. Oh, why couldn't she make this man happy? Would she ever make him happy? Could she ever make him happy? She could climb a mountain trail that many would give up on—enduring heat, pain and crippling exhaustion—but she could not make this man happy. Marriage had given him a license—a license to mistreat her. Marriage put him in the most powerful position of all—enabling him to dole out hurt and pain to the most vulnerable person of all: a person who had given herself to him and loved him. Were he her boss, she would quit the job; were he her friend, she would break off the friendship; were he her student, she would kick him out of her class. But would she ever, ever, find the strength to leave him?

Chapter 35

Heart Attack

She woke with a start when she heard a shot. She looked over and saw that Jace was out of bed. What was going on now?

She rose and looked out the window. It was still grey outside, as the sun was just coming up over the mountains. She could see a large black dog lying in the pasture. Immediately she knew what Jace had done. He had shot the neighbor's dog. Jace entered the bedroom and put the gun in their closet. "That'll take care of him."

"Couldn't you have called them first and told them their dog was in our yard?"

"I don't need to call the a-hole neighbors," he yelled. "If they want a damn dog, they need to keep it in their yard."

Dawn was embarrassed every time she saw the neighbors up the road. They never said anything to her. She wasn't even sure they knew what happened to their dog, but Dawn was too afraid and embarrassed to approach them. She also didn't want to deal with Jace's anger if she did.

One night they had an especially bad argument over Ethan. It began at dinner again, when he refused to eat the dinner Dawn had prepared. She had gone to a lot of trouble to prepare a stroganoff recipe she had been given. She tried to ignore what went on at the dinner table, especially with Ethan. It had always been a losing battle with Jace, and Ethan usually got what he wanted. This particular night, though, Dawn was tired of ignoring it all. As she sat down to eat what she prepared, she thought it was delicious and that the extra time she had taken to prepare it was worth it. "You don't know what you're missing," Dawn said. "This is really good. It's a low-fat recipe, too, so it's good for you."

"He doesn't have to eat this shit, and neither do I," Jace bellowed, rising from the table. He walked over to the garbage can and scraped the contents of his plate into the can. Dawn couldn't believe it.

"Do you know how long this took me to make? I'll never cook for you again!" she said, taking her plate and running upstairs to her room. She was so angry that she dissolved in tears. She wished that when she got angry that she wouldn't cry, but one always seemed to accompany the other.

Later that night, after putting the children to bed, she ventured downstairs to watch TV. Jace controlled the remote each night and so controlled what they watched. She usually tried to do something else while watching television. She really wasn't fond of many of the programs Jace watched and thought it was a waste of time. Ethan asked for a cookie. When Dawn said, "You didn't eat your dinner," Jace again became angry.

"I'll get you one, son," he said, as Dawn's resentment of Ethan increased.

"You could at least make him taste it," Dawn said. "He might like things if he gave them a chance. He doesn't eat anything healthy—just junk."

Jace didn't answer but stared straight ahead. Dawn could tell by the look on his face that something wasn't right.

"What's wrong?"

"I … I think I'm having a heart attack."

"Should I call an ambulance?" Dawn asked, immediately forgetting the previous argument.

"No," he said, putting his hand on his chest.

"Then I'll take you to the emergency room," she said rising. "I'll get my coat.

"Wait a minute," he said. "I'm not sure I want to go."

Dawn stopped. "What do you mean? Are you saying you want to die?"

"I'm not sure. Why not?"

Dawn felt terribly guilty. She shouldn't have argued with him. She shouldn't worry about what Ethan eats. Maybe all of this was her fault. "I'm getting the car keys. Do you need help to the car?"

Jace shook his head as he walked slowly up the stairs and headed for the car. He told Ethan to go to bed and that he would be back later. Dawn drove as fast as she could, worried that Jace might pass out in the car. Twice before, she had taken Jace to the emergency room. His pulse had been racing on those occasions, which turned out to be apparent panic attacks. This time it seemed different.

When they got to the parking lot, Dawn walked with him into the lobby. She found the nearest attendant that she could find. "I think my husband's having a heart attack," she blurted out.

The attendant immediately took Jace back to a room while Dawn stayed out front and gave the clerk insurance information. By the time she got back to Jace, he was hooked up on monitors and oxygen.

"Has he had a heart attack?" she asked the doctors nervously.

"We don't think so," they said, trying to calm her. "We're running blood tests to make sure. It will take some time."

Dawn sat next to Jace and put her head next to his on the pillow. She loved this man. He certainly tugged at her heartstrings. She put her hand in his. She was exhausted. "Just rest," she said to Jace, taking her own advice.

An hour later the doctor returned. "We've repeated the test three times. It confirms that you've had a heart attack. There seems to be very little damage, if any, which is good; but you'll probably be here for a week or so. It's hard to believe for someone as young as you are. Thirty-nine is pretty young to have a heart attack."

Dawn wondered if the attack weren't caused by something emotional rather than physical. Her husband was a walking volcano. That had to take its toll on his heart. Things had to change, that was all there was to it.

"We'll be taking you to another room," he said. "I think your wife might as well go home and get some rest. You'll be fine now."

"Go ahead," Jace agreed. "I'm just going to sleep, and you need to get home to the kids."

"Do you want me to call your parents?"

"Yeah, but wait till morning. No use waking them in the middle of the night. Call work, too, and tell them I'm sick."

"Okay," Dawn replied. "I'll be back first thing in the morning." She leaned over and kissed him goodbye. "I love you."

"I love you, too," he said.

She drove home in the dark, still in shock at the news. Jace had had a heart attack.

Chapter 36

Recovery

As Dawn walked into work on a beautiful, sunny morning, she ran into Dr. Thomas. She knew he worked in the same facility as she did, but she had never run into him until now.

"How are you doing?" he greeted her, with a big smile on his face. "I had heard you were working here. It's good to see you."

"Thanks. It's good to see you, too."

"So how are things going?"

"Well," she said, "a lot has happened. Jace had a heart attack a while ago …"

"What?"

"Yeah … I know … he's pretty young for that. But it has actually helped things. The boys have been behaving much better, so there's been less friction between us. I think they understood that any arguments about them put their dad at risk. Jace seems to have mellowed out some. I think it might have scared him, too. Anyway, we've all been trying harder, and things have been going better."

"I'm glad to hear that. Never thought a heart attack would be therapeutic! How do you like your job here?"

"Oh, I love it," Dawn said enthusiastically. "I'm learning so much. I enjoy teaching, and I learn so much in the doctor's staffings. It's really been great and works out so well for me to be able to take care of my children."

"Well, I'm glad to hear that, too. Keep me informed."

"I will," Dawn said, as she headed into the building. She had visions of going into Dr. Thomas' office one day and telling him that she and Jace were going to be sealed in the temple of her religion and that she had a wonderful family and marriage. She would show him that he was wrong to give up on them.

Chapter 37

Anniversary

Dawn was so looking forward to this anniversary. It would be their tenth anniversary. She couldn't believe they had been together for ten years. She wished she could say it had been ten years of bliss. Things had gone better after Jace's heart attack for a while; but gradually the bouts of anger returned. Dawn was able to see that she had no control over—nor was she to blame for—his tantrums. What would be okay one day wasn't okay the next, and vice versa. So Dawn insulated herself. She built a solid, impermeable wall around herself. She would outwit him! Whatever it was he became angry about, she would not react. She would think to herself, 'I will not respond to your anger any more. I don't care how much you yell, you will not make me cry or feel bad. I will still be happy, in spite of your tantrums.' And for a while, it worked. But Jace found a crack in Dawn's wall: Joey.

She was upstairs getting ready to go out that night. She hoped that they would have a nice dinner somewhere. She would have liked to go to a movie also, but it was a weeknight and they both had to work the next day. As she was changing her clothes, she heard Joey crying.

"Eric hit me!" he cried, running into her arms.

"Why?" Dawn queried.

"He said I couldn't watch cartoons. But it's my TV night, Mommy! He hurt my arm!"

Dawn immediately became angry. She had given each of the children a different day to watch their favorite shows to avoid any arguments. Eric was six years older than Joey and shouldn't be hurting him. She stormed down the stairs.

"You're twice his size! And it's his night for the TV! What do you think you're doing?"

"I don't want to watch cartoons," Eric said, irritated.

At that point, Jace walked in. "If he wants to watch something else, he can!" Jace bellowed.

Dawn was furious. "They need to take turns! It's Joey's night. And Eric has no business hitting him! He's twice as big as Joey."

"Joey, go to your room," Jace ordered. He left Eric in front of the TV, who turned it to the channel he wanted.

"Why does Joey have to go to his room? He didn't do anything!" Dawn was furious. "Why are you rewarding Eric for hitting him?"

"Joey's your little baby. You're spoiling him rotten."

Dawn was in tears again. Eric had spoiled her anniversary, and she hated him for it. She told Joey to go get Taylor and the baby and get in the car. They all spent her tenth anniversary at her parents'. When she returned the next day, sitting in the garage for her was a new bicycle from Jace.

Chapter 38

Cracks

The crack in Dawn's insulated wall deepened and deepened. Ethan was supposed to do the dishes days ago. Dawn let them build up and build up until she could stand it no longer. When she got home from work and saw the mess, she ordered Ethan to do the dishes.

"Joey!" Jace bellowed. "Get outside and pick up all the garbage in the front yard. The dogs tipped the can over and there's shit all over the yard."

"But Daddy …" Joey stammered, " … it's dark outside."

"I don't care. Get out there and clean it up!"

Dawn could see that there was no arguing with him. He was too angry with her for telling Ethan to do the dishes. Joey put on his coat and went out the front door. Dawn grabbed her coat and went with him. Soon Taylor was out with them, as they all picked up the garbage in the front yard.

And so it went. Dawn withdrew more and more from Eric and Ethan. It didn't seem to matter what she said or did, Jace became angry. Once she asked Eric to please put waxed paper over his food in the microwave so it wouldn't make a mess. Jace became furious; and so she was powerless over these increasingly bigger and meaner boys. She decided that she wouldn't look at them or speak to them unless it was absolutely necessary. Unfortunately, it became necessary.

One day Joey came running into her to tell her that Ethan was in the driveway smoking with his friend. Dawn went outside and told Ethan's friend that he couldn't smoke there.

"But I'm 19—I'm old enough to smoke," he told her.

"Well, Ethan's not," she countered. "And you can't smoke on my property. You need to leave."

Ethan's friend reluctantly got into his car, as Ethan gave Joey "the finger." Dawn knew that Jace would be angry with her, but she wasn't going to have that going on. Of course he was, and she suffered his wrath. Unfortunately, so would Joey. She had embarrassed Ethan. Joey must be punished. That weekend, Joey had his friend over to play. While they were in the backyard, Jace told Joey to go retrieve the chicken eggs.

"But, Daddy, the geese are out," Joey protested. "They peck at me!"

"I don't give a damn," Jace said, as he lifted Joey by one arm and threw him over the fence. Joey ran to get the eggs, and the geese took after him. He came back with the eggs, crying and embarrassed. "You big baby!" Jace said, taking the eggs from him.

Joey then ran into the house to Dawn. "I hate Daddy! I want you to divorce him, Mommy! Why don't you divorce him?!" Dawn continually asked herself the same question. 'It was Ethan's fault,' she reasoned. Had he not caused trouble in the first place, Joey wouldn't have been hurt.

Dawn remembered an afternoon when she had gone downstairs to do some sewing. Joey was sitting on the floor in front of the TV watching his favorite video, "Hook." A touching part in the movie showed Peter Pan, who had been a neglectful father, reconnecting with his son and embracing him. Peter Pan told the boy that all he had to do was think of a happy thought and he could fly. His happy thought was "My Dad!" Dawn looked up to see Joey with his arms wrapped around his sides, rocking and hugging himself. He, too, longed for such affection from his father.

That evening, it was Joey's turn to put a note on Jace's pillow: "Daddy, why don't you love me?" It broke Dawn's heart. Jace crumpled the note and threw it away. Denial absolved him. Denial absolved them both.

The next day when Dawn got home from work, she confronted Ethan about the smoking. "Why don't you just go away?" she pleaded. Ethan went out to the shed to skin muskrats he had trapped in the ditches. Dawn hated it. After doing it, Ethan would come into the house, blood all over his hands, and continue to spread that blood to the doorknobs, light switches and sink. "Just stay out there. Stay away from me. And don't come in this house while I'm here!" she hollered after him angrily, locking the door. She felt she had no control. Jace was gone much of the time, yet he left her with these boys while taking away any power she had. She resented them. If only they were gone, things would be so much better! She went upstairs and lay on her bed to take a nap. A while later, the phone ringing startled her out of her sleep.

"Hello," she answered tiredly.

"Mrs. Malone? This is Sergeant Hawks at the police station. We received a call from your stepson Ethan. He's at his aunt's house and says that you've locked him out of the house."

"Oh," she replied, trying to piece things together. "We had an argument about him smoking, and I did lock the door, but he has a key to the house that he keeps with him all the time. I just didn't want to see him for a while, but he can certainly get in the house."

"I understand," the sergeant said. "Teenagers can be difficult. I'll call him back and talk to him. I'll tell him to use his key and tell us the whole story next time."

Dawn was angry, and she was hurt. She called Anne. "Did you know that Ethan called the police from your house?"

"Yes," Anne replied curtly, "we told him to. You can't lock them out, Dawn."

"You're right, I can't," she replied, her voice rising. "He has a key!"

"And what are you thinking, slapping Eric?"

She couldn't believe what she was hearing. "What?! What are you talking about?"

"His cheeks were red when he got here. He told us you slapped him."

"I did no such thing! Do you think I'd ever hit those boys? They're much bigger than I am. I'd be a fool to do that. Maybe his cheeks are red because he walked two blocks, and it's cold outside!" She hung up and dissolved into tears.

She felt betrayed. Not only by Jace and the boys but now by her in-laws. How could they?! She paced the bedroom and became increasingly agitated. She didn't feel safe in her home. Both boys had guns, not to mention the several in the closet that Jace had. No ammunition was ever locked up. The more she thought about things the more agitated she became. She needed help. She called the police.

When they arrived she explained her situation. The boys were breaking laws, calling them and lying about her. She had no control. She was often left alone with them. They both had guns and ammunition. She didn't feel safe there. She wanted the police to take the guns away.

"We can't do that, ma'am. Even if they were in this room right now and loaded, if they haven't threatened you with a weapon, we can't do anything. You can leave if you don't feel good about being here."

"But this is my home!" she protested. "I have three other children." She was embarrassed. She could see that she never should have called but had done so out of desperation. She didn't know where to turn anymore.

Jace escorted the officers out the door. He was Mr. Cool, of course. "I think it's just that time of the month," he said condescendingly, and she heard the officers laugh. Too bad they couldn't have seen Jace a few weeks ago, kicking in their bedroom door. Dawn had locked the door to change. When she couldn't get to the door quick enough to open it for Jace, he had kicked it in so hard that the moulding split in two. Mr. Cool. She went to bed resignedly, hoping that none of them would shoot her in her sleep.

A few weeks later at work, the high school called to say that both Ethan and Eric were truant—again. Dawn asked the school secretary, "Could you please call their father at work? They're my stepsons, and every time I let him know, he shoots the messenger. (She tried to sound flippant.) It would be so much better if he heard it from you." Dawn appreciated the secretary's willingness to comply with her wishes.

That weekend, Jace needed to go into the crawl space under the house to run a water line. He decided to give the job to Joey.

"But, Daddy," he protested, "it's dark, and there's lots of spiders!"

"Take the flashlight and get going!"

Shaking, Joey took the flashlight. "Couldn't Eric do this?" Dawn suggested, but it was no use. Joey made it through the crawl space, covered in cobwebs and dirt with a tear-stained face.

"Geesh, Joey," Jace said, reacting to his tears. "Why don't you go put on a dress?"

"You think you're such a tough guy," Dawn said to Jace later in private. "Such a big, strong man. Well, I'll tell you something," Dawn said with all the indignation in her heart, "anyone who has to pick on a little boy is no man at all." And she walked out of the room. She hated him.

Chapter 39

Scar Tissue

Dawn's sister, Pat, was tending her children because her mother was having minor surgery—to remove a cyst from her abdomen. Her mom had gall bladder surgery six month's earlier, and some tissue had grown in its place. The doctor felt that it was scar tissue and could easily be removed. Dawn stopped at outpatient surgery on the way home from work to see her mom, but they had already released her to go home. 'That's good,' Dawn thought. 'Things must have gone well.'

When Dawn reached her sister's, Pat met her at the door in tears. Dawn could tell immediately that something was wrong. "Mom has cancer!" she blurted out.

Dawn felt like she had been socked in the stomach. "No!" she cried. She made it to the couch and sat down. "How bad?" she asked through the tears.

"It grew where they took out her gall bladder. The doctor took out what he could see. She's going to have to have radiation."

Not her mother! How could this happen? Dawn tried to gather her thoughts, but mostly she and Pat just sat on the couch and cried. She was relieved that her children were in the back room playing.

When Jace came home from work that night, he came into the kitchen and sat down to take off his work boots, as usual. Dawn walked over to him, agitated, and blurted out, "Mom has cancer!" She crawled into his lap, threw her arms around his neck, and sobbed. Jace held her. How she needed to be held.

"I was supposed to go to a class tonight for work," he said. "If you don't want me to go, I won't. I'll stay home."

Dawn was surprised. She thought that it was the nicest thing he had ever said or done for her in their marriage.

"It's okay," she said. "I'll be alright. I appreciate your offer, though. You'd better go to your class." His offer meant the world to her, and she loved him all the more for it.

Chapter 40

Last Thanksgiving

Dawn's mother had always fixed Thanksgiving dinner. And since Dawn's marriage, she had never had Thanksgiving at her parents'. She and Jace had agreed to have Thanksgiving with Jace's family (his sister Susan always made dinner) and Christmas Eve with her family. But this year was different. Dawn's mom had made it through the radiation, and all had gone well. She was declared cancer free. But it had weakened her, and she wasn't back to her old self. She had said to Dawn and her sisters, "This Thanksgiving I want my girls to cook for me." And they all wanted to honor her wishes.

Dawn told Jace of her mother's wishes, but Jace was resistant. "Please, Jace, we go to Susan's every year. Just this once. It was a special request from Mom. I need to make the potatoes and dressing and bean casserole. I have to take them in once they're ready."

But Jace wouldn't give in. It became a major power struggle. Dawn explained to his family, and they seemed to understand. She would still make the pies, as she usually did for them. Jace could still go to Susan's, since their dinner was a couple of hours earlier than Dawn's parents was. But she needed to stay home and cook. She made the pies, and Jace left with them, furious at her.

"Please come in to Mom's when you're through," she begged him. "You don't have to eat anything. Just come and be with us." But he would have no part of it. Ethan and Eric went with him.

That evening at her parents, Dawn's mother asked Dawn what was wrong. "Nothing, Mom," she said, trying to smile but not doing very well. "I'm so glad to be here with you."

"It's too bad Jace couldn't come," her mother said. "I might not be here next Thanksgiving."

"Yes, you will," Dawn said, but her mother's words seemed ominous.

"I just hope next year will be much better than this year," her mother said.

"It will," Dawn said, but somehow her heart wasn't in agreement. She drove home that night to a dark house. Jace had locked all the doors, turned off the lights and gone to bed. Dawn carried in her sleepy children, one by one, and put them to bed; then crawled into the stone-cold bed next to her husband.

Chapter 41

Last Christmas

It was Christmas Eve, and Dawn was running behind. She had just finished making treats for the children to take to the neighbors, and she was exhausted. Now she had to prepare Christmas breakfast for the next morning. Jace's parents traditionally came for Christmas breakfast, and then Jace and Dawn went to Dawn's parents for Christmas dinner.

Last year Christmas had been difficult, because she had had surgery on both feet the day before Christmas Eve. She had hoped to use less leave from work by recovering over Christmas vacation. She had still managed to fix breakfast last year for her in-laws while using a walker. She was glad for the increased mobility this year but was becoming more stressed and fatigued as the night went on. She wished she had the gifts wrapped, but Jace insisted on doing it together after the children went to bed. So it made for a very long night. She got the children into bed. They were all sleeping in Joey's bed together, in excited anticipation of Santa Claus.

Once she prepared the next morning's breakfast, so it could easily be put into the oven in the morning, she swept the floor in preparation for mopping it. Ethan lumbered into the kitchen and opened the fridge. He then sat down at the table with a glass of milk and several cookies. He deliberately dipped one cookie at a time into the milk, very slowly, and slopped it into his mouth. Dawn was mopping as quickly as she could and mopped everywhere around Ethan, who still sat at the table.

"Ethan, I need you to move, please," she said impatiently. Ethan ignored her.

'Okay,' she thought. 'I'll just mop over you.'

She pushed the mop under the table. She mopped everywhere she could and then pushed against Ethan's shoes with the mop, trying to finish up. At that moment, Jace walked into the room.

"What are you doing?" he interrogated her, angrily.

"I'm trying to mop the floor!" Dawn said in exasperation. "And he won't move!"

"So? He doesn't have to move," Jace said in his usual defense of Ethan.

"No," Dawn answered, infuriated. "He doesn't have to do anything. If he weren't so lazy, he could help me!" She had done it. She had insulted Ethan. She must be punished.

At that, Jace went to the base of the hallway and bellowed up the stairs, "Bastard Joey! Joey F-er! Useless, stupid Joey!"

Dawn glared at him with an intensity of hatred that she had never known for anyone. She wanted him dead. Had she had a gun in her hands, she could have killed him. She had a hard time killing spiders, but at that moment, she wanted to kill her husband. What did Joey have to do with any of this? And on Christmas Eve!

"I promise you," she said, with pure intent flashing in her angry eyes, "I will never spend another Christmas with you as long as I live!" She walked up the hallway stairs past him, praying that Joey and Taylor and the baby were asleep. To her dismay, they all lay there under the covers with eyes open wide.

"Daddy didn't mean what he said," she said to them all, trying to sound calm. "He's just mad at me 'cause I said Ethan was lazy."

"But you're right, Mommy," Joey said earnestly. "Ethan never does do anything to help you, and neither does Daddy." Dawn was amazed at the insight of her little boy.

"Try and go to sleep," Dawn said, as she kissed them all. "Santa will be coming soon."

As she walked down the hallway stairs, she glanced at the engagement picture of her and Jace hanging on the wall. It was a beautiful picture, framed in dark wood, inset in brown velvet. Impulsively, Dawn removed it from the wall and walked into the kitchen. She took out a sharp knife and cut a line down the middle of the picture between her and Jace. Jace saw what she was doing. He walked over to her, took the knife out of her hand, and used it to stab tiny holes in Dawn's picture. He stabbed her face and chest repeatedly, tearing the paper away from its backing. Dawn knew the intent of his symbolism and walked away. She walked wearily down the stairs and began wrapping presents, tears running down her face. Oh, why did she always have to cry! She hated it. Christmas Eve had always been her favorite day of the year. It, too, had been ruined.

At four o'clock in the morning, after taking a short shower, she put some money she had saved for Jace into a card. He had told her that she had never given him a Christmas present that he had really wanted, so she gave him money to buy his own. She climbed into bed, exhausted to the bone. Two hours later, the children were awake.

She came downstairs, and under the tree was present after present to her from Jace. As she unwrapped them, one by one, she felt numb.

Chapter 42

Invitations

She didn't know where else to turn. Her friends who knew Jace just shook their heads. But she told very few friends. She wanted to keep up the image—she was so lucky to be married to such a kind, handsome man who gave her such beautiful children.

She wouldn't turn to her family again. Her past move, and move back in, had stressed them too much. Her mom was recovering from cancer. Dawn would not stress them more. She had made her bed. She must lie in it.

But did her children also have to lie in that bed? Especially Joey? Dawn turned to her bishop. She knew he couldn't counsel her to get a divorce, but she could see the pain in his eyes as she related her Christmas Eve experience.

He told Dawn about a marriage conference coming up in a couple of months. "We have money to send a couple from our congregation. I'd like you and Jace to go to see if that might help things."

So they attended the marriage conference. Dawn was grateful for a chance to get away, but Jace was very resistant. He was resentful of the church's interference. Dawn hoped that maybe this would help them get some romance back into their marriage. Intimate relations were rare. Dawn's operation had not changed that aspect of their marriage at all. But as they lay in the hotel bed next to each other, Jace showed no interest in her still as he changed the TV stations nearly rhythmically with the remote. She hungered so much for some attention, some affection, that she forced herself on him but hated herself for it. He responded, but she resented that she had to initiate things. She vowed she would never do so again.

The speakers at the conference were excellent. At one point, they had each couple go to their rooms to negotiate solutions to problems together. As they sat down together, Jace stubbornly informed her that there would be no giving on his part. There was no compromise; not even an attempt at compromise. She married him; she must take him as he was.

They returned home the next afternoon. Jace forced Dawn to drive home. She didn't want to drive, especially when he began to criticize her driving. As they headed home, he picked up the middle seatbelt and touched the hot metal to her arm.

"Ouch!" she said. "What … why did you do that?" He had no answer, but smiled. "Why would you want to burn me?" she said. In her anger, tears appeared, which made her even more angry. She realized for the first time, from his smile, that he actually felt pleasure when he hurt her.

When they returned home, her anger was kindled even more. They had left the children with Jace's niece. She informed Dawn that while they were gone, Ethan and Eric had hurt Joey. "They picked up some rocks in the pasture and threw them at him. I had to threaten to call my dad to get them to stop." Dawn was infuriated, feeling that she could never again leave her home without her children. Jace just laughed it off.

"They're just being kids," he said. "All brothers fight."

"Not when the brothers are twice his size and age!" she protested but knew she was getting nowhere in the argument.

Her neighbor confirmed what had happened when she was gone. "I saw Eric from the living room window just tearing into Joey. The babysitter stopped him."

She vowed to never leave them alone again. Eric and Ethan were patterning their father's abuse of Joey. She must stay home and protect him from now on …

Ethan was graduating. Dawn couldn't believe it. He had sluffed and/or flunked many of his classes the last two years. But Ethan had found an advocate—a coach—who offered to make up credit hours for Ethan if he and his friends would paint his house.

Dawn was livid. It was a travesty of the school system. Dawn considered reporting the coach and complaining to the superintendent. Were Ethan her son, she would have insisted that he earn the credits honestly. But Ethan was her stepson—were she to report him, she could imagine the wrath of Jace that would descend upon her. She felt the same way with Ida's assault—something else that was very wrong—but something that she also got away with because she was Dawn's stepdaughter.

Juanita and Ida were invited down for the graduation, but Dawn was shocked when they showed up at her front door. How could they? Why didn't they just go to the stadium and see Ethan there? Jace met them at the door and gave them directions to the school stadium. If she didn't know better, and maybe she didn't, she would have sworn that Juanita was flirting with Jace. She was very dressed up and had lost weight.

Dawn went downstairs and finished ironing Ethan's robe. She did not want to have any dealings with Ida. Ida had never apologized for striking her, and Dawn had nothing but absolute distrust for the girl. She wanted her to have no influence over her children. Dawn had told Ethan of her disapproval of his graduating without really earning it but was trying to make a concession by ironing his robe. Ethan wasn't ready and didn't have time to iron it. It was a daunting job as it was.

As she was downstairs ironing, she heard Juanita invite Jace out to dinner with her and Ida that night. At no time did she indicate that Dawn was invited. Dawn didn't want to be invited, but she didn't think it appropriate for Jace to go either. She was relieved when she heard Jace decline the invitation.

There would be another invitation, however, that Jace would not decline. Nor did Dawn expect him to. Ida was getting married, to a guy who was divorced and had a child of his own. 'How appropriate,' Dawn thought. Ida would know what it was like to be a stepmother. When the invitation came in the mail, though, Dawn's name was not on it.

"You're invited," Jace tried to reassure her.

"No, I'm not," Dawn replied. "If she wanted me there, she would have put my name on the invitation. It's a deliberate putdown. So go ahead and go, but I'm not going up there with all of her family. It was bad enough at the courthouse. I don't want to get hit again."

"Nobody's going to hit you," he said condescendingly. "And it's probably Juanita who addressed the invitations."

But this time Dawn would not budge. She didn't expect Jace not to go to his own daughter's wedding, but how she wished he would stand up for her. She would have loved to hear him say, "If you don't have enough respect to put my wife's name on the invitation, then count me out, too. If she's not invited, I can't come either." But she knew that was a fantasy. She wrapped a nice present for Jace to take with him. He would spend the weekend there and made reservations at a nearby motel. Taylor and Davey were both ill, and Dawn was glad for a further excuse to stay home with them.

A couple of weeks after the wedding, a package arrived for Jace. Inside the package was a video of the wedding ceremony and several pictures. Among the pictures was one of Jace and Juanita together with Ida and the boys. A family portrait. On the back Juanita wrote a note thanking Jace for the wonderful weekend they had spent together. When Dawn asked him about it, he attacked her and defended Juanita. So the tables had turned. This always-enemy had now turned ally. Dawn was unnerved by it. She tried not to be jealous, but she was. She didn't have a picture of herself and Jace with just their children. Once, Dawn had won a free coupon for an individual portrait. She had a darling picture taken of Joey riding a carousel horse. Jace had yelled at her for doing it.

There was another invitation. Taylor had been asked to give a talk about her father in church for Father's Day. At five years old, she would be the youngest of the participants. It was to be a surprise. Dawn received a call from one of the ladies in the congregation who was putting together the program. They were also preparing a booklet to give as a gift to all of the fathers in the congregation that contained quotes from their children about what they liked about their dads. The woman waited on the other line, while Dawn asked Taylor: "What do you think Daddy does best?"

Taylor's first reply: "Fights."

"No, sweetie, you've got to think of something else."

"He makes good honey," Taylor replied.

Dawn prepared a poem about Jace for Taylor to give in church. She cut out a picture for each line of the poem to help Taylor remember the words. She glued each picture to a piece of construction paper and then to a popsicle stick for Taylor to hold them up with. They worked and worked on memorizing the talk.

Dawn invited her in-laws and parents to their church meeting to hear Taylor give her talk. Jace had no idea what was going on. Dawn curled Taylor's long black hair, and she wore a beautiful peach dress. She looked like a little princess. When she got up to speak, she was not the least bit afraid. She spoke loud and clear:

"My Daddy's heads above the rest; at 6 foot 4—more or less.

I think he's the best dad there is; I'm awfully glad to be his kid.
When he comes home from work, I'm happy. He give me hugs,
kisses and candy.
With him it's fun to feed the cows and sheep and goats and
stinky sows.
He tells me that he thinks I'm pretty, and that it comes from
him, not Mommy;
But take a good look at your beard, Dad, and you'll see, I take
after the other side of the family.
He works real hard and does things quick; there's nothing that
he cannot fix.
It's seldom that you'll catch him napping; he even cooks when
we go camping.
He makes our yard look nice and neat and plants a garden
that's hard to beat.
He has a very big green thumb and fills our house with plants
by the ton.
His favorite thing is chocolate cake, a piece so big it fills his
plate.
It's fun to bounce on his full belly and play with him when he
acts silly.
He reads to me books that I've got and skips with me in the
parking lot.
I like to pat his soft, black beard and tell him that I love him
dear.
He spoils me, but that's okay; with him I always get my way.
The good thing, Dad, about being your daughter is just in
having you for my father.
You do so many things for me, but best of all—you love me.
I love you, Daddy. Happy Father's Day."

Mission accomplished. Everything in the talk was true, and Jace
appeared to be the perfect father. Taylor did a perfect job, even though
she was the youngest speaker. Dawn was so proud of her, and Jace was
so surprised. When Taylor sat down, Dawn glanced over at Jace. She
was shocked that he was actually wiping tears from his eyes. It was the
first time she had ever seen him cry.

She was glad that he was touched by it. She had hoped that he
would be pleased. Maybe since she had been so positive in pointing
out all of his very best traits, he would be good to her for a while.

Maybe there would be peace. But that night he found something else that he wasn't pleased with. Something she hadn't done right. After working so hard (and secretly) on Taylor's talk, she had neglected to vacuum their bedroom floor. Jace stepped on some of Davey's left-over crackers. A tirade of profanity was directed at Dawn.

"I thought after the nice day that we just had, you might be nice to me—just for one night," she told him disappointedly.

She walked downstairs to see Joey lying dejectedly on the couch. "What's wrong, honey?" she asked him.

Joey looked at her in tears. "Mommy, I wish I was a girl."

The statement crushed her, and her heart ached for her hurting, little boy. She knew Joey didn't really want to be a girl, but she knew his line of thinking: if he were a girl, maybe his daddy would love him like he loved Taylor. Dawn wondered if Jace actually loved Taylor as much as he appeared to, or if he lavished affection on her and Davey to hurt Joey even more. Taylor was also the recipient of all of the affection that Dawn longed for, but she refused to let Jace make her jealous of her own daughter. She loved her too much to allow him to affect her relationship with her little girl. She took Joey into her arms, wishing that she could give him all of the love that he deserved to have and needed to have from his father.

Chapter 43

Pigs and Turkeys

Dawn woke up to hear Jace ranting. 'What is it this time?' she wondered. Jace came into their room holding Joey's pet baby pig, wet and nearly frozen to death.

"Look at what your precious little boy did!" he yelled.

"What?" Dawn answered sleepily.

"He got out of the pen, and Joey didn't put him back!"

"In the middle of the night?" she asked defensively.

"He probably never even checked on him last night!"

"He's just a little boy, Jace!"

Joey woke up from the commotion. Jace dumped the limp piglet into his arms, and Joey dissolved into tears.

Dawn grabbed a small blanket from the closet. "Let's go put him on the heater vent," Dawn offered. "Maybe we can warm him up."

"Mommy, what if he dies? I didn't mean for him to be hurt."

"I know, honey. Why don't you go say a prayer to Heavenly Father?"

Joey wasn't the only one praying. Dawn also prayed. "Please don't let the pig die," she pleaded in her heart.

The pig slept all morning, but by afternoon it perked up. Soon it was apparent that the baby pig would be fine. Dawn was so grateful, and Joey had a more sure knowledge of what it was to have his prayers answered.

When they were in church the next day, Joey and Taylor were playing on the floor and started to giggle. Jace reached for Joey, pulled him into his lap by his ear and, putting his face next to Joey's, nipped it with his teeth. Joey knew better than to cry out but whimpered in pain as he covered his ear with his hand.

Dawn looked at Jace incredulously. "You bit his ear!" she whispered loudly to him. Jace just glared back at her. One of Dawn's neighbors was sitting behind them. Dawn was embarrassed and prayed she didn't see what Jace had done.

Weeks later, Dawn woke up to Joey's excited voice. "Daddy, the turkeys are out!" So much for sleeping in on Saturday, she thought.

"Well, go out and get them!" Jace said, pulling on his pants. Dawn could hear the turkeys gobbling outside their bedroom window. She disliked having the turkeys. Each fall, in November, he would hang the turkeys in a row by their feet from the patio roof and slit their throats. Blood would run all over the patio. She begged Jace to do it when the children were gone, but they were annual witnesses to the gruesome scene, much to her dismay.

Dawn could tell from the commotion that Joey was having a hard time getting the turkeys all back into the pasture. She could hear Jace swearing at him.

"I'm trying, Daddy!" he hollered. And then she heard him crying.

Dawn got out of bed. Joey came running up the stairs, Jace not far behind him. Blood was running down Joey's leg out of a gash above his knee.

"Daddy threw me into the bushes!" he cried. Dawn looked at Jace standing behind him, shaking his head.

"I didn't either," he said, unconvincingly. She knew Jace was lying.

"He was only trying to help!" she said to Jace angrily. He might abuse her, but he was not going to hurt Joey anymore. No more blood. She took Joey into the bathroom, washed his knee and bandaged it.

"It'll be okay," she tried to reassure Joey. She vowed to herself to leave this man before he hurt her son anymore.

Chapter 44

Disease

Dawn again felt hopeless. She felt trapped living with Jace and his two increasingly-difficult sons. She began thinking again about contacting an attorney. She felt like there was nothing left to do but worried what Jace would do in retaliation. She couldn't bear the thought of her children being alone with him and Ethan and Eric should she divorce him.

She sat at her desk at work. It was lunchtime. She remembered that her mother had gone to the doctor that morning. In spite of the doctor's reassurances that she was cancer free, her mother had continued to feel that something was not right. Dawn called to see what the doctor had said, and her father answered the phone.

"Hi, Dad," she said, taking a sip of water out of the water bottle on her desk. "I just called to see what the doctor said about Mom."

"Are you sure you want to know?" she heard the discouragement in his voice, and her stomach tightened.

"Yes, Dad. Tell me what he said."

There was a pause. "They told her she's dying," he said slowly. "They told her she has from two weeks to eight weeks to live."

Dawn couldn't believe what she just heard but knew by the tone of her father's voice that it was indeed true. "Oh, Daddy," was all she could say.

"I'll talk to you soon," he said, his voice breaking as he hung up the phone.

Dawn couldn't breathe. She walked out of the classroom, shaking. As she opened the door, Dr. Thomas came walking down the hall.

"Hello, Dawn," he said cheerfully. "How are you?" As he looked at her, however, the tone of his voice changed to concern. "Dawn? Are … are you alright?"

Dawn couldn't speak as tears rolled down her face. "Come in here and sit down," he said, guiding her back into her empty classroom.

Dawn blurted out, "She's dying!" Dr. Thomas looked confused. "My mom's dying of cancer!" she sobbed. Dr. Thomas took her in his arms as she wept and wept. When she gained her composure, he asked her how the rest of her life was going. When she told him she was considering contacting a lawyer, his reply surprised her.

"You can't do that now," he said. Dawn knew that he knew what she was going through at home and was the last person to encourage her to stay, but she knew he was right. "You've got to get through this first. Concentrate on your mom. You can deal with Jace later. One thing at a time."

Dawn was so glad that he had been outside her door. He even arranged for a co-worker to drive her home, and that night a bucket of chicken was delivered to her door. Dawn found out later that the same was delivered to her parents that evening. Dr. Thomas told Dawn that she could talk to him whenever she needed to. She was so grateful for the extra support. How she needed it.

The next day Dawn sat next to her mother on the sofa. Her father was on the phone, trying to make arrangements to go to a clinic states away. He was not going to accept the diagnosis. There must be something they could do. Her mother was more resigned.

"You know what's happening?" she said calmly. Dawn shook her head. "My mother wants me up there to do her hair."

Dawn chuckled, wondering at the same time at the strength of her mother making jokes. Dawn's grandmother had died the year before— at age 91—and had enjoyed good health nearly up to the end. Dawn had always assumed that her mother would live to be as old as her grandmother. As the weeks progressed, though, she would see even more strength in her mother as the disease ravaged her body. And it was a terrible time.

Dawn went to her parents every day after work, trying to spend as much time with her mother as she could. She tried to catch up on the housework on Saturdays at home and still make it into town to see her mom. Jace was inconsistently supportive. At times he would watch the children so Dawn could leave, and she was appreciative of that. At other times, he was anything but supportive, saying callously at one time, "Everybody's mother dies."

Dawn's mother was too weak to make the trip that her father had hoped for. The cancer cells, now in her liver and pancreas, had also strangled her esophagus. She was unable to swallow any solid food and lived on liquids. She enjoyed eating the popsicles with a joke on the stick. As she finished the popsicle, she could see the revealed punch line. But soon she couldn't even eat popsicles.

Then she went to bed. She would never get up from it again. She could barely swallow water, and that swallow was so agonizing that she would have to spit it up, even though she thirsted beyond anything she had ever known. Hospice came in and began a morphine pump. She could pump in morphine by pushing a button. But the misery could be seen in her eyes as she retreated more and more inside her-self. Time that seemed to pass so quickly to Dawn was torturously slow for her mother. Each morning her mother would wake to more torture and want to be gone. Yet she didn't complain. And she had taken the time to tell each one of her children goodbye.

"If ever I've done anything to hurt you," Dawn said to her, "I'm so sorry." Her mother shook her head. "No, never … and don't you cry, or I will, and it hurts my throat."

Dawn immediately bucked up. She didn't want to cause her mom any more pain than she was already in, even though all she really wanted to do was weep and weep at her feet. Her mom looked at Dawn intently as she said, "Don't let your husband …"

Dawn knew what she was going to say. "I won't," she said solemn-ly. "I promise." She knew it was a promise she must keep this time.

Chapter 45

What Makes a Man a Man

Dawn had arranged to take her students at the hospital to the nearby university. A convocation was scheduled for the public, and the speaker was Frank Abagnale, a man known as "the world's greatest con man." The presentation sounded very interesting. He had written a book, *Catch Me if You Can*, that told about his life as a con man—a very successful con man.

As Mr. Abagnale detailed his life, he talked about his parents' divorce and how he ran instead of having to choose between his parents. He told about his life impersonating a pilot, a doctor, a lawyer … and told about living in the most beautiful hotels, driving the fastest cars, associating with the most beautiful people.

He also told about his arrest and living in a prison in Europe that was dark and dank. He suffered greatly there and almost died in the process.

He then told about his life after prison. He talked about how wonderful it was to have a family of his own and to be a real "daddy"—not just a father—to his children. He talked about the love he had for his wife. He then said something that pierced Dawn's heart:

"I want to speak directly to the young men that are here," he said. "I have lived in the finest places. I have driven the fastest cars. I have lived a life of luxury. But I want you to know what really makes a man a man. What makes a man a man …" and he paused for emphasis … "What makes a man a man … is how he treats his wife."

Even though Dawn was sitting next to her students, she couldn't contain her tears.

Chapter 46

Detectives

It was Saturday morning. Dawn was busy catching up on housework at home. Jace had taken his usual Saturday morning drive to his parents' home and had taken the children with him. Eric and Ethan had gone with friends, and Dawn was glad for the time alone. Her solitude didn't last long, however, as the front doorbell rang. Dawn opened the door to see a sheriff and another man standing on her front porch.

"Hello," they said cheerfully. "Do Ethan and Eric Malone live here?"

"Yes, they do," Dawn answered, "but they're not here right now."

"Are you their mother?"

"I'm their stepmother," Dawn answered.

"Could we come in and talk to you for a moment?"

Dawn nodded her head and opened the door wide. They came in and sat down opposite her, and the sheriff introduced his partner as a detective.

"There's been some vandalism going on in the area," the detective explained. "We have reason to believe that Ethan and Eric are involved."

"Sorry to say, I'm not surprised," Dawn answered. "But I really have no say over what they do. I don't know where they've been or what they've been doing. To tell you the truth, I'm afraid of what they'll do here, but I have no support from their father. Ethan has several guns …" She thought of her encounter with Ethan a few weeks ago. He was shooting at seagulls out in the pasture. She had stormed out the back door and ordered him to put his gun away. After arguing with her for several minutes, Ethan discharged his rifle, just inches away from Dawn's foot. "I have to empty it in order to put it away," he had said belligerently.

"Could we see the weapons?" Their statement interrupted her

thoughts.

"Sure." Dawn took them down the basement to Ethan's room. On the wall were mounted several rifles. "His dad bought him a pistol for Christmas, also," she said, "but I don't see it here. Could you tell me, it's not legal for them to shoot in our backyard, is it?"

"The neighboring dwellings are too close for that. How old is Ethan?" they queried.

"He's almost 18," she told them as they walked back up the stairs. She could see the concern in their faces and was embarrassed at her lack of control of the situation she was in. "I was going to go through divorce proceedings," she continued, "but I found out my mom is dying of cancer. She doesn't have long to live. I just can't do anything about this right now."

They looked at her sympathetically. The detective gave Dawn his card as he walked out the door. "If you know of anything suspicious going on, or if we can help you, please give us a call."

'Yes,' Dawn thought, 'I've called you before.' She closed the door behind them and continued with her vacuuming.

Chapter 47

Separation

Dawn wearily walked into her mother's dim room after work that day. The drapes were pulled so that she could sleep, but her mother's eyes were open. They seemed hollow as she stared at the ceiling and didn't acknowledge Dawn's presence.

Dawn sat on the floor next to the bed and put her hand on her mother's arm. Again, there was no acknowledgement that Dawn was there. Dawn watched her chest rise laboriously, making sure she was breathing. She rested her head on the bed, next to her mother's body. Tears filled her eyes. How was she going to live without her mother?

She stayed next to her for a long time. Then she slowly rose from the floor. Stooping over her, she kissed her on her cheek. "I love you, Mom," she said as she turned to go out the door.

The quietest, sweetest words came whispering back to her: "I love you, too."

She had heard her! She knew she was there! But those words took such effort, were nearly imperceptibly silent. They would be the last words Dawn would ever hear her speak.

The next day she stopped at her parents after work. It was Friday. It felt like Friday. It had been an awfully long week. When Dawn arrived, Hospice was in the back room bathing her mother in bed. They reported that she was in a coma now; her temperature was 106 degrees. Dawn sat in the living room, waiting for them to finish, when she heard an unearthly groan, coming from the depths of pure misery. It was her mother! They had turned her to bathe her and had exposed a gaping bed sore in her hip. Dawn was horrified that her mother could still feel such pain, supposedly in a coma and with a continuous morphine pump. For weeks she had pleaded with God to save her mother. Now she pleaded with Him to take her; she could watch her suffering no longer.

That night, as she lay next to Jace, she began to cry. Grief overcame her, and she thought her heart would burst. She cried and cried till she could bear it no longer. She put her head on Jace's chest and sobbed, wetting his naked skin with her tears. He put his hand on her back. She wanted him to take the pain away but knew he couldn't. Eventually, she turned away from him and cried herself to sleep.

Dawn wasn't the only one having a hard time separating from her mother. Her mom had been Davey's caretaker, nearly since he had been born. She had always been there for him. He was upset and confused at the change he saw in her—and in the reaction of those around her. Dawn was dismayed when he began soiling his pants, something he had never done. She had asked Dr. Thomas about him at work one day.

"That's a normal reaction," he reassured her. "That's how children react to stress. He'll be okay as time goes on and he adjusts."

Saturday morning, Jace took the children with him to run errands while Dawn stayed home and did the laundry. As she was loading clothes in the washer, the phone rang. It was her father. "She's gone," he said. "She died this morning."

"I'll be right there," Dawn said. Oh, where was Jace? She wanted him there. She didn't know how to get in touch with him. She thought about leaving him a note but didn't want to take the time. She ran out to the car and drove quickly to her parents' home.

When she walked into her mother's room, she was alone. She didn't know what to expect, but one glance at her mother and she knew for a certainty that she was gone. Her face was contorted and her head twisted to one side, in testament to her torturous death. She looked nothing like the waxed, dead bodies she had always seen at viewings. But it was also testament to Dawn of the reality of the spirit, that it did indeed exist, for it was conspicuously absent. Her mother's body was empty. She didn't look at all like she was sleeping.

As Dawn was standing there, her father and sisters entered with two men from the mortuary. They were wheeling in a stretcher. They opened a large, black leather bag on the bed and lifted her mother into it. They then did something that horrified Dawn. They zipped it up. It was over. Her mother was zipped up into a bag. Dawn dissolved into heavy, heaving sobs, grasping her sisters for support. It was, indeed, the most terrible moment of her life.

She spent the day there with her father and sisters. Jace called when he got back home, and Dawn told him the news. "I'm sorry," he told her. He stayed home with the children. When Dawn got home, she was disappointed, but not surprised, to find a stack of messy dishes in the sink. Exhausted, she went to the sink and did the dishes, as tears ran down her cheeks. She wondered if she would ever stop crying.

Chapter 48

Wallpaper

Dawn's mother had divided some extra cash that she had between all of her children. Dawn wanted to do something special with it. After thinking about their needs, she decided to redo and rearrange the children's bedrooms. Taylor needed a room of her own. Even though Eric and Davey shared a room, Eric basically spent all of his time in Ethan's room. He often slept in it in Ethan's absence and basically only used his own room to change his clothes. He and Ethan's beds were once bunk beds. They could easily recombine. Then she could buy a set of bunk beds for Joey and Davey to share in the room that Joey and Taylor now shared, and Taylor could have a room of her own.

The entire arrangement made sense. Taylor was getting older, was the only girl, and needed her own space. Joey and Davey played together and Eric spent the majority of his time with Ethan. But it wasn't Jace's idea. He had been good to Dawn for a few weeks following her mother's death, long enough for her to become hopeful. But her hopes would again be crushed. Jace was against moving Eric's bed in with Ethan. "It won't give Ethan enough room," he said firmly.

"Ethan's never home anyway! What difference will it make to have a bunk bed over the top of his own? He's not losing any space. The only space he'll lose is from Eric's dresser, and it's not large. Eric doesn't hang up any of his clothes—he doesn't need any closet space—but if he has a couple of things to hang up, there's room for that, too."

But it didn't matter how much she reasoned or how much sense it made. Jace had made up his mind. The more Dawn thought about it, though, the more she was intent on doing it. The older boys were seldom home, and then it was usually only to sleep. Ethan had threatened to move out long ago, and Dawn didn't think he would be there much longer as it was. Then Eric would have the entire room to himself. She wanted to use her mother's money to do something lasting.

She knew that her mother would love to see Taylor with a cute room all for herself and the boys sleeping in a nice bunkbed set that her money had paid for. She kept thinking about her final conversations with her mother. *"Don't let your husband …"*

She wouldn't. She would stand up to him, no matter what the consequences. Wasn't he in control of everything else? He had designed the yard just how he wanted. Dawn had no input there. In fact, most of their backyard was pasture, and she disliked how closely the fence came up to their home. They had only a few feet of grass between the fence and the house. He had so many animals stuffed into the pasture that the flies were often uncontrollable. He controlled what they watched on television every night. Dawn read a book most of the time while he flipped the channels. He had controlled her in many ways, because it was easier to do what he said than to deal with his wrath. But the tantrums always came anyway.

"Unless you can give me a really good reason not to do this," she mustered up her courage one day, "I'm going to move the rooms. I asked Ethan and Eric if they cared about changing rooms. They said they didn't care." She knew he had no good reason.

"Then you're on your own," he said flatly. "Don't ask me for any help."

"Fine," she said.

As she spent the money for paint and wallpaper and beds, it was gratifying to her to be able to use her mother's money for the project. Things would be much better this way. She did have some obstacles, though, in moving the heavy furniture. Joey helped her as much as he could. Because she couldn't move Eric's bed in one piece, she had to take it apart, and that took her days to do. Jace had made the beds himself with heavy, large bolts, and it wasn't easy for her to get it apart. Putting it back together and getting it on top of the other bed was another matter. She did what she could and left it up to Eric to get his own mattress on the top bunk. She had lugged it down the stairs on her own, and that was all she could do. When it came time to put up Joey and Davey's bunk beds, Joey and she were able to manage with difficulty.

She loved wallpapering Taylor's room. Every time she walked by it, she thought of her mother. She was at peace now with her mother's death. She was so glad she wasn't suffering anymore. She had had a wonderful relationship with her and was able to have the time to tell her how much she loved her and to tell her goodbye. That meant a great deal to Dawn, even though she missed her terribly.

Still, Jace was so hard to deal with. He was angry that Dawn had changed the rooms; so, of course, he upped the odds. Even though the heat was sweltering outside and in, he refused to hook up the swamp cooler. And then there was the yard. He refused to mow it, refused to water, basically refused to do anything. "*Don't let your husband …*"

He also came up with another unique punishment: He wouldn't let Dawn pull the front drapes at night. She had always pulled the drapes when the sun went down. She was a private person and hated feeling like she lived in a "fishbowl," but Jace wouldn't relent. As a result, she stopped watching TV with him at night and went upstairs to her room. She didn't want the neighbors or anyone else looking in at them as they drove by—it made her very uncomfortable. If the children joined her in her bedroom, though, which she often wanted them to do rather than watch inappropriate programs with Jace, he would come upstairs and berate them for being in their bedroom. She couldn't stand for this. Her favorite memories were of lying next to her mother on her bed at night, discussing the day's events.

He didn't stop there. Jace soon wouldn't allow her to close the drapes in her own bedroom at night. As their window faced east, Dawn would be hit in the eyes with the morning sun much earlier than she wanted. She couldn't sleep in. She went to a lingerie store and bought some eye masks to wear at night to block out the sun but hated wearing them. "*Don't let your husband …*"

One day, as Dawn was washing the dishes, she noticed that there were very few spoons in the sink. She opened the silverware drawer, and there were none there. She suspected that they were in Ethan's room. She had suspected him of doing drugs for quite some time. She was aware of spoons being used in drug use, and so she went on a "spoon-finding   mission."

In Ethan's room, Dawn lifted up Ethan's mattress and saw a large, open box in the back corner, underneath the wooden slats of the bed. There was also something she hadn't bargained for—pornography. Ignoring the magazines, she reached between the slats and scooted the box out from underneath the bed.

She sifted through mounds of garbage and found several spoons. She also found a small box. She opened it to find some seeds of some sort. It had a distinctive odor—she guessed it was marijuana.

She put the box back under the bed and took the spoons and small box upstairs. She put some of the seeds in a baggie—she was going to check it out with a drug counselor at work. She put the spoons in the dishwater to soak. She felt like she was dealing less and less with a rational person in Ethan and more with drugs and alcohol.

When Jace got home, she got the reaction that she expected. He was angry with her for going into Ethan's room. "But we had no silver-ware!" she retorted. When she showed him the seeds, Jace took the box and put it out in the garage. "Aren't you going to throw it away?" she asked him.

"No, that's good stuff," he said sarcastically.

When she took the baggie to work, the counselor verified for her that it was, indeed, marijuana. It wasn't all that Ethan was doing. He regularly came home late with bloodshot eyes and reeking of alcohol. He smelled so bad of cigarette smoke that Dawn had to spray Lysol in the bathroom after he had used it. She often went into his bedroom and sprayed the room and his sheets, so the odor didn't permeate the house. This wasn't the environment in which she had wanted to raise her children! She and Jace had more arguments over Ethan, and she blamed Ethan for all of the trouble in her marriage. 'If Ethan would only leave,' she thought, 'things would be so much better.' He had always been the cause of so many of their arguments. In blaming Ethan, she could ab-solve Jace of any wrong doing, salvaging her feelings for her husband and thereby saving her marriage.

One weekend Ethan didn't come home. Dawn didn't dare ask about him, as the mention of his name usually started an argument. Jace left on Sunday afternoon and mentioned to Dawn in passing that he was going to pick Ethan up from jail. He had been arrested for being "under the in-fluence" and for "public disturbance."

Ethan's drug use certainly didn't make him any more cordial either. "Did you get that phone number?" he said to Dawn in passing one day.

"What number?" she asked naively.

"1-800-ASK-JENNY," he said smugly. It was a number advertised on TV for weight loss. Dawn hated him for the comment. It was espe-cially hurtful to her as she had put on close to 20 pounds and wasn't happy with how she looked.

She remembered sitting in the car next to Jace not long ago, waiting at an intersection while an attractive woman walked in front of them in the crosswalk. "Look at her fat a-," Jace had said. "What a fat pig!" Dawn thought the woman looked much thinner than she was. 'What must he think of me?' she wondered. As much as she would have liked to lose weight, she lived in too stressful a situation to be successful at dieting right now.

Things weren't much better with Eric. He had resented Joey ever since he was born, as Joey had taken away his status of being the youngest child. He probably also resented the love that Dawn had for Joey. She had tried to love Eric, but the feelings she had for him weren't the same as they were for Joey. Eric was so possessive of Jace that he often monopolized his time, which Dawn also resented.

One afternoon, she heard Joey crying. "What's the matter?" she asked, coming to the front porch.

"I was taking Salty for a walk, and Eric took him away from me." Dawn was livid. Joey seldom had the dog to himself. She stormed down the road and caught up with Eric.

"Give me that dog!" she ordered, grabbing the leash. "I told Joey he could walk him!"

Eric grabbed onto the leash. "No! I want to walk him now!" A tug-of-war began, but Dawn was no match for this 16-year-old's strength. He ripped the chain out of her hands, slashing the skin of her palm and making her bleed. She felt helpless. She was incensed.

For some strange reason, a thought crossed her mind. She had seen on the news the previous night that someone had been sued for spitting, but the court found that it could not be considered an assault. She wanted to strike Eric but knew that she couldn't hurt him. So she did something she had never done in her life, even in fun. She spit at him. It shocked him for a moment, but only for a moment, and he spit back.

She turned and walked down the road in tears, feeling more angry over her reaction than at Eric's actions. She couldn't believe what she had done and felt terribly guilty. She was so ashamed at her actions. What was she becoming?! The instant Eric returned home, she apologized for spitting at him.

That night she took out a notebook and made a chart. After writing in calendar dates for the next few months, she wrote in categories to check off: not looking at Ethan; not looking at Eric; not speaking to Ethan; not speaking to Eric. She would beat this. She would have no interactions with them, and she would chart her progress. She would concentrate only on her children and Jace.

She made another chart. On this chart were numerical categories for each day: 0 = horrible day; 1 = she cried; 2 = bad day; 3 = fair day; 4 = good day, no criticisms; 5 = excellent day. She would be diligent about writing in her journal. She needed perspective on how bad things really were. She would beat this.

Chapter 49

The Specials

Jace was a force to reckon with in the wallpaper war. Instead of being happy that Dawn was working through her grief by working on the bedrooms, he became increasingly jealous.

"So, are you spending the night with the specials?" he said, his voice dripping with sarcasm. And he didn't let it go. Her children—their children—became "the specials." It didn't matter if she were taking them to a soccer game or helping them with their homework. They were "the specials." Part of her punishment, she guessed, for getting her way with the bedrooms.

She had totally withdrawn from Eric and Ethan. She didn't speak to them. She didn't even look at them, for Jace could misconstrue a look. She had nothing to do with them. She isolated herself totally from them. They didn't exist. She was true to her chart and marked it consistently each day. But it made no difference to Jace. He continued berating her with "special" talk any time she did anything with her children.

One day she confronted him. "Jace, they're your children, too. How do you think it makes them feel to hear you say that? What if I called Ethan and Eric …" she tried to think of something insulting, "… the spics? They're both Mexican. Would you like it if I said that?"

It didn't matter that their conversation was private. Ethan and Eric had not heard what she said. Jace became incensed and launched into a tirade of insults toward Joey, loud enough for him to hear outside. So she would play his game, she thought angrily. Enough withdrawing. Enough being nice. Enough turning the other cheek. She would fight fire with fire.

That evening Jace was gone, and Ethan was in the kitchen as Dawn wiped off the counters. "Please move your plate," she said to Ethan. "I need to get this spic and span. Maybe I'd better go buy some 'Spic and Span' so I can get it really clean." With the emphasis she gave the word, and the glare she received from Ethan, she knew she had made her point. Ethan had heard Jace call the children "the specials" more than once. It was his turn. Ethan went upstairs to take a shower. As he did so, Dawn ran the kitchen water as hot as she could, so that Ethan's shower would be a cold one. She would get back at him one way or another!

But it wasn't in her to be this way. She felt guilty. She had stooped to a level that she didn't want to stoop to. She must go back to marking her chart. She would not speak to them. She would not look at them. They did not exist.

Chapter 50

Charity

As Dawn looked at her chart, she realized something. It made no difference. She blamed Ethan and Eric for so many of their problems, and they certainly didn't help things, but since she had gone with her "no contact" goal, nothing had changed. Her days were still horrible. She counted up the days that had been "good"—only five days in three months! It was seldom that she had a day without criticism or harassment from Jace. Most days were "bad;" several rated "horrible."

Oh, how she didn't want a divorce! So many conflicting thoughts went through her mind. She had heard the sayings so many times: "It takes two to tango. There are two sides to every story. You married for better or worse. It takes two to argue. No matter how flat the pancake, it still has two sides. Forgive seventy-times-seven." They were all guilt trips for her. She must be doing something wrong to cause Jace's anger. She thought often of their wonderful dating relationship. That was the man she married. That was the relationship she wanted. Why couldn't she have it? If she loved him enough, returning all of his hurtful attacks toward her with love, wouldn't he eventually become loving in return? Couldn't she soften his heart? Couldn't she love him into changing?

Then there was the fear. She was so afraid of what would happen in a divorce. Jace had told her of so many things he would do to her, should she divorce him, the least of which would be to "put a beehive in the living room"—he knew she was terrified of bees, which is probably why he invested in beehives and made honey. She thought of all of the murderous threats he had made toward Juanita—after they had been apart for so many years and in different relationships—what would he do to Dawn? What would he do to the children?

And then there was Joey. Joey was his scapegoat. What about Jace's relationship, though, with Taylor and Davey? He didn't punish them and at times was a doting father to them. Even though they were afraid of his anger, they loved their daddy; but was he good to them with the intent of hurting Joey even more?

She fasted Sunday with a prayer in her heart about what to do. She spent a great deal of time on her knees, pleading for help. She went downstairs in the morning to prepare her Sunday School lesson for the children at church that afternoon. She turned on the television to a church program while she searched for appropriate pictures for her lesson in the file cabinet. A woman was delivering a sermon about charity.

Dawn grabbed a file of pictures and sat down on the couch to go through them. As she glanced at the TV, suddenly the woman delivering the sermon seemed to be speaking only to Dawn. The words she heard were embedded into her spirit: "Don't ever accept abuse in the name of charity. *A most important love is love of self.* Charity, the pure love of Christ, is the supreme love; but to accept His love and to be able to love others, you must love yourself. If you allow someone to abuse you, you are not being charitable to yourself."

'Nor are you encouraging them to be charitable,' Dawn continued the thought in her head.

She had her answer, and she knew it. She knew the answer had come from her Father-in-Heaven in answer to her fasting and prayer. She hadn't ever felt that she could divorce Jace and still live the law of charity. Divorce was just too mean and ugly. How could she ever do it? But what about her spirit? What about Joey's spirit?

Still, as strong as the answer was, it wasn't the answer she had wanted. As she sat in church that day next to Jace and her children, she thought, 'This is heaven: to have your family all in church together and have peace. This is heaven.' This must be her answer. They were meant to be together. She must learn to stand up for herself and not let the abuse continue. She would raise the wall that was around her in order to survive.

Chapter 51

Conference

A brochure had come through Dawn's mail at work advertising a conference for those working in the mental health profession. The three-day workshop was on abuse, and it looked excellent. Her supervisor had told her that he would pay the cost of the conference for those wishing to attend, and Dawn signed up. She had told Jace at the beginning of the summer that she would have to be at work those days—that they were paying for her to attend—so that he could schedule with his extended family and his employers the date for their annual camping trip. Dawn always looked forward to camping. It reminded her of her first, wonderful camping trip with Jace when they were dating. Because Jace was around his family, he was usually good to her and the children during that time. The children loved going to the mountains, fishing, and playing with their cousins.

Jace came home from work one night and announced that he had scheduled time off work for the camping trip. When he told Dawn the dates, she realized that it was the same week as the conference.

"I told you, Jace, I couldn't go those days. I told you! I have to be to work. They have already paid for my registration at the conference."

"Well, they can un-register you then," he said flatly. "Dave, Susan, Missy and Mom and Dad are all planning on it."

She couldn't believe it. She had told him weeks ahead of time. She had so wanted to go to this conference—so needed to go to this conference—how could he? *"Don't let your husband ..."*

"Well, I guess you'll have to go without me then," she said resolutely. "I can drive up Wednesday afternoon after the conference." She was afraid of telling him no, but she knew somehow that she must go to the conference.

"I'm not going without you," he yelled at her as he walked out the door.

"Why can't you go up earlier?" she followed him. "Your family will be there, the kids will be there. Two days won't matter that much," she tried to reason with him. But it was a stalemate. He wouldn't budge. The weekend before the camping trip, he stormed around the house angrily and wouldn't speak to Dawn. He packed their tiny trailer and made preparations for the trip, so Dawn assumed that he would go ahead and leave Monday morning. He had made her life miserable for weeks, and she was so tired of arguing with him. She was almost glad he wasn't speaking to her anymore. Anger permeated the house.

She dressed and drove to the conference Monday morning. The morning sessions were excellent, and she was so glad to be able to attend, but it was hard to keep her mind on things. She was worried about what Jace was doing and about the children. At lunch, she called her neighbor.

"Has Jace left with the trailer, yet?" she asked. She had confided into her neighbor, Nora, the troubles she was having.

"No, he's still there," she answered. "The children are out playing in the front yard," she said.

"Thanks," she said, hanging up the phone. So he didn't leave. She wondered what game he was playing, and when she returned home she found out.

"Mommy, Daddy says it's your fault we can't go camping. Why can't we go camping? He told us he wasn't going to take us. He said he was going to leave us here alone. Can't you not go to work, Mommy?"

She was so angry at him for involving the children. He was making her into the bad guy once again. She had often been the wicked stepmother, but now Jace was doing it with their own children. "Why don't you just go and take them with you? You don't have to wait for me. You don't like me anyway," she said to him.

No answer. She was so frustrated with him. She remembered something the counselor had said to him once—that not taking a stand was the most powerful position of all. That was so true. That way she was always off-balance. When she didn't know where he was coming from, she had no control at all. It was very unnerving to her. "*Don't let your husband …*"

As she sat in the living room that night reading the paper, Jace walked up to her. "I never thought I'd say this," he started. "You threaten to leave me all the time. Well, honey, this time I'm thinking about leaving you. I was even thinking of taking you to the temple before you started this shit."

More attempts to control her. More punishment for not being submissive. But she had had enough punishment this summer. Enough war. Enough.

Before she left for the workshop the next morning, she walked out into the garage with the phone and called her lawyer. "I'd like to make an appointment for next week," she said. She'd had it. She could take no more.

Again, she called her neighbor from work at lunch time to check on things. "He's still here," she answered. "Your children have been playing over here all morning."

That morning, in one of the sessions, a handout detailing abuse was handed out. Dawn went through a self-questionnaire designed to let someone know if they were being abused.

To the question, "Has your partner ever done any of the following?" Dawn answered in the affirmative to:

Shoved you
Neglected you when you were sick or pregnant
Burned you
Caused bruises
Thrown you down the stairs (almost)
Threatened with objects or weapons
Criticized your sexual performance
Accused you of being a "whore"
Minimized your feelings about sex
Withheld affection as punishment
Manipulated you with lies, contradictions or promises
Blamed you for things
Criticized you
Threatened you, your family or your friends
Called you names—"bitch, whore," etc.
Ridiculed your most valued beliefs, religion, etc.
Undermined your sense of power or confidence
Told you to leave
Refused to work or to provide for the family
Tried to intimidate you
Threatened to take away your children
Made jokes that demean
Made you feel inadequate or worthless

Ignored your feelings or ideas
Threatened to commit suicide
Prevented you from sleeping
Humiliated you
Insulted you
Put you down
Forbid you to work, handle your own money, make decisions,
etc.
Tried to isolate you
Broken furniture, pictures, etc.
Punched holes in doors or walls, broken windows, etc.

Dawn was surprised that she had answered 'yes' to so many of the questions. She could think of specific examples for each 'yes' answer. So she was abused. She was one of those abused women she had always read about, but she had no bruises to prove it.

She read more of the handout: "A woman who has been abused over a long period of time is afraid. Not only is she afraid that she, herself, will be seriously hurt, but if she has children, she fears for their safety also … by being angry, the abuser is saying, 'As long as I am threatening to you, I can have my way.'"

In addition to the questions Dawn answered affirmatively, there were several categories of verbal abuse listed. Dawn could think of specific instances for each category listed: denial, demanding, forgetting, threatening, name calling, undermining, trivializing, criticizing, blaming, diverting, disguising as joking, discounting, countering, withholding. She approached the presenter after the meeting.

"What do you do if he does all these things to you, but he's too smart to leave any bruises?" Dawn asked intently. "I'm so afraid of losing my children … or of losing my mind … or of losing our lives. I'm so afraid of what he'll do."

The presenter looked at her sympathetically. "That's really hard. What I would do is get yourself a good counselor to help you work through these things."

'Been there, done that,' Dawn thought.

"The YCC is an excellent place to go for help," she added as Dawn thanked her and walked away.

When she got home that night, she was welcomed with more disdain from her husband and more questions of why she was being so mean from her children. Her stepchildren didn't speak to her either, but she had long been the "bad guy" with them.

She fixed a nice dinner that night, cleaning out the fridge of any items that would perish while they were gone. Ethan was rarely there for dinner anymore. Eric regularly showed up for dinner but turned up his nose at Dawn's efforts that night.

After dinner, Dawn walked upstairs to speak to Jace. "I'll try to leave early tomorrow, so we can get to the campsite before dark," she offered.

"If I'm still here," he said, walking away. "I've used two of my vacation days sitting around this house."

"You mean you've waited two days, and now you're going to leave?" she said, following him down the stairs. "You could have gone two days ago! Don't blame me for your vacation days—I told you long ago." She couldn't believe what he was saying and was so exhausted from his games. Didn't other married couples have conflicting schedules at times? Why couldn't he respect her wishes and support her?

He looked at her, full of contempt. "I'd love to slap your face off," he said to her as he walked out of the room.

As Dawn walked upstairs to the kitchen, she noticed that Ramen noodles were boiling on the stove. She was angry that Eric was making more dishes after refusing dinner. She yelled down the stairs at Eric. "Your noodles are done!"

He sneered at her as he came out of his room. "Go to hell," he yelled back. Like father, like son.

The next morning she was in a workshop about the detrimental effects of spanking. The presenter had divided everyone into groups. The members of her group introduced themselves and told about their places of employment. A woman across from her caught Dawn's notice when she said that she had an administrative position at the YCC.

Dawn left shortly after lunch, missing the final session of the workshop. She remembered that she was out of contact solution and film for her camera. She stopped at the grocery store and ran in quickly to retrieve the items. As she walked down the aisle, she was surprised to see the same woman from the YCC who had been in her group. Something told Dawn that she was supposed to run into this woman.

Dawn was in a hurry but talked to her briefly. In their short conversation, the woman gave Dawn the name and phone number of a counselor at the YCC. "I think it would be good for you to call and make an appointment with her." She also wrote down some names of lawyers that she recommended. Dawn thanked her and went to the check-out counter.

Jace was home when she got there and ready to leave. Dawn grabbed her pillow and some clothes, threw them into a bag and got in the truck. The ride to the campsite was long and silent as several thoughts went through Dawn's mind. Jace interrupted her thoughts. "Look at them," he motioned toward the children in the back of the truck, lying on sleeping bags among camping items under the camper shell. "They're so excited. They live for this. And you kept them from it, just so you could attend your precious workshop. You make me sick. You're dumber than hell."

Dawn didn't reply. After a couple hours of driving, Jace pulled off the freeway and stopped at McDonalds. It was the last stop before heading into the mountains. As they stood in line waiting for their dinner, Dawn told Jace that she was going to go use the restroom.

"I don't care," he said disgustedly, looking down at her with total disregard and hatred. The tone of his voice and the look in his eyes gave her chills. As she stood in the restroom booth, she tried to compose herself when tears came to her eyes. 'I will not cry,' she vowed.

More silence on the way to camp. Dawn was relieved when they drove into camp. She stretched as she got out of the truck. Soon Dave and Anne and Susan had joined them. As they stood there catching up on news, Jace said to her sweetly, "Why don't you go sit around the campfire with them and relax. I'll go unload the truck." Dawn looked at him incredulously and could only shake her head as he walked away.

Chapter 52

Ride Home

The iciness that preceded the camping trip continued. Jace might have tried at first to put up a good front before his family, but Dawn couldn't keep up the pretense. She isolated herself from him for most of the time. She spent a lot of time in the trailer alone and away from him, playing solitaire and thinking … and thinking …

As the week and then the weekend came to a close, Dawn took pictures of everything she had loved about camping before leaving. She took a picture of a large rock that she often sat on in front of the river. She took a picture of the bed in the trailer where Jace had once made love to her. She took a picture of the campsite and the mountains and her in-laws. She approached Susan.

"I think it's over," she said calmly to Susan.

"Things haven't seemed to go too well for you this trip," said Susan.

"Just don't hate me, Susan," Dawn said.

"Oh, I could never hate you," Susan replied affectionately. However, Dawn would never have the relationship again that she once had with Susan. Susan had once told Dawn that Jace had been hurt "really, really bad" (she had emphasized the really's); but she would never confide in Dawn what that hurt was. Dawn suspected that the source of that hurt was Jace's mother, Mary, but she would never know for sure. Because of that hurt, though, that Susan was so keenly aware of, Jace could never really do any wrong in her eyes. Susan had a soft spot for him that would never become hard; but Dawn was the recipient of all of that hurt and all of that pain and all of that anger, whatever it was and wherever it came from, and she was tired of it. She was losing her soft spots.

Dawn sat in the truck as Jace finished his goodbyes. He talked to Susan for quite a while. Dawn decided that she would try one last time.

Maybe they could have a really good talk on the way home. It was a long drive, and there were just the two of them.

But she couldn't penetrate the wall. He wouldn't look at her. His tone of voice was angry and sarcastic. More ice. She gave up.

The next morning after Jace went to work, Dawn called the number for the YCC and asked for the counselor that the woman in the workshop had recommended to her. The counselor told Dawn that she had an opening the following afternoon. Dawn told her that she would be there. It wasn't far from her attorney's office, and Dawn also had an appointment with him the next day.

Dawn used the day to clean up from the camping trip. She did the laundry, aired out sleeping bags, and unloaded the trailer. She caught Eric as he went out the door. "Eric," she said firmly, "the night before we left for camping and I told you that your noodles were done cooking, you told me to 'go to hell.' I think you owe me an apology for talking to me that way."

"I'll never apologize to you," he said stubbornly, anger and resentment flashing in his dark brown eyes.

"That's fine," Dawn replied calmly. "I just want you to know, though, that until you apologize I won't cook for you anymore. Don't show up for dinner tonight, or any other night, until you apologize to me." Eric stormed out the door.

Dawn knew that Jace would be angry if Eric told him what she said to him, but she knew that she needed to stand up for herself and that Eric needed to respect her. She dreaded Jace coming home that night. Eric apparently had gotten to him before he even walked in the door. He stormed into the kitchen.

"You *will* fix his dinner!" he demanded angrily, standing over her.

"Then tell him to apologize," Dawn answered.

"He doesn't have to apologize to *you*," Jace said demeaningly.

"Then I won't fix his dinner," Dawn answered. She was proud of herself for standing up to him but cowered inside. She was very afraid of what he would do. Jace had punished her for years when she didn't have his dinner ready when he got home from work, even though he never came home at the same time. It had been a stressful guessing game for Dawn.

Jace stormed out of the room. Dawn fixed the children and herself sandwiches, and they went outside and ate dinner. Jace made dinner for himself and Eric, and they ate inside. Dawn knew that he was plotting his next revenge against her and knew that there would be extreme punishment for what she had done. She just hoped that he would leave Joey out of it. That night as she went to bed, she glanced at the phone, its long cord dangling over the side of their headboard. A fleeting thought went through her mind of Jace grabbing the cord and strangling her in the middle of the night. Above their bed, anchored to the wall, was a gun rack full of rifles. In the closet were more weapons that wouldn't fit in the rack. Then there were always Eric and Ethan with their arsenal of weapons in the basement. She hated living in her own home and feeling so vulnerable. She had to get out of there …

Dawn sat in her attorney's waiting room, wishing she were anywhere else but there. Oh, how she didn't want to go through a divorce! Why couldn't Jace just die? Then she could be a grieving widow, and no one in Jace's family would hate her. They would surround her and support her. It would be so much easier on the children, and she would be so much better off financially. And there wasn't the stigma. Being a widow was much more acceptable, in her church and in society in general, than being a divorcee. Oh, those evil divorcees! Even she had judged them in the past. But her wishes for things to be easier only left her feeling more guilty. How could she wish for another human being, least of all her husband, to die? Even so, there had been moments she had questioned her *own* will to live, but she knew that she could never desert her children. Her eyes wandered to the sign on her attorney's closed door: *My lawyer can beat up your lawyer.* Oh, how she hoped it was true!

The door soon opened, and Jeff Gregory emerged, greeting her warmly and taking her hand. He was a man much shorter than Jace in stature with thinning, blonde, unruly hair and blonde mustache. He was a very attractive man with a deep, deep voice and a confident air about him. He certainly dressed like a lawyer, she thought. He hadn't seen her for a very long time. Dawn was sure that he didn't remember her and her oft-broken appointments; and that was fine with her.

As she told him of her experiences, she felt that he heard her, but she also felt that he had heard so many other stories of how terrible the "other half" is that he most likely didn't realize the real pain and danger she was in. He talked to her about cost and what papers she needed to file and the time it would take.

"You mean I have to live with this man for two more weeks?" she asked. She wasn't sure she could do that. She knew that real punishment awaited her for refusing to fix Eric's dinner.

"I'm afraid so. Unless you have grounds for a protective order," he said. "Then a sheriff can remove him from the home immediately."

"And he can't come back?" Dawn asked.

"You'll have a court hearing within a few days. If the protective order stands," he continued, "he can only come back with a policeman to get his things, and child support will automatically be arranged."

"Maybe I should just move out," Dawn thought aloud.

"I would never advise you to leave your home," he said. "Not with three children."

The whole thing made Dawn's stomach hurt. The vision of a sheriff escorting Jace away was more pain than she could deal with at the moment. She just couldn't do that to him. She couldn't hurt him that way. And she didn't want her children to see a sheriff taking their daddy away. But she didn't have the strength and energy to move either. She had done that before.

She left the lawyer with time to spare for the appointment at the YCC. She sat in her car for a few minutes in the YCC parking lot, trying to get up the nerve to go in. Just by going in the door, she knew she was admitting something. She didn't want anyone to see her. She wasn't one of those women who let themselves be beat up. She had more self-respect than that. As it came time for her appointment, she slowly got out of the car and walked in the door to find a woman sitting behind a desk. It reminded her of a desk clerk in a hotel—but this hotel was an old building. She motioned for Dawn to sit down while she summoned the victim advocate.

The advocate's name was Janice. She wasn't quite what Dawn expected. Middle-aged and worn, but attractive, Dawn felt like the lines in her face were lines of strength. She shook Dawn's hand and asked her to follow her. They walked up a steep staircase and entered a small room with a small corner dresser and two chairs. As they sat down, Janice said to Dawn, "So tell me why you're here."

Dawn wasn't sure where to begin and rambled between her horror stories. She ended with the latest dinner war with Eric.

The advocate straightened and said firmly, "I shouldn't say this, but if that had been my son and my husband, they'd be out on the front porch."

Dawn felt ashamed at her weakness, but it was exactly what she needed to hear.

"Tell me why you want to stay with this man," Janice continued.

"I … I love him," Dawn said.

"And what is it that you love about him?"

"Well," she answered slowly, "sometimes he's really nice to me. Usually on holidays."

"I'd feel better if you said that that was the only time he wasn't nice," Janice replied. "He's a package deal, Dawn. You take him; you take the package. By telling you that you have to fix the boys' dinner, he's elevating them over you."

Dawn knew what she said was true. "I'm so afraid," she started to cry. "I'm so afraid that he'll take the children, that I'll never see them again. He's made so many threats against me, against his ex-wife. I'm afraid he'll kill me. I'm even afraid that he'll hurt the children. He can be so mean. He won't talk to me, so I wrote him a long letter. He refused to read it."

"I do believe that you are genuinely afraid of him," she said. "Has he ever hurt you physically?"

Dawn recounted the story of the stairs and the bruises on her arms and threats to hurt her. "He told me that he'd love to smash my face in." Dawn told her of the different schemes he had to kill Juanita. The more she talked to the counselor, the more she wondered why she was still with Jace. Then she told her what she had never told anyone.

"One day, when he was talking about how he hated Juanita, I said to him, 'Oh, you wouldn't really kill her. You're just mad.' He looked at me with a look that was pure evil and said, 'Nothing would give me more pleasure than slitting her throat and pissing in it while I watched her bleed to death.'" Dawn dissolved into more tears at the thought of the man she was married to and what he was capable of doing. She told Janice about the counseling they received and how Dr. Thomas gave up and counseled her to leave.

"That tells me right there, Dawn, that there was really no hope, because there is always some change a counselor can affect in someone. Counselors rarely give up. If you would like to get a protective order, I have one here. I'll help you fill it out right now, but it's up to you to file it with the court. If you want me to go to court with you, I can do that, too."

Dawn nodded and answered Janice's questions through tears as she filled out the form. That night, as she ate alone again with her children, she told them that she was going to divorce their father. Joey seemed relieved, and Taylor seemed to understand. But as she tucked Davey in that night, while Jace watched TV downstairs, Davey sobbed.

"I don't want Daddy to leave," he cried over and over again. "I don't want Daddy to leave!"

Dawn's resolve was shaken. 'What am I doing?' she thought to herself. She pulled out her journal and read some of the entries:

"Davey sneezed at the table tonight. Jace yelled at him and swore at him, telling him to cover his mouth. When I put Davey to bed, he said to me, 'Daddy was being mean to me. I want a new daddy.' He then said, 'Mommy, when Daddy starts talking to you, just don't listen, because he's being mean …'"

"Eric hit Joey in the leg as hard as he could. Jace was standing right there and didn't do a thing to Eric. Joey said, 'Mommy, Eric could shoot me, and Daddy wouldn't care.' I told Jace if Ethan and Eric ever hurt me or the children again, I would call the police. He said, 'That will be the last thing you ever do …'"

"Ethan tried to insult me in every possible way, turning to a stream of profanities directed at me and Joey. I told him to leave the room. He refused. I was ironing and held up the iron, telling him to leave. He said he was going to 'shove that iron up your a-.' I tried to grab the phone. He pulled it out of the wall and walked out of the room. I locked the door …"

"Ethan walked into my room tonight as I was changing. I had the door closed tight. When I asked Jace to put a new lock on my door, he called me a b-ch …"

"Jace yelled at me for buying him a hamburger. Called the food I make 'sh- …' and told me I 'wasn't worth pissing on …'"

"Yelled at me when I asked him to put the groceries away …"

"Yelled at me when we ran out of mayonnaise …"

"Bit my head off for leaving the flashlight on the counter …"

"I have a patch of eczema on my upper leg several inches in diameter. I'm sure it's just from stress. My arthritis has flared again. I don't want to go through another surgery. I've had so many surgeries …"

"Jace wrote checks again when he knew we had no money—now we have $100 in bad check fees …"

"Jace made Joey sweep the floor (Taylor's job) when I mentioned that Eric hadn't done the dishes …"

"Threatened to slap Joey's face …"

"Hit Joey twice on the backside of his head …"

"Pulled Joey's ear …"

"Shut Joey's head in the freezer when he was getting ice out of it. Joey cried and Jace said, 'You're not hurt …'"

"Jace got angry tonight when I was talking on the phone. I told him to go ahead and eat without me, but he refused. Pat was on the other end and could hear him yelling. I told her I had to go and would talk to her later. I was so embarrassed …"

"Today was Valentine's Day. Jace didn't go to work. He told me he quit his job—that he was tired of working and supporting me. We got into an argument, and I left for work angry and hurt again. Later, I found out that he had 'use-or-lose' leave from work that he had to take. He brought a huge bouquet of red and pink balloons to work for me. Everyone was so impressed. Another roller coaster ride …"

"I needed money to pay the bills. Jace told me he didn't have any. While he was downstairs in his sweats watching TV, I looked in his uniform pants for his wallet. It wasn't there. I found it hidden in his clothes hamper. I opened it up. It was full of cash ..."

"We drove by a house tonight that had a boat out in front of it for sale. 'Oh, how I'd love to have a boat,' I told Jace. 'You could have had one,' he said, 'if you'd been a good girl. I was going to buy you one …'"

She sat downstairs in the living room, long after everyone was asleep, and wrote to herself:

Do you want to be married to a man who:
1. Doesn't support you?
2. Constantly criticizes you?
3. Lies to you?
4. Swears at you and your children?
5. Insults you?
6. Hurts Joey?
7. Shows you no affection?
8. Never initiates sex?
9. Never compliments you?
10. Doesn't care about your feelings?
11. Always puts your needs last?
12. Gets pleasure from harassing you?
13. Doesn't keep the commandments?
14. Doesn't want to take you to the temple?

15. Can't express feelings—only anger?
16. Never lets go of the past?
17. Blames others for his actions?
18. Does one percent of the work?
19. Won't attend the children's events?
20. Never supports you with his children?
21. Punishes you when you do what you want?
22. Keeps money all for him and lies about it?
23. Is mean?
24. Watches horrible shows?
25. Ridicules you for your beliefs?
26. Treats you the worst when you are ill?
27. Has continual temper tantrums?
28. Threatens you?
29. Writes bad checks?
30. Orders you around?

The list could have gone on, but the truth was in front of her. No, she did not want to live with this man anymore. She couldn't live with this man anymore. Whatever might happen was not worth what it took from her to stay with him. Let him kill her—she was all but dead as it was. And he was killing Joey, inch by inch. She had done all that she could and more. She was the only one trying. He had worn her down. This was not a marriage. They were not partners. She had been his doormat long enough. She must overcome her fears. She must find the strength somehow to get out and stay out.

Chapter 53

Order

The next day Dawn mustered up all the energy she could to get herself to work after her week's vacation. After she was done teaching, she stopped by Dr. Thomas' office hoping he would have a minute to spare. Dawn was grateful that he was free and told him of her latest plans.

"I could go one of two ways," she explained. "I could file for divorce, or I could get a protective order."

"I think a protective order would be the way to go," he counseled, "given all the circumstances."

"He'll never see the children again!" Dawn sighed. "He told me if I ever left him, that was it."

"He's not a very nice man, Dawn," Dr. Thomas replied.

Dawn returned to her office and phoned Jace, not really knowing why but hoping for a miracle to occur over the phone. More iciness. Her resolve strengthened. Then she called Nancy. Nancy could hear the desperateness in Dawn's voice, as Dawn told her she was going to drive to the courthouse.

"Stop by and get me," Nancy said firmly. "I want to go with you."

Dawn was grateful for Nancy's support. Her knees crumbled under her as she walked up the courthouse stairs. She was shaking and sobbing. Nancy held onto her. "You can do this," she said firmly.

The judge was a very kind, old gentleman with a full, gray beard and big, blue eyes. He reminded Dawn of Santa Claus. Dawn was afraid that there wasn't enough physical abuse documented for her to get a protective order.

"If you don't get it," Nancy offered, "then it's not the right thing to do. If you do, then you'll know it is."

The judge didn't need any more evidence. All he had to do was look at the pitiful, broken, sobbing, shaking woman in front of him. "I don't want him anywhere near you," he said. "Is he mean to the children?" he asked intently.

"He is to my oldest son," Dawn said. She considered adding Joey's name to the protective order but decided otherwise. That would just give Jace even more fuel to target him. She didn't want him treated differently from the others. She asked about Eric and Ethan. Would they be able to come to the house?

"If their father doesn't live there, they have no reason to come to the house," he assured her.

The judge signed the order and sent her to the sheriff's office to have it served. They told her that they would have it served at his work. She didn't want to embarrass him at work, but that would be better than having the children involved.

"How long will it take?" Dawn asked the clerk.

"It should be served this afternoon," she said.

Her knees again crumbled. Nancy followed her to a pay phone. She was intent on calling Jace. He answered, his tone turning icy when he realized it was Dawn.

"I want you to know," she said shakily, "that this is killing me. I love you. Please do something to fix all of this and come back to us."

"Whatever," he said.

"Goodbye, Jace," she said, and hung up the phone.

Nancy held onto her as she walked her to the car. Dawn dropped her off before heading for home. "Let me know if you need me," she said, outside the car window. "I'm here for you."

"Thanks so much," Dawn replied appreciatively.

Dawn returned home exhausted. She called her neighbor, Nora, who was watching her children. "Could you keep them a little longer?" she asked. "I'm trying to get some of my composure back."

"Sure," Nora replied. Dawn was grateful for good friends. She lay on her bed and cried and cried, hoping to get it all out of her so she could be decent later for her children. Soon she drifted off to sleep and was startled when the phone rang. It was Jace.

"Have you done something?" he demanded. "Have you started some-thing?" Dawn realized that he must have realized things were not quite right when she called him. She also realized he hadn't seen the sheriff yet.

"Yes, I have," she said.

"Then there's no going back," he said angrily. "You started it, I'm going to finish it."

"Okay," Dawn said resignedly, as Jace hung up the phone. She glanced at the clock. Jace would be home in an hour.

She called the sheriff's office. They checked and confirmed that the order had not yet been served.

"But he's on his way home and knows something's up!" she said desperately, panic rising within her. "I thought he would be served! I called and told him goodbye!"

The clerk advised her to leave the home. "Take your important papers with you and leave the house. We'll send a sheriff out tonight, and then you can return to your home later."

Dawn went hurriedly through the house and took what she didn't want to lose. She took the photograph albums and pictures off the walls, as she knew Jace still had all of Juanita's pictures from their marriage. She went through the file cabinet and grabbed papers on the house and any other papers she thought were important. She took clothes for herself and the children for the next day and took their pajamas—she didn't want to stay there alone that night. She would stay at her sister's. She didn't want to worry her father. She put everything in the trunk of her car and went to Nora's to pick up the children.

She did her best to be composed and calm in front of them. She took them out to get hamburgers and ate inside the restaurant with them. She explained to them that their father would be leaving that night, as well as Eric and Ethan. She did her best to reassure them and comfort them. She was glad that Davey had gotten over his crying and seemed fine.

Nora called her at Pat's later that evening. She informed Dawn that the sheriff had come and that Jace and the boys had left. "I talked to the sheriff," she said. "He came to our address first by mistake. I told him that you had good reason to be afraid of him. Jace loaded up your little trailer and took it down the road to his brother's. I can see it on their lot out my back window. I'm sure the protective order caught him off guard. He was probably expecting to get served with divorce papers but not a protective order."

Dawn thanked Nora, put the children to bed, and tried to sleep. She awoke off and on through the night, often in tears, but managed to make it to work the next morning. She hadn't been there long when Nora called again.

"Ethan and Eric are at your house and are taking things out of your yard," she told her excitedly. "You'd better call the sheriff."

Dawn immediately called the sheriff, who told her their office would have to speak to the judge about the order. The judge called her back. "Have the boys ever been mean to your children?" he asked her.

"Yes, they have," Dawn answered. "I was afraid to leave my children there with them alone anymore."

"I'm afraid that you're going to have to fill out another protective order against your stepsons, in order to prevent your husband from sending the boys to your home," he said resignedly. "Let me know if you have any more problems."

So Dawn went to the courthouse again. Anne told her later that Jace was furious when the sheriff served the orders and said that he was going to sue Dawn for having a minor served. Dawn felt especially bad for having to involve Ethan and Eric but knew deep down that it was Jace's doing. He was the one who sent them back to the house. The protective order against Jace was also his own doing: she had not kicked him out; he had kicked himself out of the house. It was his doing. Had he been even the least bit decent, she would not have been able to get a protective order without lying. She had not lied.

When Dawn returned home that afternoon, she took stock of what she was missing. The boys had picked up several of the animals, and that was fine with her. She couldn't take care of them. She soon came to realize, though, that some of her most precious things were missing. Her camera was gone, along with the roll of film she had taken of the campsite and trailer. Jace had also taken one of the pictures she had in her drawer of herself with her mother and father on her wedding day. What would he want with a picture of her parents except to hurt her? She thought it was especially mean.

Her dad and brother came out that evening and installed new security doors on her front and back entrances. She was so grateful for their help. The locks were changed, and Jace and Eric and Ethan were gone. They could not return without a policeman's escort and then only to pick up their belongings. Now she just had to get Jace out of her heart …

Her only experience with court had been sitting outside the room when Jace was involved with Juanita. This time she would go inside. Jace had always made fun of his sister, Missy, for taking her father with her when she divorced her first husband; so Dawn was intent on doing this alone. Her lawyer, however, would be at her side. Jace was not alone though, as Ethan and Eric sat at his side.

The hearing went well. Dawn had hoped that the judge would order Jace to go to anger management classes, but her attorney discouraged her hopes. "It's the usual consensus that if he's ordered to go, it will only increase his anger. That's something he needs to recognize and take care of on his own."

Dawn understood. Certainly her attempts to force counseling had not helped in the past, but how she had hoped that something would help her situation.

The commissioner made the protective order permanent, in spite of Jace's protests. He had never hit her! She had no need of a protective order! Dawn wished that she had the same judge in front of her who had issued her protective order. He had been so compassionate, so understanding. This commissioner was much younger and seemed jaded, somehow. "We have our own stories," Jace told him. Dawn wondered what their stories were. Had they ever feared for their lives? Was she terrible because she wanted the drapes pulled at night to keep the sun out of her eyes in the morning? Or was it because she asked them to cover the food in the microwave so she didn't have to constantly clean up their messes. She decided their stories were merely that—stories.

The commissioner also set an amount for Jace to pay child support and part of day care costs, allowing Dawn to stay in the house with her children, "until it's decided who gets the house," the judge said, "if the divorce goes through. Maybe this is just a lover's quarrel," he quipped.

"Is it possible that he'll get the house?" Dawn whispered to her attorney. Her stomach began to hurt.

"Don't worry," he reassured her. "It's not likely." She was grateful that she had filed the protective order and had stayed in the house. Had she left, she was sure that she would have lost the house. She was glad her attorney had advised her to stay there.

She came home exhausted from the hearing and went next door to Nora's to get her children. She told Nora that the next step would be for her to file for divorce, but she couldn't afford the fee.

"Then why pay it?" Nora asked her. Dawn looked at her questioningly. "No, really," Nora continued. "You've got him out of the house—that's the hardest part. Child support has been set, so you've got that. Let him file for divorce and pay the fee. That puts the ball in his court."

As Dawn thought about it, she thought that it was a good idea. Why should she file? She had gotten the protective order—that was hard enough. If Jace filed, that would help him save some face, help him feel like he had some power in all of this, and it might help assuage some of his anger. She could just hear him telling everyone that he was the one who filed for divorce, implying that it was all her fault. But she didn't care. That was okay. Those who really knew her would know the truth. The rest didn't matter. And it just might save her life.

Chapter 54

Light Bulbs, Plants and Pinball

It had only been a few days since the hearing, and Dawn was exhausted. Everything had taken such an emotional toll, which then expended a physical toll. She tried not to cry, but she usually dissolved into tears each night. In spite of his cruelty, in spite of the perpetual ice, she still missed him. Loneliness consumed her. More than once she had gone to his side of the closet, where some of his clothes still hung, and smelled his flannel shirts. Would she ever get over him? She had fantasies of him coming back to her on bended knee, of apologizing for the first time in his life, of apologizing to everyone for how he had treated his wife and children. She longed for him to realize what he had done, to take some responsibility for the whole mess, to be a loving husband and father. She had lain on her bed for a few moments to gather strength to get up and fix dinner for the children. She could hear them fighting downstairs. In fact, there had been a great deal of fighting between them lately; along with a fair share of disobedience. She had asked them to pick up their toys before dinner. She came downstairs to messes everywhere.

"Okay," she shouted down the basement. "Everybody up here. I want to talk to you."

Joey, Taylor and Davey lumbered reluctantly up the stairs amid protest. "What's for dinner, Mommy?" Taylor asked.

"I'm hungry," Davey added.

"We'll eat in a minute," Dawn answered. "Come sit down. I want to talk to you."

Dawn sat in the brown rocking chair her parents had given her for her birthday—the chair she had rocked all of them in, despite Jace's protests. She looked steadily at the three of them. "Listen," she began.

"I know all that has happened lately hasn't been easy on any of you. I know you miss your daddy. But I also know that you all know how hard this has been on me. I never wanted this to happen. But your fighting and not minding me are only making things worse. Why are you treating me this way?"

Taylor looked at Dawn intently and answered calmly, "Well, how do you expect us to treat you, Mommy? How do you think we've watched Daddy treat you all this time?"

From the mouth of babes! A light bulb went off in Dawn's head. A huge light bulb. She had taught her children, by accepting Jace's mistreatment of herself, to mistreat her also. She must turn things around. She must earn her children's respect. Things must change, and they must change now …

Dawn knew that Jace would soon be returning to pick up the rest of his things. When he came back, she wanted the house to be spotless. He had often criticized her house-cleaning efforts along with everything else. She also wanted things put away that were special to her that she was afraid he would take. She expected him to come that weekend but wasn't ready for him. She purposely didn't answer the phone on Saturday and cleaned all day. The next day, the call came. Dawn arranged for Nora to take the children to the park. She didn't want them there in the middle of it all.

Jace not only showed up with a policeman but with reinforcements. He had both of his sons, his brother Dave and his two sons, and an empty flat-bed trailer hooked to the back of his truck. The policeman was little help with six people in six different places. The policeman stuck close to Jace. As Jace went to load up the house plants, the policeman looked at Dawn for her permission. Dawn nodded that it was okay. She wanted no reminders left of him. "They're probably all dead anyway," Jace said as he approached the fern in the corner. "I'm sure they haven't been watered." As he picked it up, the bottom of the pot separated to reveal two inches of water. "Do you think you watered this enough?" he said sarcastically to Dawn. "Root rot," he said disgustedly, shaking his head. She didn't answer him but thought to herself, 'First not enough water, then too much. Never could win with him.'

She walked to the back door to see Ethan and Eric loading up all the tools in the garage. Dawn was grateful that she had wheeled the lawn mower, along with rakes and snow shovel, over to Nora's earlier in the day and put them in her shed. She still needed to mow the lawn, rake, and shovel her driveway. She then walked to the front door to see what was happening in the front yard. As she stood there holding the door, Jace brushed by her angrily carrying things out the door, pinching her arm. The policeman was not there. Dawn walked out front and sat in the swing that hung from the large cottonwood tree. Jace had made it for her one Mother's Day. With the trailer loaded, the policeman came over to her and asked her if everything were okay.

"Um, I just bought that case of toilet paper at the store yesterday that's sitting on the back of their trailer."

"Oh, he didn't mean to take that, did you sir?" the policeman addressed Jace.

Ethan picked up the box and put it back in the garage.

The policeman addressed Dawn in the swing. "Every time I do this, it makes me appreciate my wife and marriage."

"Never again will I have to hear him swear at me, threaten me, put me down," she said with resolve, as Jace's truck pulled away. Dawn sat and sat in the swing …

When the children returned, Dawn told them what had happened before they noticed things amiss. "Daddy took the three-wheeler, Mommy!" Joey cried.

"It didn't work anyway, honey," Dawn comforted him.

"I know, but I could've fixed it!"

Dawn felt bad but was so relieved that part was over.

Later that night as she tucked the children in bed and kissed them goodnight, Taylor said to her, "Mommy, you know that game where you pull a knob and a ball goes up and hits something and it dings and lights up, and then it hits something else and goes ding?"

"You mean a pinball machine?" Dawn answered her.

"Yeah. That's kind of like Daddy," she continued. "Something comes along that he doesn't like and he gets mad and yells … and then something else and he gets mad again … and he's just always getting mad and going ding."

"That's a good comparison," Dawn said, amazed at the insight of her smart little girl.

Chapter 55

James

Jace traded trailers for a larger one and moved a block away and across the street. It was on property they had bought a few years earlier at a time when Jace had hoped to open his own car repair business. The neighbors had protested their plans, however; so to spite them, Jace had placed as many pigs as he could on the property. He purposely stunk up the place.

Now in addition to the pigs, he added a trailer. Dawn could see the fifth-wheel from her front porch. She hated having him so close and figured that that was his purpose in moving there—along with the convenience of it all; but she told Anne that she was glad he was there. "That way the children can see him more easily," she had told her. Anne expressed to Dawn how difficult it had been for her and Dave to have Jace reside with them on their property. Apparently, Jace and sons hadn't been the ideal tenants. She knew Anne understood her reasons for leaving him.

In spite of his proximity, Jace seldom saw the children. Dawn had decided long ago that she didn't want them to ever blame her for not being able to see their father. So she placed no restrictions. She told her children that they could see him as often as they wanted—and she never restricted Jace from seeing them. And because of that, he saw them very little. Had she told him that he couldn't see them, she figured, he would have been knocking down her door. It was always a game to him, she had decided.

Soon after he had bought the fifth-wheel trailer, the children wanted to go over and see it. They called him up and he allowed them to come, but still he had to be in control. The only way he would see them was if Dawn walked them over and came and picked them up. He would not come pick them up or bring them home. So Dawn walked them down their street and across the busy highway to his trailer. She stood feet away and watched them go in the door with a prayer in her heart. Jace was prepared when they came to fill their heads with information to get back to Dawn and hurt her.

He had bought new clothes—new levis, shirts, new cowboy boots—and laid them out on his bed for them to see. Jace never bought clothes when he was with her. Whenever she had money, she had tried to buy nice clothes for him to wear. He had been content to wear his work uniform all day and put on old sweats at night. He told them he had a girl friend and had to buy new clothes to take her out. Of course the children came home with this report, as well as other derogatory things he had said about her. And of course she was hurt by it, as much as she tried not to be. Another night crying herself to sleep.

"Maybe you could tell Daddy that I don't say bad things about him and that you don't like to hear him say bad things about me," she offered after hearing their report. But then she realized—from the panic on Joey's face—that that was wrong. It would be so hard for Joey to stand up to his imposing father; and she was putting them in the middle, something she didn't want to do to them.

Anne had told her that Jace's intent was not to see the children at all—and that it was only James who convinced Jace to continue to see them. "Don't you punish the children," he told him. "They're your kids." But all of that was to change. Anne called Dawn one day with the news: James was in the hospital and wasn't doing well at all.

Dawn went directly to the hospital after work that afternoon to see him. When the elevator doors opened to his floor, she was surprised to see Susan and Missy standing in the foyer. When Susan saw Dawn, she threw her arms around her and wept. "He has cancer," she sobbed. "He's dying."

Dawn felt so bad. In fact, it tore her up inside. She knew how much Jace loved his father. And she loved James, also. She wished she could go to Jace, to comfort him, but she knew that was impossible.

Dawn walked down the hallway and into James' room. Mary was standing at his side. He smiled when he saw Dawn, and she took hold of his hand. "I want you to know that I love you," she said to him, lowering her head to kiss his cheek.

"I love you, too," he said to her intently. Dawn left the room with tears in her eyes but grateful to hear that he still loved her, in spite of everything. She didn't realize that those would be the last words he would say to her. As she walked down the hallway, Missy approached her nervously.

"Dawn," she said, "you know when the sheriff came and made Jace leave the house?" Dawn nodded her head. "How did you do that?"

Dawn looked at Missy. "Missy, is your new husband abusing you?"

Missy started to cry. "I'm so afraid," she continued. "He dragged me across the room by my hair … and when he gets drunk …"

"What I did," Dawn explained, "was I went to the YCC, and they helped me get a protective order. Oh, Missy, if you want me to, I'll go with you. In fact, I can go right now if you want."

Missy nodded. They walked to Dawn's car, and Dawn drove her. They met with one of the counselors there, and Missy told them what she had been going through. She helped her fill out an order, but it was still up to Missy to file it. As Dawn drove Missy back to the hospital, she told her of some of her struggles with Jace.

"I know he has a temper," Missy acknowledged. "He's always had a bad temper."

The next morning, Anne called Dawn and told her that James had died during the night. Dawn felt so bad. She wanted so much to call Jace but knew that he hated her. So she did what she could for the rest of the family. She went and bought buckets of chicken and delivered them to her soon-to-be-ex in-laws.

The next morning on her way to church, she grabbed the morning paper. As she read the obituary, she noticed her name purposely missing. She was in tears as she walked into the building. After the service, she asked to speak to the bishop.

"How could they do that?" she said to him. "I'm still his wife. His dad told me that he loved me two days ago! His mom told me that I meant as much to her as her daughters! How could they do that?" she said in tears. "How can I go to the funeral?"

"Dawn," he tried to comfort her, "down the road people will see what kind of man he is and what kind of woman you are. You need to not let anyone keep you from doing what you want to do and what you know is best."

Anne called Dawn later that day. "I told him that would hurt you," she said, referring to the omission. "I told them all that your name should be in there," she said, "but Jace would have no part of it."

Dawn tried in her heart to not hold their family responsible. She knew how stubborn Jace could be. She had hurt him. He must retaliate. Still, she felt so left out of things. She wanted to be with their family.

She wanted to hug her sisters-in-law. She wanted to be there for Jace. She should have waited to divorce him, she told herself.

She decided that she would indeed attend the funeral. She would take her children to honor their grandfather. That morning as she dressed, her father called.

"I'm going with you," he told her firmly.

"Oh, Dad, you don't have to do that," she said.

"I'm not going to let you go through this alone." She was so grateful for his support.

She drove to her father's home and picked him up. He walked out and looked very handsome wearing a tan wool sports coat. Dawn was so grateful that he was with her. She was going to go be with her family, but they weren't her family any more. She hated the feeling in her stomach.

It was December and was a cold, gray day. She remembered driving up the winter that they were first married to bury Jace's brother. Jace had not let her in any more at that time than he would this time. As she arrived at the church where the service was held, she got into line to walk through the procession. Jace's cousin Jim, a cousin that Dawn had been especially fond of, came over and put his arm around her. "Are you going to be okay?" he asked her affectionately.

"I don't know if I'll ever be okay," Dawn replied, slipping her arm around him and squeezing him.

Mary was standing at the beginning of the line, next to James' coffin. Mary was glad to see the children but seemed very distant to Dawn. Dawn hugged her and continued through the line. Jace was standing at the end of the line, looking very handsome, dressed in slacks and a sweater vest that Dawn had never seen before. More new clothes. When she got to Jace, he refused to look at her, but she spoke to him anyway. "I'm so sorry, Jace," she said. "I love you." No response. She moved on. All the eyes in the room were on them. Anne told her later that several had made bets on whether they would speak to each other.

She remained in the room for the family prayer that was offered. Susan's husband said a very nice prayer. As the family filed into the chapel for the service, Dawn told her children they could go and sit up front with their father. Dawn sat in the back, grateful for the presence of her own father next to her. After the service, the children got into her car with her father. Dawn glanced to her left and saw Ethan standing apart with his cousins smoking. James' brother, whom Dawn was also very fond of, came over to her. Dawn hugged him, and he started to cry. "I don't understand this at all," he said to Dawn, who wasn't sure whether he meant the death of his brother or her impending divorce.

"I don't understand it either," Dawn said.

Then she saw anger flash in his eyes. "It's a bunch of bullshit," he said angrily and turned and walked away.

Dawn had decided not to go to the cemetery for the burial. The funeral had been stressful enough. After James' brother's reaction to her, she knew for sure that she should leave. She had paid her respects to James. She knew he loved her and that she loved him. That was enough.

As she lay in her bed, exhausted after the day's events and fighting the inevitable tears, she was surprised to hear a knock at her door so late in the evening. When she opened the door, a grinning young man asked if she were Dawn Malone and handed her an envelope. Dawn then realized that she had been "served" papers.

She walked up to her bedroom, sat on the bed that she had shared with Jace for eleven years, and opened the envelope. It was from Jace's lawyer. Jace had filed for divorce. Dawn was certain that he had given explicit instructions for the papers to be delivered on the night his father was buried.

Chapter 56

War

So it was war. Dawn was almost relieved that Jace had filed. She knew now the direction they were headed. She had put the ball in his court, and he had served it.

Jace called on Christmas Eve and talked to the children. He told them he had some presents for them and to come over and get them. Dawn obediently walked them over to the trailer, and when they called she walked them back home. Jace gave them a video (the movie 'Babe') and some candy. Even though they didn't know it (but Dawn suspected), they would not visit their father again. With James gone, Jace had become even more bitter and had written them off. It was his retaliation against Dawn.

That evening, after the children went to bed, she got Christmas ready. Her thoughts went back to the previous Christmas Eve. 'This has to be better than that,' she thought. She made all the same preparations as she would have had Jace been there, without the turmoil. They would still keep their traditions. She wanted the children to have a sense of security and unity and family. Santa would still come, and Christmas breakfast would be ready. What she missed most was the presence of her mother. That was a void that couldn't be filled.

The first hearings that were scheduled for court seemed to always be cancelled, as the lawyers arranged and rearranged schedules. And in the meantime, Dawn received unsolicited phone calls.

The first call was from the cattle auction. Dawn's lawyer had subpoenaed the auctions records to document how much cattle Jace had sold since their separation. The report came back: $5,000! Jace was furious when he found out and had one of his famous intimidation tantrums at the auction offices.

"I'm just calling to warn you," the man on the phone said. "He was very angry. I know him—I've known him for a while. I told him,

'Jace, calm down,' but he was out of control."

"I've put up with that for years," Dawn told him.

"Lady, I wouldn't put up with that for one minute." Dawn wondered why she had.

The next call came from the bank. Dawn had taken her name off of the joint account, and when he found out, Jace was very angry. "We're just calling you to let you know," the teller had said. "He was really, really mad." Dawn thanked them.

The doctor's office called. "Your husband said he would not pay the bills and not to use his insurance," they told Dawn. "And he was very angry."

When she went to rent a video from the video store, they informed her that she no longer had an account there and would have to open another one. "Your husband told us to take your name off the account." Dawn almost laughed. He wouldn't keep her name on a video rental account but expected her to keep her name on their bank account!

Dawn slowly began to realize the battle she was in for. And she began to line up her ducks. She was not going to give into him, no matter how afraid she might be of his wrath. "That's what he wants you to do," her bishop had told her. "He wants you to curl up in a ball and give up." Jace had neglected to take a large box of things stored from his first marriage. Dawn decided to take a long and thorough look through those things.

Dawn was surprised, as she went through the papers, to find other things Jace had hidden while they had been together. She found bonus checks from his work that she had never known he had. Of particular interest were a bundle of receipts—$7,000 worth—from the sale of cattle. As she studied the dates, she realized that he had this money at the same time she was working nights for the paper so that they could afford Christmas. He couldn't afford to give her money for milk while he was hiding $7,000! He had certainly never spent any of it on her. He had been continually deceitful to her throughout their marriage. Was her whole marriage a lie? Had anything been legitimate? Did he ever even really love her at all?

As she continued her snooping, feeling fully justified as she was arming herself for battle, she came across medical receipts for testosterone shots he had received while married to Juanita. What was up with that? Why would such a large, masculine man get testosterone shots? Did that make him even more angry? More aggressive? Did he get them to increase his sex drive? Was that the reason he never touched her—he just didn't have the hormonal desire? Her search left her with more questions than answers.

Of particular interest to her was a letter from Juanita. She sounded very different from the Juanita that Dawn knew of or the Juanita that Jace had painted for Dawn. The letter was written during their separation. In it, Juanita pleaded with Jace for him to let her see the children, to have some decency. "How do you think it makes them feel," she pleaded, "when you won't let them see their own mother? Ida already is beginning to resent you," she wrote. "Please let me see my children."

As Dawn added up her weapons, she began to fear Jace even more, not because of his reinforcements but because of his lack of them. With Juanita, he got the house, he got the children, and he got the child support. With Dawn, she had the house, she had the children, and she got the child support. He couldn't lose like that. His hatred of Juanita had been enough for him to fantasize about killing her. His hatred of Dawn must be much more intense. Surely, he would kill her, one way or another …

And there were more worries. Dawn was worried about the effect the divorce would have on her children. She had taken them all to see a counselor through her work—she had a few free visits as a benefit of her employment. She went to see the counselor first and gave him a synopsis of the past several years.

"I wish he were short, fat, bald and ugly," Dawn lamented to the counselor. "It would just be easier somehow." She told him about his winning the beard contest—that she knew he would—and that he could have been a model.

"He's lethal," the counselor, a young nice-looking man himself, told Dawn. "Guys like that are lethal. And I bet he gave you flowers when you were dating."

Dawn wondered how he knew this. "Yes, he did," she said, "when all I had was a sore throat."

"I swear, it's a bad sign," he continued. "I know there are legitimate reasons for giving flowers, but I know of more abusers who sweep their wives off their feet when they're dating. And I also bet you never had an argument before you married."

Dawn wondered how he knew this, but he was right.

"People need to have disagreements before they marry—it helps them work things out after they're married." Dawn remembered Jace being agreeable to everything she wanted before their marriage.

"I don't understand why I'm having such a hard time getting over him," Dawn continued. "I loved my mom more than anything and miss her more than anything, but I have peace with her being gone. But with Jace I have no peace."

"Bad relationships are always harder to get over than good ones," he counseled. "You had a good relationship with your mom, and you've been able to put that loss to rest. Your relationship with Jace has only brought you pain and turmoil. That takes a while to get over. Had you stayed with him, what do you think your life would be like ten years from now?"

"Much the same as it was when I left, only I don't think I'd be any kind of person at all. I would be reduced to nothing. I nearly feel that way now. And my children … Joey would have been destroyed. He would have no self-esteem. My children wouldn't respect me. They would be like their father."

"Remember that," he told Dawn. She felt much better after talking to him. She brought her children to her next appointment and was slightly nervous as she sat outside the room they were in, wondering what they were all telling him. He opened the door with a big grin on his face. "You've got great kids," he said. "They've got a good handle on things. You've done a good job. I don't think you need to worry."

But Dawn did worry. She worried that Taylor would grow up to marry a man just like her father. She worried that Davey would never get over the abandonment or all his losses. And she worried that Joey would grow up to be Jace. She worried about the effect that all of the abuse Jace heaped on Joey would have. He had been so cruel to Joey, and Dawn had put up with it much longer than she should have. One night, after fighting with Davey, Joey dissolved into tears, saying, "Mommy, I'm becoming Daddy."

"No, you're not," Dawn reassured him. She resolved to get him some help. She would not ask Jace to share the expense; she didn't even want him to know. She decided to take him to Dr. Thomas. She wanted someone who knew what Jace was capable of to see Joey. And she knew that Jace would never agree to that.

Dr. Thomas worked on gaining a rapport with Joey. One session that Dawn was a part of was especially hard for her to hear.

"So, Joey," Dr. Thomas began, "on a scale of one to ten, with one being the worst and ten being the best, tell me where you were after your father left." Dawn thought he would reply with a fairly high number.

"Two," Joey replied. Tears came to Dawn's eyes.

"That's pretty low," Dr. Thomas said. "Why a two, Joey?"

"I thought my dad was going to come and kill my mom," he replied sincerely.

"That would be very hard," Dr. Thomas agreed, "to live with that threat. And where are you now?"

"I guess about an eight," Joey said.

"What caused the improvement?"

"My mom," Joey replied. "She's talked to me a lot."

"You have a really good mom, Joey," Dr. Thomas said. "I really think the world of your mom." Dawn was honored and relieved to hear that Joey was feeling better.

A few appointments later, Dr. Thomas told Dawn that he didn't need to see Joey anymore. "I don't think anything I would do would be any different from what you're already doing."

"Joey's worried that he'll be like his father," Dawn told him.

"No," said Dr. Thomas reassuringly. "He's got his mother's heart."

Chapter 57

Tennis

Court reminded Dawn of a tennis match—the ball was on his side of the net; the ball was on her side of the net; but the score was never love. There seemed to be hearing after hearing after hearing—an order to show cause here, a subpoena there, and money flying out the window. And when court didn't go well for Jace, the threats increased.

Summer came, and still nothing was resolved. It was July 4th; Dawn could not recall a pleasant July 4th since she was dating Jace. For some reason or another, it had always been a horrible holiday between them. So she resolved that this July 4th would be a good one. She got the children up early. They attended the local parade, participated in the events at the park and had a wonderful time. It had been a perfect day. They were thrilled when Joey won first prize in a foot race. They had come home after the events of the day, rested, and planned on driving back to the park to watch the fireworks. The only unpleasant thing about going to the park was that Dawn had to drive by Jace's trailer. She hated him living there. Often she would pass by him in the car and was subjected to "the finger"—whether the children were with her or not.

The children had called him at times, and he talked to them momentarily when they called, but that was all. He had nothing more to do with them. More than once, Dawn's lawyer brought up the fact in court that he refused to see the children, but it was no use. He was not going to be a good father. He was not going to be a father at all. She felt bad for her children, who would stand at the end of the road waiting for the school bus and were just feet away from their father's trailer. The bus passed it on their way to school and on their way home each day. How hard for them! At times they would see him drive by, and there would be no acknowledgement. It was like he was still in their face, and there was nothing they could do about it. She couldn't believe his cruelty to his own children.

As they rounded their street corner and headed toward the park for fireworks, Dawn was dismayed to see Jace in his truck headed toward them. He stopped opposite his trailer ready to turn into his property. He waited to turn in until Dawn was nearly opposite him. At that point he turned the truck into her car, forcing her off the road to avoid colliding with him. It frightened her, and she was furious. It also frightened the children.

Her tires spinning in the dirt, she pulled out onto the road and continued driving to the park, which was only a mile or so away. As she drove into the parking lot, she noticed two sheriff cars parked there. The sheriffs were standing outside their cars and visiting, enjoying the evening. Dawn put a blanket down for her children nearby, told them to stay there, and walked directly over to the sheriffs. She explained to them what had just happened.

"Did anyone else see what he did?" they questioned. "My children!" Dawn said firmly.

"We hate to bring kids into it," they responded. (As if they weren't already in it, Dawn thought.) "We'll take down the information," they offered. "If we go over and talk to him, he'll just deny it," they continued. "It's best just to make a report and build a case against him. Eventually, he'll mess up."

Dawn felt that they were trying to placate her. She was becoming less and less satisfied with the justice system and felt more and more victimized by Jace.

In talking to Anne one day, Anne let it slip that Jace had a girlfriend. Dawn knew the girl, as she had such a poor reputation in their town. She had three children by three different fathers, and none had married her. That Jace would be dating someone like her, the same age as his daughter, Ida, sickened her. Word had it that he had even bought her a trailer.

"Oh, yuck," Dawn said. "He must be pretty desperate. Actually, that's good—it seals things with me. I would never want to touch him again."

"That would do it for me," Anne agreed with her.

Jace became less and less attractive in Dawn's eyes. Since they were still married, he could add adultery to his list of indiscretions. Anytime she yearned for him to come back or blamed herself for his actions, she read her journal. She would only have to read a few lines before becoming sickened. She knew she did not want to be back in that situation.

Anne also filled Dawn in on Mary's status. Her behavior was becoming more and more erratic. Dawn was aware before leaving Jace that Mary was stalking Susan's daughter—accusing her of molesting Missy's daughter. There was no basis to the allegations, and both Susan and Missy were stressed at what to do with their mother. A counselor Mary went to see suggested the possibility of paranoid schizophrenia. After James died, Mary moved to a trailer, asserting that she couldn't live with the people residing in her basement—there were no people in her basement. After trying to piece everything together many times, Dawn came to the conclusion that Mary had abused Jace—possibly even sexually. When Dawn had suggested it to Jace one evening, the volcano had erupted most fiercely, making her even more suspicious. When Jace stopped seeing the children, so did Mary.

A few weeks later, Dawn and her children attended an annual summer concert and fireworks show at the nearby university, accompanied by the local symphony. She was looking forward to meeting her family there and listening to the music. She had backed her car out into the driveway and loaded up her trunk with blankets, chairs, and treats, unaware that Jace was watching her with binoculars the entire time. They would be gone for hours. They had to go early to reserve a place, as the event had grown more popular and crowded with each passing year.

The concert was wonderful, the summer air was refreshing, and the fireworks were beautiful. The traffic, however, was very heavy, and they got home very late and went straight to bed.

The next evening, after having been gone for most of the day, the children went out to play in the backyard and found things amiss. Joey came in with the report that there were large pieces of wood thrown into the dog pen. A week earlier they had torn down an old barn that Jace had built, so there were several large logs lying around the pasture. Dawn wondered why the wood would be in the pen. A large tree trunk had also been thrown in the pen. The pen had previously been used for fallow deer that Jace had raised and had a six-foot fence around it. Dawn had acquired a dog named Chance, who had become the new resident of the pen.

Another thing that Dawn noticed was that an old lantern of Jace's was also missing. Dawn had put artificial flowers around the lantern, which didn't work, and used it as a centerpiece for the outside table on the patio. The lantern was missing, but the children found the flowers, smashed into the dirt, out by the dog pen. The lantern had been sitting next to Dawn's radio, which was still on the table. Had it been common thieves, they would have taken the radio. She knew that Jace had been there. She immediately called the sheriff.

It took several hours for the sheriff to get there. By the time he came, she had already put the children to bed, and it was too dark to show the sheriff anything. She told him that she had noticed the lantern gone and told him about the smashed flowers and the wood. She didn't understand why there was wood in the dog pen, but due to the six-foot fence, knew that it would have taken a very large, strong man to throw the large logs and tree trunk over the tall fence. She had often watched Jace toss bales of hay onto his truck with no effort at all. She was worried that it was Jace, who lived less than a block away.

The sheriff was non-plussed. Again before her was a placating, condescending man who dismissed her fears as unfounded. "You have no proof that it was him," he explained.

"Who else would it be?" she asked. "And why would he throw wood in the dog pen?" she wondered.

Again, he told her he would take down the information and that it was best for her to "build a case." He told her goodnight and she went to bed, exhausted, frustrated and in tears.

The next day her father came out to visit. Dawn fixed him lunch, and as she was sitting at the table in the kitchen, she looked outside and noticed that Joey had not finished mowing the lawn. She saw the aisle of lowered grass where the mower had been, and then it just stopped and there was very tall grass.

"Joey, did you put the lawn mower away?" she called to him.

"No, Mom, it ran out of gas," he called back. "It stopped right there on the back lawn where I left it."

"It's not there," she said, rising out of her kitchen chair and heading out the door. The children and her father soon joined her in the search. The mower was nowhere to be found. She began to take stock of other things—anything that Jace felt was his was gone. Jace's father had given them an outdoor thermometer that was attached to the side of the house. It had been ripped off its bracket. Lawn tools were missing. What was even more disconcerting was that the apples had been stripped from the apple trees. Even though they weren't ripe, apparently Jace felt they were his. He had planted those trees. Dawn walked out to the dog pen to take a better look at things there. What she saw dismayed her.

Among the several long logs that had been thrown into the pen was Chance. He ran over to see them, and she could see that the fur on his back had been scraped off and he had been injured. All of a sudden, a scenario came into her mind. Jace knew that they had gone to the fireworks. It would have been easy for him to watch them leave. He came over with the intention of getting things that he felt were his—things he didn't get the first time. The back of their lot connected with a lot his nephew owned. He could have come in that way. But he hadn't counted on Chance. He probably didn't even know that they had the dog, as he was kept in the back pasture. Chance had probably barked and barked, which accounted for all of the wood in the dog pen and the scrapes on his back. He most likely had tried to silence or kill the dog. How could you hurt your own children's dog? Chills ran up the back of her neck.

She immediately called the sheriff again. The dispatcher said she would send someone out. Dawn's father told her that he wanted to be there when they came, but after waiting and waiting, her father finally left. Dawn was disappointed when no one came. She wanted them to come before dark so she could show them the dog. She called again the next day. Again, no one came. She was furious. She would take matters into her own hands. She grabbed her camera and went outside and took pictures. She took a picture of the grass, which showed plainly where the mower had been. She took a picture of the flowers smashed in the dirt. She took a picture of the apple trees and of the torn bracket on the side of her home where the thermometer had been. She took several pictures of Chance and of all the wood in the dog pen. Then she wrote a letter to the lead county sheriff—a very long letter—detailing the whole experience. "Since I can't get anyone to come out and take a report," she wrote, "I am making a report of my own. Please file these pictures along with it." She went on to explain the condescending comments of the previous sheriff and her increasing frustration with Jace and all that he was doing.

A few days after the letter, she received an apologetic call from the sheriff's office, with the offer to come out to her home.

"No," she said. "That's okay. I've already taken pictures, and there's not much evidence left now. Please just keep the report."

Chapter 58

Small Claims

Dawn was headed to court again, but this time it was with Nora. Jace owed Nora money. He had been ordered to pay child care and had made no payments at all. Nora had kept track of it for months, had sent him several notices, and had finally petitioned small claims court. Nora had told Dawn that she needed her for a witness—to say that Jace had not given Dawn any money for child care either and that Dawn had not reimbursed Nora.

As Nora's case came before the commissioner, Nora presented all of her written notices and evidence. Nora was standing right before him with Jace on the other side. Dawn was sitting on the row behind her. The commissioner asked Dawn if Jace had given her any money, and Dawn stood and replied that he hadn't. She then sat back down.

The commissioner ruled in favor of Nora. As he dismissed them to go, Dawn stood up, waiting for Nora to reach her so they could leave. But Jace reached her first. As he walked behind her, he leaned over and whispered in her ear, "You're dead."

She must have had a horrendous look on her face, as the bailiff came immediately over to her. "What did he say to you?" he asked intently.

"He said, 'You're dead!'" Dawn answered him.

"He can't do that," the bailiff said firmly. He ran out the door after Jace, but Jace was gone. He came back to Dawn who was waiting outside the courtroom. "He's gone," he told her. "I think you need to report the threat to the police."

Nora concurred. Dawn needed to return to work. She told Nora she would call from there. Dawn phoned the police just before leaving work that day. A woman officer took down the information. The same woman later called Dawn at home.

"I've talked it over with some of the other officers," she told

Dawn. "We want to charge him with witness tampering, since you were there only as a witness for your neighbor. It's a more serious charge," she said. "It's a felony, but we'll need your testimony."

"I'm so afraid of him," Dawn told the officer. "I'm afraid that it will make things worse. If he were to go to jail, I know he would kill me when he got out. And they always get out," she said nervously. She started to shake.

"But you also need to build a case against him," the officer said, "or we can't help you."

"I've been trying," Dawn said desperately. "That's all I do is make reports and build a case, but he always gets away with everything!"

"Well, we won't let him get away with this," the officer said firmly. "But we can't do anything if you don't help us."

"Okay," Dawn said weakly.

"Think it over, and I'll call you later," the officer replied.

It was nearly midnight when the phone rang. It was the officer. "We've talked it over some more. We talked to the bailiff who was at court. Apparently, he saw your husband speak to you, but he didn't hear what he said. Was there anyone else who may have heard him?" she asked Dawn.

"He whispered it in my ear," Dawn said. "No one else would have been able to hear him."

"I'm afraid, then," the woman explained, "that it would just be your word against his and the case would be dismissed." Dawn understood. Would this man she married ever be accountable for anything he did? The officer was very sympathetic to her position. "Please call if I can ever help you in the future," she offered. Dawn dissolved into tears of exhaustion and then went to sleep …

A few weeks later, Nora knocked on her door late in the evening. The children were in bed. Dawn invited her in, but Nora stood at the door."

"I just came to tell you something," she said anxiously. "I just went grocery shopping and ran into Jace in the store. When he saw me, he started yelling out rude comments—stuff like 'There's a bitch for you.' I moved aisles but decided to check out and go home. When I went to the checkout stand, he was at another one in front of me. He pointed at me and said to the clerk, 'You'd better watch out for her. She'll rip you off.'"

"After my groceries were loaded and I went outside to get in my car, I noticed that the whole side of my car had been keyed. You should see what he did—he scraped the whole side of it as he walked by! I went back into the store and called the sheriff—they came out. The officer said that he could see the paint specks on the ground, but no one actually saw him do it. The clerk told the sheriff what he had said, and he took a report. But, still, we have no proof."

Another report, Dawn thought. "I'm so sorry, Nora. I hope your insurance will cover the repairs."

Nora nodded. "You just be careful," she said. "Make sure you've got your protective order with you all the time and that your cell phone is charged," she cautioned Dawn as she walked across the street toward her home.

But that wasn't the end of it, still. One morning Nora walked outside to find all of the air let out of her tires. "If Ned catches him," she told Dawn that morning, "he'll kill him. At least then your troubles would be over."

"Yeah," Dawn agreed. "And yours, too."

A few weeks later, Dawn was downstairs watching an old movie on television. She had been too tired to get up and go upstairs to bed. She was startled when the phone rang. It was Nora.

"There's a truck parked a few feet down the road," she whispered to Dawn. "I've watched them ride up and down the road more than once."

Dawn turned off the TV, so there was no light, and looked out the window. She couldn't see anything, but Nora told her she could see two people walking toward the truck. They got in and pulled away.

"Sorry to scare you," she told Dawn.

"Thanks for looking out for me," Dawn replied. "Nora, do you know … could Jace shoot me from where he is … could a bullet make it clear over here from his trailer?"

"Sorry to say, he probably could shoot you with a high-powered rifle if you were standing on the front porch."

"Thanks for telling me the truth," Dawn told her. She wouldn't be spending much time out front anymore. More intimidation.

There were way too many nights like that one. Not with Nora calling, but with dogs barking and Dawn leaping out of bed, her heart pounding, to look out the window. She was so afraid that Jace would harm her. It was rare now that she slept through the night.

She wasn't the only one who was afraid. Dawn had never told her children about Jace's threats and had talked to the police from her work or when the children were in bed. Joey must have had a sixth sense. He began sleeping on the floor at the foot of Dawn's bed. He had assumed the role of protector; not a role Dawn wanted him to assume, but one he had assumed nonetheless. He knew, firsthand, the rage that seethed within his father.

Dawn had typed up instances of abuse from her journal should she need them in court. She hadn't kept a journal for most of her marriage—she was just too worn down—but in the time that she had written she had the following documented:

> Threats of physical harm to Joey – 9;
> Physical harm to Joey – 15 (3 from stepbrothers), including slapped head, socked stomach, dragged by arm and ear, kicked, dropped over fence, thrown across room, spanked;
> Name calling Joey – 11;
> Yelled at Joey – 17;
> Punishing Joey for other's misbehavior – 9;
> Threats of physical harm to Dawn – 4;
> Threats of isolation – 6;
> Isolation – 20;
> Name calling – 6;
> Yelling at Dawn – 80;
> Trouble with Ethan and Eric – 34.

She was ashamed and sickened when she added up all the instances against Joey. She had not realized there were so many. Jace had never left marks on him that Dawn was aware of—with the exception of the cut when he pushed him into the bushes—no bruises, no broken bones, nothing she could report; but definitely a broken heart and spirit.

Chapter 59

Trial

The day had come. No more pre-trial hearings and "orders to show cause." This was it. They had been separated a year and a half. After today, Dawn's marriage would be over and her divorce would be final.

Dawn had bought a dress weeks ago in preparation. Even though she was a bundle of nerves, she wanted to at least look her best. To her, the dress was symbolic. Jace had always told her about black roses that were beautiful but had never given her one. The dress had tiny, black-ribbon rose buttons down the front of it, fitting for the end of her marriage.

She met Mr. Gregory in his office, which was a block away from the courthouse. "How nice you look," he greeted her. Dawn was grateful for the compliment. Now if her knees would only quit shaking. They walked together to court.

Dawn carried a large, maroon binder. In the past year, with every notice from Jace's lawyers were lies upon lies upon more lies. Dawn had always been a very organized person who kept excellent records. Now it would pay off. For every lie, she had the records to prove that they were indeed that—lies. From bank records to charge cards to taxes to retirement accounts to medical insurance: In her binder was the proof, organized and alphabetized, to refute his claims. Her attorney told her, "The best ammunition we have is in that binder. You know better than I what the answers to the issues are. Just turn to it to answer the questions, and you'll do fine." He marveled at her organizational skills. What was most ironic to her, though, was that what meant the most to her—her children—was not even an issue. Jace had given her full custody with no argument.

Dawn was grateful when she got to court to see Nora and Nancy there. Her father wanted to be there, but Dawn knew that he would be upset by Jace's lies and antics. She told him she would come see him directly after the trial. She was disappointed, though, to see Missy there. Had she come to support them both, it would have been different, but her lawyer told her that she was there to testify for Jace in behalf of his taxes. 'How could you?' Dawn thought. 'Especially after my spending the day helping you get a protective order?' That's what she thought and would have liked to have said to her; but she only smiled bravely and said, "Hello, Missy, how are you?" as she walked by. Missy must believe Jace's lies, even on his taxes, and he could be quite convincing. Anne had told Dawn that Missy had never filed the protective order and was still with her abusive husband. Dawn could only feel pity for her. Dawn's attorney informed her that Missy would not be permitted to testify about taxes, even though she was a certified tax preparer, since she was a member of the family.

Someone who wasn't there, however, was the man from the auction who had called Dawn on the phone to warn her and tell her about Jace's tantrum. He had been subpoenaed to testify about the cattle Jace had sold. Jeff Gregory told Dawn that they had called him from judge's quarters to ask where he was. He told them he was afraid of Jace and would not be there. It was explained to him that he was in contempt of court and could go to jail for not showing up. He replied, "I'd rather go to jail."

Dawn recalled a time when Jace came home late from work. When he drove in the driveway, Dawn noticed that the back of her beautiful car, Rocky, was smashed in. Jace told her that when he was driving home, a car full of men commuting had cut him off. Whether it had been intentional or not, Jace became immediately angry and began playing cat and mouse with them. He passed them and pulled in front of them, slowing down to a crawl on the freeway. The game ended with Jace running them off the road, with the back fender of Dawn's car taking the damage. When both cars were off the freeway, Jace jumped out of the car and ran in a rage toward the other car. The men wisely locked their doors and refused to get out of the car. Jace stormed off. The men later called the highway patrol, but since there were no witnesses to file a report, the incident was dropped.

Dawn had hated riding with Jace in the car. Someone invariably made him angry in one way or another. He was constantly giving "the finger" to someone or cutting them off, and Dawn was invariably embarrassed. His car had broken down a few times, and she had to tow him home. She hated it, too, as he always raged at her for not driving fast enough or slow enough to suit him. She was grateful that she would never have to be in a car with him again. She knew that there were many people afraid of Jace. As long as her lawyer wasn't. *My lawyer can beat up your lawyer …*

One of the first issues of the trial was child-care costs. Nora testified for Dawn this time about Jace's non-payment, threats and damage to her car. The judge issued a no-contact order between them, and Dawn thought that it gave the judge, at the beginning of the trial, a good idea of the kind of person Jace was. Dawn actually knew the judge—he was two years younger than Dawn and had grown up in her neighborhood, attending the same church and school. Dawn didn't know him well but thought that he would be a fair judge.

The morning of the hearing went by slowly, as the lawyers argued issue after issue. At one point Jace took the stand. Dawn's attorney questioned him about his lack of involvement in his children's lives. Dawn looked at Jace intently as he told excuse after excuse, lie after lie, about his abandonment of them.

In Dawn's binder was a song that Taylor had written about her father. Dawn had recently found it when she was helping Taylor clean out her room. "What's this?" she had asked her at the time. "Oh, just a song I wrote," Taylor told her. As Dawn read the song, in her little girl's handwriting, her heart ached for her. At the same time, she was amazed at Taylor's insight. She wrote:

> I see you standing in the doorway.
> I see you standing in my eyes.
> I see you standing everywhere.
> I see you standing in my heart.
>
> Why did you have to be so rude to me, Papa?
> I loved you. You did not.
> So I gave up, I gave up.
>
> Now you're just a man,
> Never to be known
> In my heart, in my heart.

How different this poem was from Taylor's Father's Day poem a few years before. Dawn could no longer stand to listen to anything else Jace said. She began copying the words to Taylor's song, over and over again.

There was a short break at lunchtime. Dawn was too upset to eat but uncharacteristically drank a Coke from the pop machine. She disliked carbonated drinks, but the Coke helped refresh her. Jeff Gregory had several copies of auction receipts that he had subpoenaed. He asked Dawn to help put them in order for him. Dawn spread them out on the table in front of her, and as she did so, Jace returned from lunch. He sat down just feet away from her and glared at her. He didn't take his eyes from her, and Dawn could feel the hatred for her pouring through them. She shook as she organized the papers but didn't look up at him or return his stare.

Directly after lunch, Dawn took the stand. Jace's lawyer was menacing, even cruel, as he fired question after question at her. Dawn did her best to keep calm, turn to her binder, and answer the questions. At one point, his lawyer badgered her to the point that Dawn wanted to throw the binder at him. She glanced at Nora who gestured to her to keep her cool. The attorney had a picture of the vehicles that were in question but instead held up a picture that Jace had taken of the family room when it was messy and the children had been playing.

"Oh, this isn't the picture of the car," his lawyer said condescendingly, "this is a picture detailing your wife's housekeeping skills—or lack of."

'How cruel,' Dawn thought. She wondered why an attorney would even mention that, but then she realized that he was just playing mind games like Jace had done. Anything to unnerve her. His lawyer was also irritated that the trial had gone on so long—after all, he had wanted to leave early to attend an RV and boat show that afternoon.

When Dawn stepped down from the stand, her attorney leaned over to her. "You did great," he said affectionately. She could feel Jace's eyes on her. "Don't faint when you see this next part," he warned her, rising to address the judge.

It was good he warned her. Dawn almost fell off her chair. She felt that she had done much of the work for this trial—supplying records and refuting arguments and organizing it all. But when she saw the itemization of lawyer fees, she couldn't believe it. She had paid the retainer and more along the way—but the fees totaled $8,000! How could she ever repay this?

"Your Honor," Jeff Gregory began, "because of the sheer volume of records we have had to subpoena, much of it because of the plaintiff's unwillingness to be forthright, we are requesting that he be required to pay the defendant's attorney fees."

Jace's attorney immediately shot to his feet, refuting the claims.

What happened next she had never seen nor had any idea that it could actually happen. Jace's attorney put Dawn's attorney on the stand. Dawn felt she was watching a circus. Weren't these guys friends outside of court? Apparently, they weren't as friendly as she thought. Jace's attorney grilled her attorney about the fees. But Mr. Gregory stayed professional and answered the questions sincerely. When he sat down, Dawn leaned over to him, "Does that usually happen?"

"No," he answered, and Dawn could tell that the incident angered him.

At this point, the judge spoke to everyone. "Due to the lateness of the hour, I'm going to review these things over the weekend. We'll have to reconvene Monday morning at 9:00 a.m."

Dawn was devastated. Now she had to worry the entire weekend about the judge's decisions. She wasn't sure she could do that. She had wanted it to be over today. Oh, why couldn't it be over?

Chapter 60

Reconvene

Dawn tried to gain her composure before going to her father's. She didn't want him to worry. Her sister had kept her children and met her at her father's. He took them all out to dinner, and exhaustion consumed Dawn afterwards. She just wanted to go home and crawl in bed. Fearful of spending the night at home alone though, Dawn had arranged to stay with her friend Erin in a nearby town. She put her children, who enjoyed the diversion, to bed in Erin's spare bedroom and recounted the day's events to Erin, a kind and sympathetic listener. Dawn was so grateful to be able to "unload" to someone so supportive and understanding.

Still, another night crying herself to sleep. Would she ever stop crying? She was so frustrated. The events of the day played over and over again in her head. They would play over and over for weeks to come: what she should have said; what she didn't say; what she should have done differently. The next morning as Dawn finally slept, Erin took Dawn's children out to play and have breakfast at McDonalds. How grateful she was for good friends!

Monday morning Dawn dressed in her favorite pantsuit—it was a beautiful beige suit that had belonged to her mother, who had worn it only a few times before her death. It felt comforting to her, somehow, to have something of her mother's enveloping her. Again Jeff told her how nice she looked as she met him in the courtroom. She was glad that her attorney was such a nice guy.

As the judge read his decisions, she was glad for some and not so glad for others. He ordered Jace to pay $2,000 of the fees. She was hoping for more. She had absolute proof that Jace had cheated her out of money he claimed the past year on taxes. That was not resolved. Jace had spent his retirement money—it didn't matter. She "must have benefited from it" because they were married at the time. Yeah, right.

Still, he got credit for half of her retirement. She was grateful that she was awarded the house. If she remarried or when Davey turned 18, Jace would get $8,500 equity. The more the judge talked, the more she realized that he was actually just trying to make both lawyers happy. A great compromise. Great, but not when one of the parties was a cheat and a liar. Is that what judges do? Just try to make the lawyers happy? She had been a fool to argue about everything—to try and prove Jace's allegations false. It didn't matter. The judge just tried to make everything even. Victimized by the abuser, she thought, and then by the justice system. But take out the justice. Apparently the judge considered them the winners, as her attorney had to write up the decree.

Still, when it came down to everything, she did win. She did not have to spend another day, another hour, another minute being the victim of his criticism, threats and harassment—toward her or the children. She had a nice home to live in, a good job to pay for that home, and most of all—most wonderfully of all—three beautiful children.

Chapter 61

Roof

Dawn needed to get her home ready for the winter. Fall was in the air—she could feel it—and she knew that her swamp cooler needed to be winterized. She called her dad, who had hooked it up in the spring, and he was able to tell her over the phone what she needed to do. Dawn got Joey, told him the procedure they needed to follow and, after turning off the water line that led to the cooler, headed to the roof.

Dawn didn't mind heights, but climbing up the ladder was another matter. Joey helped her onto the roof, and they began the process of draining the cooler. It was early evening and had been a beautiful day. Joey removed the side and unplugged the motor as they waited for all of the water to exit the cooler. Then they replaced the side and covered the cooler with its heavy canvas cover. They tied extra twine around it to make sure it was secure.

Dawn knew that she had only to reverse the procedure to get the cooler running in the spring. She wished she had known this earlier, when Jace refused to hook up the cooler to punish her. It had been a horribly hot summer that year. She would have shown him! But no matter. She knew now. And it was only the beginning of her and Joey's education. She would learn skills she had never known. And Joey learned right along with her. The following summer they would both do an admirable job replacing the patio roof.

The evening was beautiful. They could see everywhere. Dawn loved being on the roof.

"We did it, Joey! We fixed up the swamp cooler!"

They both felt quite proud of themselves. Dawn knew that she would be all right. She knew that Joey would be all right. What she couldn't do and Joey couldn't learn, they would get help with, but there was much they could do on their own. Together they sat on the roof and watched a beautiful sunset paint orange across the sky.

Chapter 62

Home Sweet Home

Dawn was awarded all of the property that remained at her home. Jace had collected a great deal of junk. Dawn had boxed much of it up—including all of Jace's old papers—and put it all in the garage. She had asked Dave and Anne to come and pick it all up for Jace. They came and loaded up their pickup.

When they cleaned out the shed, the children found an old suitcase. When they opened it up, they came running to Dawn. It was full of pornography. Dawn was sickened by it and realized all of the hours that Eric and Ethan had spent out in the shed. She was grateful that her children had immediately closed the suitcase and gotten her. They burned it all in the fire pit in their back yard.

In an effort to get some money, Dawn put everything worth anything in the paper for sale. It wasn't long before she heard from Jeff Gregory. Jace's attorney had contacted him with the complaint that she was selling all of his property. Anne had also told her that Jace and Ida were conspiring to send a derogatory letter about her to her employers to try to get her fired.

Dawn couldn't afford more lawyer fees. She decided that she would take matters into her own hands. She wrote a letter to Jace, detailing the dates and contents of all the property he had already taken. She listed everything she had given Anne to give to him. She reminded him of the court order, giving her everything that was left at the home. Then she brought up the threat from him and Ida to try and slander her. She documented everything and sent a copy to her lawyer, so Jace would know that she had a witness.

Dawn's lawyer wrote her, upon receipt of the letter, and told her that it was an excellent letter and that he agreed with everything she had said. Dawn was glad that she was able to save herself some money.

She was so tired of Jace's antics but also determined not to let it get to her. What she hated most of all were Jace's midnight visits and that the children were so aware of it all. They came outside often, every few weeks or so, to find something else amiss in the yard—hoses cut, sprinkler heads off, flowers pulled out. That was his favorite—pulling flowers out of their holes, ever so neatly, and placing them on the sidewalk or in the driveway.

She thought it ironic that he usually pulled up a pansy. So many times when she was in tears, he would discount her feelings, calling her a "baby" or a "pansy." Yet pansies were one of Dawn's favorite flowers. Although very delicate, pansies were hardier than many flowers, thriving in cold weather, surviving the harsh winter, and coming back to bloom in the spring. Like the pansy, she, too, would survive.

Even worse than pulling up plants were all the animals that died. He left three fallow deer behind. All died; their pet pot-bellied pig—healthy one day—dead the next. When Joey's dog died mysteriously, Dawn vowed to get no more animals. She couldn't afford expensive autopsies and inquiries into their deaths. She and Joey just dug more holes in the pasture.

Dawn talked with her church leaders about the possibility of setting up a video camera. She wanted to catch him on tape. "I don't just want a picture," said the bishop. "I want bells to go off and lights to come on."

Dawn followed the scenario out in her mind. Then what? He's arrested, spends a few nights or even weeks in jail. Then he's released. Then she's dead. Jace's byword was revenge. He lived by it. It was an integral and inseparable part of him. He would have to get revenge, which would be much worse than just coming into the yard. Death would come to more than an animal.

The bishop referred Dawn to her home teacher, Brother Anson, a man assigned by the bishop to their home. He was there to help out with whatever might be needed. Each family in her church was assigned a home teacher, some who fulfilled their calling very seriously and some who fulfilled it not at all; but in Dawn's case, her home teacher was one who greatly magnified the calling, even though he had a wonderful wife and family of his own. He had been her home teacher through most of her marriage and throughout the divorce. He knew Jace well and of what he was capable.

Dawn asked Brother Anson for a blessing—not for herself or her children—but for her home. She knew that church buildings were dedicated to God for his purposes, and she had heard of others who had blessed their homes when first moving in. So she asked her home teacher to bless her home.

As they knelt in prayer that night as Brother Anson blessed her home, she knew that she had made the right decision. She felt God's power firmly as he prayed for their home to be a place of personal safety. She felt comfort and peace. She hoped her children did as well.

Jace still continued the night visits and mischief in the yard, but the visits became fewer and farther between as time went on and incidents were ignored. What Dawn was most grateful for was that their home was truly blessed and was never touched. Nothing ever penetrated their home. Eventually Joey would stop sleeping at the foot of Dawn's bed and would move to the basement bedroom for a room of his own. Their home became a safe haven for them all.

Dawn did all she could to keep them together as a family unit. After hearing Davey say soon after the separation that they weren't a "family" anymore, Dawn did all she could to make them feel like one. She continued traditions as before. She designated Sunday night as family night. They spent time together, read together, sang together and played games together. They participated together as a family to raise money for the Multiple Sclerosis Society. This time it was a walk. The children collected pledges and donations as Dawn drove them around the surrounding neighborhoods. They walked miles on a beautiful Saturday, enjoying each other's company and feeling good about the service they were doing.

Dawn came up with a family song, with a verse for each of them, sung to the tune "Row Your Boat" to further boost her children's esteem. They sang it often:

> Ma—Ma—lone's are great! What a family!
> Loving and giving, kind, honest, and happy are what we want to be.
>
> Joey is so neat—fishes till there's no sun. Gorgeous blue eyes— and a great personality makes him lots of fun!
>
> Taylor is so sweet—smart and pretty, too. She's always giggling, smiling and singing. Cartwheels she likes to do.

Davey's great big smile lights up the cutest face. He likes to play outside, running, riding bikes. He's our little Davey!

Last is dear Mommy. She loves us all so much. She tries to teach us to be the best we can be. She's awfully proud of us.

A few years later, a bookstore in their area had a contest for Father's Day. The father who won the prize would win a trip overseas. Dawn and her children entered the contest. They filled out the application: "My Dad deserves a vacation with a good book because … he is always there when we need him and is full of kindness. He gives us blessings, takes us camping, and on daddy-daughter dates, and helps with our pinewood derby cars. He comes to our basketball games, takes our pictures, gives us birthday and Christmas presents. He fixes things when they break and even gave us new carpet for our bedrooms. He tickles us, plays with us, spends time with us and gives us hugs. The most special thing about him is that he does all this but isn't our dad. He's our home teacher. Our dad left four years ago and won't see us, so Brother Anson "adopted" us. And even though he's not our real dad, he's the best father we could have." Brother Anson didn't win the trip, but the bookstore sent him a beautiful art book along with the following message:

Before Father's day this past June someone that loves you entered your name in a contest called "My Dad deserves a vacation with a good book because …"

We had hundreds of applicants for this vacation, as there are exceptional fathers who are loved deeply by their children everywhere. Although another father won our trip, the letter sent to us about you was so touching, we wanted to send you a little gift.

Have a wonderful day and thank you for being such a great example not only to your children but also to the rest of us here. Thank you for your incredible example. I can't tell you how touched we all are by your Christlike acts.

Chapter 63

Bills

The school had called Dawn to tell her that Davey had an eye infection and that it was going around in the school. She would have to take him to the doctor and get it cleared up before he could return to school.

Dawn left work, picked up Davey at school and went to their insta-care facility. Davey apparently wasn't the only one who was ill; something must be going around, as the office was full of people. After waiting for more than an hour with sick people coughing everywhere, they were finally called up to register. When the receptionist pulled up Davey's name on the computer, she informed them that they weren't covered by insurance there anymore.

"We had a call from your ex-husband," she informed Dawn. "It's written here that apparently his company has changed insurances, and you're not covered here anymore."

"But he's supposed to let me know if the insurance changes!" Dawn was livid but knew that it wasn't the receptionist's fault. She also felt bad that Davey was witness to his father's mean-spirited conniving. They left the facility, and Dawn took Davey to the facility covered by her insurance. Again, they had another hour's wait. She determined then that she would never use Jace's medical insurance again. She did use his dental insurance, however, as the children were partially covered for orthodontic services under Jace's coverage. Still, Jace refused to pay his part for anything and threatened to cancel the insurance if Dawn pursued it.

Dawn remembered last year's Christmas when Joey wanted to give Jace a chocolate orange. Even though Jace had written off the children the previous Christmas, Joey felt the need to reach his heart out to his father at Christmastime. Fearfully, he had run up to his doorstep while Dawn waited in the car with a knot in her stomach. No one answered the door, so Joey left the orange on his porch and ran back to the car. There was never any acknowledgement from Jace for the gift. No "Merry Christmas" to his children. No "Happy Birthdays." Joey gave up any further hope for acknowledgement from his father.

"Tell Dawnette that if anything happens to her," Jace told Anne one day, "not to count on me. She'll have to find someone else to take care of the kids."

They had been to court again to settle questions about the water shares on their properties and other matters, but Jace never fulfilled the terms of the court orders. This time, he was able to get a supervisor at his work to say that he didn't make as much money as he used to—that he was slow and didn't get the jobs done on time. That's why they won a trip to Hawaii—because he was so slow!—but it worked for him, and the child support was lowered. Dawn was amazed at how little she received. Her attorney said he would like to subpoena Jace's salary records later, sure that there would be a discrepancy, but Dawn just wanted to let it go. Rather than continue to get in arguments with him and pursue money that he owed her (and continue to pay attorneys, though Mr. Gregory hadn't charged her any more for his services), Dawn decided to keep records and settle it all when it came time for Jace to receive the equity due him from their home. Jace was now on his fourth attorney; apparently they didn't like dealing with him any more than she did. Jeff Gregory, who had been practicing law for years, told her that Jace was indeed the worst he had ever dealt with.

She left the draining court hearing, frustrated and angry at having her child support reduced. She sat in the car alone and cried and cried. She hoped she would be all cried out by the time she got home but walked into her bedroom and cried and cried some more. Taylor came in and wanted to know what was wrong.

"Oh, nothing, honey," Dawn replied.

"Something's wrong, Mommy. What's wrong?" Dawn didn't want to worry her, but she had never been good at lying. 'Why am I trying to protect him?' she wondered.

"I just went to court, honey. Your dad got the child support lowered. I'm just frustrated … we need the money so bad." She couldn't fight the tears.

Taylor looked at Dawn intently and then said, "I hate Dad, Mommy."

Dawn looked back at her. "I hate him, too," she said.

Dawn had prayed a great deal before every court hearing, wanting justice, but she never seemed to get it. She wondered why she seemed to always come out the loser in court and why Jace got away with everything. She then realized, however, the answer to that question: the Lord was indeed watching over her. Had she won, as she should have, she would have been the object of his revenge. She probably would have been dead. If Jace felt that he had won, though, he would leave her alone. Yes, she lost monetarily, but she won everything that was important: her life—a good life—with all of her children.

Chapter 64

Cockfight

Jace had moved. Dawn was so relieved. No longer did they have to look at his residence when leaving theirs. Anne told Dawn that he had bought a small house that sat on a chicken farm in an adjoining town. It was on the exact same west that Dawn lived on, which unnerved her—you could draw a straight line directly south from their house to his—but at least it was miles away.

With the move came the end of most of the yard visits, another blessing. Anne had told Dawn that Jace was now in the business of raising fighting roosters for cockfights. Since it was illegal, he was traveling to Indian reservations and to other states for the activity. Dawn felt sorry for the roosters and knew it was wrong but was glad that his aggression was focused on something rather than her. He had owned mean roosters while they had been married; Dawn had always wondered what the point was of having birds that were so mean they had to be kept in a cage. She was never aware of Jace using them for fighting, though.

Dawn sought closure to everything. She was getting on with her life but still had bitter feelings. Right after Jace had left, she had written him a letter asking him to forgive her for any offense she had caused in their marriage. She decided she needed to do the same with the boys. Anne had told her that Ethan had moved back with his mother, because he was "sick of all the lies" his father had told him. Dawn wrote him an earnest letter, apologizing for any pain she had caused. She explained to him the reasons she had to take out a protective order against him and Eric. She asked him to share it with Eric and Ida and wished them all a happy life.

In reality, Dawn felt much more pity for her stepchildren than her own. Jace's children had spent most of their lives in the middle of a war between their parents and then between her and Jace. She held nothing against them. They were only a product of their environment—an angry father, an absent mother, and an ineffective stepmother. She could never be the kind of mother she wanted to be to them, as Jace placed her in an impossible position. Without his support, he was always the good guy and she the bad guy, with resentment on all sides. She was determined that her children would be the product of a very positive and nurturing environment, with or without a father.

Dawn never heard back from Ethan, nor did she expect to, but she received a scathing letter from Ida who had definitely turned on her and blamed her for everything. Dawn's first impulse was to return a searing letter in return but decided instead to let it go. Dawn had done what she could to make amends. If Ida didn't accept it, that was her choice. Dawn could do nothing more about it and, in view of Ida's animosity and unstable nature, decided it was best to end any contact at all.

Eric continued to live with his father, after dropping out of high school. He had fathered a child and refused to marry the mother; still, she moved in with Eric and Jace and became their housekeeper in exchange for room and board. Dawn felt pity for the girl. "All that women are good for are cooking, cleaning and having babies," Jace had said.

One spring night, as school was about to end for the summer, Davey and Dawn were lying on her bed watching the evening news. "We have breaking news …" the report began. It reported that a cockfight ring had been busted that evening west of their town. "Over forty dead roosters were found, and sixty wounded. Razors were attached to the roosters' legs, and blood was everywhere. Large amounts of cash were found as several people, believed to be illegal aliens, fled the scene. Two young men were arrested. The wounded roosters will have to be put down."

When Dawn heard it, her first thought was that it was Jace. She wondered if one of those arrested were Eric. It was, indeed. Anne later told her that Jace was partners with the guy who owned the building they were using and was hiding in a trailer while they arrested his son. "What a great father," Dawn thought, although she already knew what kind of father he was. Dawn didn't tell her children about their father. It unnerved her that he associated with such low-life people. She could imagine him hiring someone very easily to kill her.

A few weeks later, a detective called Dawn, seeking information. Davey was sitting next to her watching TV when he called. Joey and

Taylor weren't home. When Dawn realized who it was, she walked into the bathroom and shut the door to continue the conversation.

"I need to tell you," Dawn said, "that if he knew you were talking to me or that if I had any information at all, he would kill me. I mean that literally. He is capable of it, hates me, and has threatened my life in the past."

"I understand completely," the detective said sincerely. "I deal with guys like him all the time. I assure you that he won't know I've contacted you."

Dawn told him everything she knew that might possibly help him but admitted that she didn't know much. "I do my best to stay away from him," she said.

"If you think of anything else, even if it's in the middle of the night, please call me. I'm going to get these guys if it takes me all year. They're doing dogs, too, and that's a felony."

Dawn wished him luck, and as she opened the bathroom door, discovered Davey sitting on the floor by the door, listening with eyes wide. "Was that Daddy who killed all those roosters?"

Dawn knew there was no use hiding it now. She nodded her head.

Davey started to cry. "Oh, Mommy I'm scared!" he exclaimed. "Is he going to come over here and shoot us?"

"Come sit down," Dawn said to him, pulling him onto her lap and comforting him as best she could. "You weren't supposed to hear that conversation. I didn't want you to know. Daddy isn't going to come over here, honey. He doesn't even know that we know about this. It will be okay."

"Will they put him in jail?"

"If they catch him doing it, they will. But he probably wouldn't stay there long."

"Oh, Mommy, I wish he were dead!"

"I'm so sorry, honey."

When Joey and Taylor got home that evening, Dawn shared the news with them. They weren't surprised at all by it. A year later, Jace had still not been arrested and, according to all accounts, still continued his covert activity. Dawn had wanted him arrested, in part, so that everyone would know what a mean guy he really was. She wanted the validation, especially from those who thought he was such a nice guy and wondered why she would divorce him. If his picture were on the front page of the paper, then they would say, "No wonder Dawn divorced him! I bet she's glad she's not with him anymore!"

Chapter 65

Disneyland

It had been a rough time by any standard. The loss of her mother and father-in-law to death and the subsequent loss of her father (to dementia) and mother-in-law (in support of her own son's abandonment) along with most of her in-laws was hard enough to handle on its own, without the separation that the divorce brought. Dawn had also changed jobs. As much as she loved teaching at the hospital, teaching for the school district would pay more. And even more importantly, she would have the summer off. That way she could be home with her children and not have to hire a babysitter.

Today marked another anniversary of her mother's death. It had been a hard day for Dawn. She missed her mother so much. She had put her children to bed and was downstairs doing the laundry when the phone rang.

On the other end was Lori, a good friend of hers from California. She and Dawn had been good friends during their college days. Lori and her husband Nate had been in town a few months previously and had stopped by to visit Dawn. Lori hadn't seen Dawn's children since they were babies and had since had a baby girl of her own; Dawn had never met Nate, so they had had a really good visit. Dawn was surprised that Lori was calling but was glad for the diversion.

"Hey, how ya doin?" Lori asked in her usual casual way.

"Good," Dawn replied. "It's a surprise to hear your voice."

"I know," Lori acknowledged. "We really should get together more, ya know."

"We should," Dawn agreed.

"Which brings me to the question … how much leave do you have? Could you get a couple of days off of work?"

"I have two day's personal leave," Dawn answered. "That's all I have since it's my first year teaching there. Why?"

"Well, I'd like you guys to come down here and see us."

"Oh, I'd love to, Lori, but my old car would never make it to California."

"Is it in good enough shape to make it to the airport?"

"Well, yeah, I could probably make it to the airport. Why?"

"We want to fly you and your children here—and take you all to Disneyland. All expenses paid."

"Oh, no! You can't do that! It's too much!" Dawn exclaimed.

"I've already called and reserved the tickets—for the end of the month. I just need to call back and confirm. We would need to go before spring break here, or it will be really crowded."

"But Lori …"

"We won't take no for an answer! After we visited you, I felt prompted to do this. We have the money—we've been blessed—and we need to share our blessings. Nate is all for it, too. There's just one condition," Lori continued, "you can't tell the children where they're going. We want it to be a surprise."

"Then you'll have to let me pay you back," Dawn replied, thinking of the expense.

"No way. We want to do this, Dawn. I remember my dad taking me to Disneyland when I was a kid, and it was a total surprise. Do it for your children."

Dawn was in tears. "Lori, do you know what day this is? You just helped me get through a really hard day."

So Dawn made plans. She arranged for time off of work and wrote notes to excuse her children from school. She told her children that she had a wonderful surprise for them and that they were going to miss two days of school. They tried to guess but couldn't imagine what was in store for them. Dawn packed their bags and her bags and had everything ready; but the day before they were going to leave, Joey came down with a fever and sore throat.

Dawn took Joey to the doctor as soon as she got off work. The doctor examined him and did a throat culture. "Call us in a couple of days," he said. "We'll let you know if he needs antibiotics." Dawn asked the doctor if she could speak with him out in the hallway. She explained to him that they were flying out the next evening to go to Disneyland and that it was a surprise. The doctor graciously sent her home with a prescription for antibiotics to take with them.

That evening Joey still wasn't feeling well. Dawn called her home teacher, Brother Anson, who came over and gave Joey a blessing.

Brother Anson knew of the surprise and had arranged for his oldest son to take them to the airport the next afternoon.

The next day Joey was feeling much better. Dawn was so relieved. She was so excited. She had been smiling for two weeks, just at the thought of the adventure that awaited her children. The only vacation they had ever taken was to go camping in the nearby mountains. They had never been on a plane. They were all bursting with curiosity. Dawn hadn't had so much fun in years, maybe in a lifetime. This was better than Christmas Eve! Brother Anson's son, Justin, arrived to transport them to the airport. As they drove farther and farther down the freeway, the children's guesses increased.

"We're going to the zoo!" Taylor guessed.

"No, I know," said Joey. "We're going to stay overnight at your friend Erin's."

Dawn kept shaking her head and smiling. When Justin took the freeway exit that led to the airport, the children still did not realize where they were going. When he drove into the airport entrance, however, Joey called out, "Mommy, are we going on a plane?"

Dawn nodded. They all shrieked with excitement, "We are!?"

"Would you like to take a plane ride?" she asked them all. Joey nodded decisively as he said, "Yes!" Taylor added an excited "Yes," but Davey shook his head.

"Oh, you'll love it," Dawn said to Davey. "It's not too scary."

Dawn thanked Justin for the ride as they jumped out of the van. The children hurriedly followed Dawn up the escalator and down the long walk to their gate. Eyes wide, they kept repeating, "We're really going on a plane?!" Dawn couldn't do anything but smile and wanted to memorize the moment. Davey was the only one a little apprehensive, but the fear soon left him as he got caught up in the excitement of the others.

They were able to get a seat close to the front of the plane, and Dawn was grateful that they were able to sit together. The children could hardly sit still and had large grins on their faces. Davey cuddled up next to Dawn as the plane gained speed and took off up into the air. She told them that they were going to go to California for a few days to stay with their friends, Lori and Nate.

When they arrived in Los Angeles, Nate met them at the gate and escorted them to pick up the luggage. The children were fascinated by the luggage turnstile. They waited as Nate went to get the car. By now it was nearly midnight, and they were very tired. As Nate drove them to their home, Dawn turned around to see them all fast asleep in the back seat.

The next morning Lori woke them up early while Nate fixed pancakes for breakfast. "I thought we'd go for a ride this morning," she said to the children, "and show you around the town."

They sat in the back of the van, taking in all the sights. Lori's baby, Mandy, in her car seat, was thrilled to have the young company. Dawn noticed when Nate took the Anaheim exit, and there were signs here and there advertising Disneyland; but if her children took notice, they most likely dismissed the thought as too improbable. The signs became more and more numerous, though; and as they entered the parking lot to Disneyland, her children sat in the back with eyes and mouths wide open in disbelief. This time it was Lori's turn to smile, and Nate and Dawn joined in, in the pure enjoyment of her children's ecstasy.

The day at Disneyland was perfect. The weather was perfect. The crowds were not too numerous, and they had time enough to take in nearly all of the park. "I can't believe we're in Disneyland!" Joey kept repeating, smiling broadly. Dawn took pictures galore. This would be an event they would always treasure. They arrived home late and went straight to bed, exhausted and cheeks aching from all of the smiling.

The next morning Lori woke them all again and announced, "We're going to the beach. It will be too cold to swim, but you'll probably want to wear shorts." So they dressed for the beach and put sunscreen on in the car. Dawn's curiosity was peaked, however, as Nate drove farther and farther, eventually taking the San Diego exit. She couldn't believe it when they drove into the parking lot of Sea World. This time her mouth was open as wide as her children's.

"Lori, this wasn't part of the deal!" she exclaimed.

"I know, but if I'd told you, you would have resisted. Just enjoy the day," she grinned.

And they did enjoy the day. Joey even said he liked Sea World better than Disneyland, and he loved Disneyland. She couldn't get over the generosity and loving spirit of her wonderful friends.

The third day was spent at the beach—one beach in the morning and a different beach that evening. The morning beach was rocky, and the children had a wonderful time exploring the rocks and finding seashells. The evening beach was beautiful. It was flat and smooth with white sand stretching as far as you could see. Dawn loved the fire pits that were set up all along the beach. As the sun went down, they sat around the fire cooking hot dogs and marshmallows and having the time of their lives.

As they woke the next morning, they were struck with the realization that their wonderful vacation was over but also realized that they were taking wonderful memories home with them. Lori drove them to the airport, and as she pulled into the side parking to let them out, she turned to the children in the back seat and said to them:

"I know that sometimes life is really hard, and you probably feel bad that you don't have a dad, that he won't see you. But I want you to know something. I want you to know that you do have a Father in Heaven, and He loves you very much, because He is the one who told us to give you this vacation. And we love you very much, too."

Dawn couldn't contain her tears as she, and each of her children, hugged Lori goodbye.

Chapter 66

More Blessings

Disneyland was only the beginning of their association with Lori and Nate. As Joey got older, he spent a few weeks on his own in California and had a great time with Nate. Taylor also would spend time on her own with Lori. Several times they all drove a few hours away where Nate and Lori had a summer cabin and spent time with them and their children there. They always kept in close touch.

There was also a couple from their congregation who became surrogate grandparents to them. The love, nurturing and support they gave Dawn's children, who lost all their grandparents in nearly one fell swoop, gave them support and security that they would not have had otherwise. Dawn's family became a part of their family, and they were blessed greatly by the association. When Joey got old enough to work, another man in their congregation offered him a job with his company, an engineering firm. Joey stayed and grew with the company, eventually becoming an excellent surveyor in his own right.

And then there was money. Somehow, they always had enough money: none for luxuries, none for all of their wants, but always enough for their needs. When Dawn received the $6,000 bill from her attorney (minus the $2,000 that Jace had been ordered to pay), she didn't know how she would ever pay it back, but the money somehow came. She was able to sell an old water share that they couldn't use for $2,000. She got a good tax return that she used to apply $2,000 more on the bill. As she reviewed the tax return, she found a mistake from the previous year and received another $1,000. It was amazing to her how quickly she was able to get out from under the attorney debt.

Christmases were another matter. While working at the hospital, Dawn received three large, unexpected Christmas bonuses. Money appeared in their mailbox anonymously. Gifts were left on their doorstep. Someone gave them the fixings for an entire turkey dinner more than once. Their church installed vinyl windows to replace their old, drafty aluminum ones. And each Christmas, for three years in a row, someone also gave the bishop $400 in cash anonymously to give to Dawn and her family. This was in addition to the kindness from their home teacher and adopted grandparents, who never failed to remember them at Christmas and birthdays, and who were there for them whenever they needed anything.

One Christmas in particular, Dawn and the children came downstairs to a room full of presents provided anonymously. Joey was thrilled to receive an expensive pair of Nike shoes he had been wishing for. There were also several nice gifts for Dawn.

"We're so blessed, Mom," Joey said over and over again that day. "We're so blessed."

An unexpected blessing came with the death of Dawn's father. Even though she missed him terribly, his death was a blessing in Dawn's eyes, because he no longer had to suffer from the horrible dementia that had engulfed him and because she knew he was back with her mother. Since Dawn's mother's death, he had become less and less able to care for himself, to the point of hospitalization. Dawn couldn't bear to see her confident, outgoing, happy father become a shell of what he once was. It was as hard to bear his mental and emotional torture as it was to bear her mother's physical suffering. He did for Dawn in death what he couldn't do in the last years of his life—take care of his daughter and grandchildren. He left her with enough money that she was able to get totally out of debt, pay off her car, put some money in savings for her children's future, and make needed repairs to her aging home.

Most of all, she was blessed with good children. When she compared Joey to the boy he might have been had Jace still been there, she knew she had made the right decision. Jace was in the business of jealously destroying Joey as his scapegoat. Joey was now a strong, happy, well-adjusted young man. He was constantly helping other people and doing what he could to keep their own home in good repair. He had gained many skills and a maturity that he would not have had otherwise.

Taylor was becoming a beautiful young woman. Dawn admired her spunk and zest for life. Davey's nickname became "Smiley," as he always had a smile on his cute, happy face.

Another indirect blessing was the love Dawn further developed for her Savior and Father-in-Heaven. She spent a great deal of time on her knees, so much so that her relationship with God was much, much closer than it would have been. When her mom died, and with the subsequent falling apart of her life, Dawn had been angry at God. She was mad at Him; but the more time she spent on her knees, the more she realized the love He had for her. He couldn't save her marriage—that was something that depended on both people involved—but He could bless her with unimaginable blessings and strengthen her and protect what she cared about the most. She knew undeniably that she was loved.

One night as Dawn was preparing dinner, a discussion somehow turned to heroes. "I know who my hero is," Joey said decisively. "My hero is my mom." Dawn counted her blessings as her eyes filled with tears.

Chapter 67

Flowers

It was a beautiful spring day as Dawn drove home from work. Music on the radio was playing, and she was humming along. She enjoyed her job but so looked forward to coming home to her children. She loved them all so much; and she loved coming home. No knot in her stomach anymore as she neared the street she lived on. No worry. No apprehension.

She thought of the night before and the time she had spent helping her next-door neighbors, two cute ladies from South America. They had a difficult time speaking English and had an even more difficult time maintaining their aging home and large yard. Dawn had helped them several times over the years, mostly with their English. Last year she had helped them plant flowers. Now she was helping them remodel their bathroom. She had patched and smoothed their subfloor with adhesive and helped them lay self-sticking tile. She helped them tear out an old mirror and towel racks and puttied holes, sanded and painted. As she showed them how to take a block of wood, put it next to a tile piece and hammer it so it was flush with the adjoining piece, they said in amazement, "How do you know how to do this?" They said the same thing when Dawn showed them tips for a professional wallpaper job.

Dawn felt good that she could help them as much as she did. As she reflected on the night before, she realized that most of the skills she had used to help them with had been acquired after her separation from Jace. She did not know how to do many of those things before he left. She was grateful for all of the things she had learned. She actually enjoyed working outside now and became much more knowledgeable about gardening and taking care of her yard and home with each passing year.

She was a much stronger person and, in many ways, more than in just practical skills. She knew who she was, and she was at peace with the person she had become. Never again would she take responsibility for someone else's anger. Never again would she allow someone to mistreat her. Never again would she be the fragile woman, tiptoeing around everyone trying to appease them, that she once was.

She realized that no matter what she had done, no matter who she had become, it never would have been enough for Jace. She couldn't make him happy, because *he* wasn't happy. It was that simple. Whatever anger he displayed nearly everyday of his life came from somewhere and sometime that Dawn would never know about. It came from a place and time long before she came into his life—most likely, long before Juanita came into his life. He had never dealt with it; and as long as he didn't, he could continue blaming others for his miserable, bitter life.

Not Dawn. She realized the part she played in their mutual misery by accepting it in the first place. She was wrong to do so. She did so at first in wanting so much to please him and in thinking things were her fault—she must be doing something wrong for him to treat her that way. Then, she thought that she could change him—if she loved him enough and forgave him enough, he would surely be good to her.

Finally, she accepted mistreatment out of fear—fear for her own life and her children's safety. But, with God's help, she got beyond it all. They were alive and well. She forgave Jace. She forgave his children. She forgave herself. She could never regret the marriage or the divorce when she looked at her wonderful children.

Most of all, there was peace. She was grateful to be going home where there was peace; not perfection, as she and her children were far from perfect, but no more walking on eggshells. No yelling. No criticism. No coercion. No threats. No intimidation. Just peace. Peace in her home. Peace in her heart. Peace of mind. Peace of spirit.

As she turned the car into her driveway, she noticed the row of sparkling daffodils, pansies and tulips in full bloom, splashing yellow cheer across her front yard. She was home.

Afterword

When I attended the domestic violence conference mentioned in Chapter 51, I filled out an inventory, much like the one that follows in the Bonus Section. Under a section titled "Psychological Abuse," I answered 'yes' to *every* question. There was no more denying to myself then that I was an emotionally-battered woman. I knew in my heart that there was nothing more I could do to try to save my marriage.

For most of my marriage, my focus was on my husband and what he was doing. I hoped and prayed that he would change. He truly was the one in control, until I took the steps I needed to take to get out. Although I thought about leaving many times during my marriage, I only had the courage and energy to put those thoughts into action on three separate occasions. Some statistics state that an abused woman tries to leave her marriage an average of seven times, and often more. I would like to see those statistics change. I believe that when there is real abuse, there will be no change on the part of the abuser as long as their partner remains. Disrespect should never be accepted: women only continue as a victim and increase the risk to themselves and their children when they return without trained intervention. *He will not change.*

When I finally got out for good, eleven years later, my focus gradually shifted away from my husband (and eventual ex-husband) to myself. I had some difficult questions to answer. Why did I stay with him for so long? Why did I accept disrespect in the first place? Why did I come back? Why did I take upon myself the responsibility for his happiness and disregard mine? Reading old journal entries sickened me. I felt angry and ashamed for accepting his abuse. After much introspection, I now know the answers to those questions. Although there are several answers, I believe that one word is at the root of them all: fear.

I was so afraid of so many things. I was afraid of hurting him, though I came to realize that I was not the cause of his pain. I was afraid for my children. I had financial fears. I feared losing my home and my children. I worried about being shunned in church and the stigma of divorce. I feared losing my extended family. I was totally intimidated by lawyers and the court system. I was afraid of loneliness. I think the biggest fear many women face is being alone, so they choose to accept abuse instead. Some of my fears were invalid; some were very real. I was afraid for my own life. My ex-husband is still a viable threat to me physically and most likely always will be. The difference now, though, is that he has no control over me. The opposite of fear is faith. Through my faith in God, who has strengthened me all the way, I have been able to overcome the fear. My life is one of happiness and peace.

I am so glad that I was advised to get a protective order, though I didn't feel justified at the time. If anything were to happen to me, it would place my ex-husband first on the suspect list; and he knows it. That piece of paper is a great protection to me and may have saved my life. I'm also grateful I kept a journal. Not only did it give me perspective in helping me to get out, when I read old entries, it helped me to stay out.

When my ex-husband left, I wept through many nights. I wanted him to return and be different. He was supposed to be my true love. I had devoted my life to him and our family. I had given him everything I had. I mourned the death of my marriage, but the pain eventually subsided. Time truly was a healer and a teacher, and I learned much.

Driving home from work, I used to have to pass my ex-husband's residence. At first it was painful. I wondered about him and how he was doing. At times I hated him. After a while, though, as my eyes truly became focused and my thinking became clear, the pain turned into peace. I was truly so relieved, when I drove past his house, not to have to participate any more in his misery; not to have to be a part of his manipulations, his criticism, his anger, his blame. I am so happy to be free of all of that. That is what I wish for you. That is what I pray for you and yours: to have peace in your home and in your heart; to never accept the least disrespect from anyone, least of all from yourself; to be free.

—Jane D. Bryant

Author Bio

Jane D. Bryant has a Bachelor of Arts degree in English, a Secondary Teaching Certificate, and a Special Education Endorsement. She has taught in the public school system as well as in the private sector for twenty years, working with the handicapped and in the Youth-in-Custody system. She has worked as a sportswriter and written many articles for several area newspapers. A single parent, Jane most enjoys her time spent at home with her children.

Bonus Section—Now What?

"Life is just a mirror, and what you see out there,
you must first see inside of you."
— Wally "Famous" Amos

Following are a self-help guide and therapeutic commentary. Throughout these pages you will find insights and tools which can benefit any relationship, assist you in evaluating yourself and your partner, and help you in making needed decisions. I would invite you to read these things and ponder them in your heart.

Many who have read "He Never Hit Me" have shared with me how impacting and real Dawn's story was for them. They have disclosed having similar experiences, feelings, and fears or have known someone close to them who has experienced the same. My hope is that if Dawn's life has in any way been a mirroring or reflective experience for you or someone you care about, that it would encourage you to act—even if it is just passing this on to a loved one. Doing nothing only allows the abuse to continue and intensify toward partners and children. Please share your feelings and thoughts with someone. Talking is the first step to building awareness and the eventual hope of getting help.

—Joel Brandley

Bonus Section Contents

IT IS NOT YOUR FAULT

Research has shown that whether or not a woman will be beaten depends upon whether her partner is abusive and not on any characteristic unique to her. (Lenore Walker: The Battered Women Syndrome, 1984.)

Abusers remain abusive: 93% of men in treatment programs have abused their former partners. (Joan Zorza, Clearinghouse Review, Vol. 29, April 1996.)

Most women will recover from the effects of repeated traumatic abuse, after they are in a violence-free environment, especially with the support of an abuse or domestic violence program.

YOU ARE NOT ALONE

It has been said that when it comes to the damage and impact on a life, there is no real difference between physical, sexual and emotional abuse—all that distinguishes one from the other is the abuser's choice of weapons.

The Center for Disease Control and Prevention (May 2003) study finds that health-related costs (including rape, physical assault and homicide) committed by an intimate partner exceed $5.8 billion each year.

A woman is beaten every 15 seconds by an intimate partner. (Uniform Crime reported, 1994)

Domestic violence is the largest single cause of injury among women seen at hospital emergency rooms. (Stark, E. & Flitcraft, A (1985) "Spouse Abuse," Surgeon General's Workshop on Violence and Public Health Source Book.)

One out of every four American women report that they have been physically abused by a husband or boyfriend at some point in their lives. (Lieberman Research Inc. Domestic Violence Advertising Campaign Tracking Survey. (Waive IV) Conducted for the Advertising Council and Family Abuse Prevention Fund.)

Nationally, 75% of battered women say that their children are also battered. (Giles-Sims, J. (1085). "A longitudinal study of battered children of battered wives." Family Relations, XXXIV, April, p205.)

CHAPTER REVIEW OF RELATIONSHIP DYNAMICS

Please read and review carefully the chart on the following pages. It is amazing how much we accept, ignore and miss in our own lives. The chart is a look back for Dawn. See what she missed and what you may have missed, also. Can you find other signs of abuse that are not in the chart?

As you are reviewing the information and going back into the chapters, I hope you will become aware of the language of emotional abuse as well as how the batterer works to convince his victim that she is responsible for *his* thoughts, feelings and actions. I hope as you do so, you will also begin to review your own life and begin to see what you, or someone you love, might be missing.

The chart is divided by chapters. The columns list the red flags that Dawn missed or discounted, his hurtful behavior and abuse, her fears and her negative and positive actions. As you review the chapters, I hope that you will begin to put into context the items in the chart. You may even begin to notice additional emotionally-abusive language and other abuse which may have been left out of the chart.

RELATIONSHIP DYNAMICS

Chapter	Red Flags--Missed/ Discounted	His Hurtful Behavior/Abuse	Her Fears	Her Actions (-Negative/ + Positive)
2	Strong physical attraction Bad feeling His reputation Quick physical involvement See each other every day		Won't see him again	- Ignores deep feelings, intuition
3	Hates ex-wife Dreams that he met her—"meant to be"			
4	Promiscuous with other women "*Only* woman respected" Bullet Cries, bad feelings Not religious Siblings left home early Parents "crazy"		Having another relationship not work out	- Discounts difference in values - Dismisses second thoughts
5	Proposes *first* day back at work Jealousy—bad dream Shy—not social			- Misconstrues jealousy for love
6	No religious ceremony No arguments Elevates her— "you're perfect"			- Complete compliance on his part not realistic, dishonest
7	Juanita calls Ida wedding day No friends, few family Doesn't look at her Off-balance from the start			- Excuses his shyness, social ineptness, comments
8	Angry over nothing "Monster" Wants her things off her dresser	Anger Demeaning term Devalues past, sentiments		- Excuses his behavior - Wishes she "obeyed" him - She obeys, avoids his displeasure
9	Loud alarm, bright light Mean to Ida Pregnant soon after married	Devalues her desires, needs Elevates male children over female child Control		- Rationalizes his behavior

Chapter	Red Flags--Missed/ Discounted	His Hurtful Behavior/Abuse	Her Fears	Her Actions (-Negative/ + Positive)
10	Doughnuts for boys Won't buy house Didn't disclose bankruptcy Ida's note—"things better now"	No support— elevates boys Implied threat Discounts her reality—lies	May lose him, home Questions his past	- Rationalizes his behavior - Accepts disrespect - Takes responsibil- ity for obtaining house
11	Socks	Anger, rage, intimidation	His rage	- Rationalizes his behavior, discounts her own feelings
12	Doesn't support with kids Doesn't care about assault Pornography Wakes her when he had keys	Discounts her Devalues her	He doesn't love her	- Continues to try to please him
13	Doesn't want time alone w/her No personal gift	Devalues her/relationship		- Gives up on romance ideals
14	Distant when home with her Gun in his pocket	Isolates her emotionally Implied threat	Lack of love	
15	Can't name Joey Criticism Jealous of Joey Ida – "you don't treat her well"	Negates agreements Devalues her Jealousy, Controlling	Not being a good mother	- Buys into his accusations, criticisms - Cares for Joey alone, exhausted + Realizes Ida is correct
16	Brother dies— no tears Sleeps with children	Negates her needs		
17	Mary abused Mike		Jace abused	
18	Pornography Refuses counseling Ida warns him	Devalues, isolates her	His immorality	+ Goes to counseling on own
19	Argues on vacation Goes back on agreement	Withholds affection Won't let her sleep	He doesn't love her	+ Sleeps instead of taking boys to store
20	Criticizes then gives her gift Puts up fence for her but wants her in it Throws fork Meal not good enough His parents argue in front of others	Roller coaster cycle Isolation, Control Physical threat Criticism	End of marriage, family, her dreams, image	+ Confronts him on criticism + Leaves situation, moves out

Chapter	Red Flags--Missed/ Discounted	His Hurtful Behavior/Abuse	Her Fears	Her Actions (-Negative/ + Positive)
21	Yells when she moves back Ida—"should have told you" Jace—"I'd never let another woman…"	Anger, rage Projects past hurt on her	Hurting him	- Comes back before counseling + Insists on counseling, gains insight - Excuses his pain, tries to remedy
22	Ida promiscuous and acting out Jace denies lying about scar Jace spanks Ida with belt Neighbors alarmed	Lying Physical abuse to Ida	What neighbors, DCFS think	
23	Ida runs to mother J. distant when Taylor born Undermines breastfeeding Boys elevated Jealous of Joey Mean when she is ill Jealous of friends, undermines, denies invitation	Rejects own daughter Demeaning Anger, rage, jealousy Mistreats her when ill Isolates from friends	His anger	+ Gets care for Joey in spite of his anger - Decides no more friends to appease him and avoid anger + Leaves situation, moves out + Does not disclose location
24		Verbally abusive threats	Her safety Her family's safety	+ Calls lawyer - Wants him back
25	Won't go to counseling unless together	Controlling, his terms	End of marriage	- Moves back before counseling + Contract, goes to counseling
26	Assault at court Boys ignore, demean her She has to demand compliance to contract	Makes her demand his support rather than insuring it	Ida's anger	+ Demands compliance to contract
27	Has to plead for basic needs Stairs	Physical abuse, rage Threats while pregnant	His rage For her life End of marriage	+ Leaves house, tells Nancy + Shows Nancy evidence + Calls counselor - Rationalizes his behavior again - Goes back home
28	No apology or acknowledgment Takes out to dinner, movie	Roller coaster cycle	Her safety	- Accepts cycle

Chapter	Red Flags--Missed/ Discounted	His Hurtful Behavior/Abuse	Her Fears	Her Actions (-Negative/ + Positive)
29	Counselor sees no hope He's relieved, contract void		End of marriage	
30	Threats of violence to Mary	Implied threats	For her life	- Denies counselor's viewpoint - Stays because of fear
31	Denies her illness	Cruelty when ill	Her well-being	
32	Surgery to please him	Discounts her needs	No affection	- Puts his needs before hers
33	Won't support her employment Won't watch children	Undermines her efforts Refuses care for children	Not enough money	+ Sticks with job despite his anger + Gets a better job
34	She's hurting—he wants cake	Discounts her pain		+ Doesn't make cake for him
35	Heart attack	Raging	Losing him Causing it	- Feels it's her fault
36	Things better temporarily			- Hopes things will change
37	Argument on anniversary Boys pattern his abuse to Joey Buys her a bike	Boys elevated above Joey, herself Gift replaces decency/cycle	Change only temporary	+ Left situation - Only temporary
38	Jace mean to Joey Boys mean to her	Physical/emotional abuse Elevates boys	His sons	- Continues to stay and take it
39			Her mom's cancer	-Rejects his offer to stay and comfort her
40	Inflexible about Thanksgiving	Denies her needs	Losing mom	+ Goes to mother's in spite of him
41	Argument over Ethan Hurts Joey who is innocent Stabs her picture Lots of presents next morning	Elevates boys/ denigrates her Verbal abuse to son Implied threat Roller coaster cycle	For safety For her & children's well-being	- Gives him card - Accepts abuse because of holiday

Chapter	Red Flags--Missed/ Discounted	His Hurtful Behavior/Abuse	Her Fears	Her Actions (-Negative/ + Positive)
42	Refuses to try at conference Burns her with seatbelt Makes her drive—criticizes Boys mean to Joey Not invited to wedding Angry at crumbs Joey wants to be a girl Extra attention to Taylor	Withholds affection Physical abuse Criticism, control Discounts harm to Joey Expects her to attend Blame—unable to please Withholds affection to son Inflicts more pain on Joey	End of marriage Joey's safety Emotional harm to Joey	+ Talked to clergy + Stayed home with children - Tried to please with talk, present good image - Continues to stay despite Joey's pain
43	Cruelty to Joey	Child abuse		+ Tries to protect/ comfort Joey
44				+ Promises mother
45				+ Hears message in her heart
46	Stepsons' delinquency		Jace & sons	+ Shows detectives weapons
47	Dirty dishes when mom dies	Lack support/care for needs		
48	Disregards her wishes No drapes No children on bed/ in room No swamp cooler Ethan does drugs Dawn/Eric spit	Denies basic needs of temperature and sleep Undermines relationship with children/Control Substance abuse Physical abuse	Jace & sons	+ Fixes rooms in spite of him + Disengages from boys + Keeps chart for insight + Keeps journal - Engages inappropriately with Eric
49	Calls children "the specials" She tries to play his game-he rages at Joey	Verbal abuse, attempts to control and isolate Double standard—unable to win	His rage What he will do to Joey	+ Maintains chart and journal
50			End of Marriage Hurting him	+ Fasts, prays + Hears message in her heart - Still afraid to act on message
51	Undermines her workshop Nice around family Blames her for not camping Regards her with loathing Eric swears at her	Control, only his agenda Selective abuse Hurts her relationship with Children Disrespect from stepson	What he will do to children	+ Stays with plan to attend conference in spite of threats + Takes self-inventory + Talks to person from YCC

Chapter	Red Flags--Missed/ Discounted	His Hurtful Behavior/Abuse	Her Fears	Her Actions (-Negative/ + Positive)
52	Orders her to cook No need for apology Abuse in journal entries	Intimidation Disrespect, elevates son	What he will do to her and Joey For her safety	+ Stands up to Eric, demands apology + Refuses to cook dinner + Goes to lawyer + Goes to YCC, fills out order + Reviews chart & journal + Writes out resolve + Talks to children
53	"I'm going to finish it" Takes keepsakes Sends boys to steal Denies abuse at hearing	Threats Harm to property Denial	For her and children's safety	+ Files order with judge - Says goodbye, pleads for fix + Takes children + Takes important papers + Changes locks + Filed order against boys
54	Criticizes watering of plants Hurts her when getting things	Criticism Physical harm	For safety of home and belongings	+ Protected belongings + Prepared for visit + Went through receipts, records + Removed children from scene
55	Refuses to see children Doesn't acknowledge her Files on day of funeral	Abandonment Denigration; demeaning	Loss of extended family	+ Counseling on own + Counseling for children + Counseling for Joey
56	Last Christmas gifts Tantrums in community	Abandonment of children Rage, threats via others	For safety	+ Documents everything + Prepares binder for court
57	Runs her off road Finger whenever he passes Flaunts girlfriend Comes into yard; steals Hurts dog, tries to silence him	Physical threat Verbal abuse via gestures Demeaning Harm to property Harm to pet	For safety of person and belongings	+ Reports to sheriff + Makes own report + Obtains cell phone + Keeps order with her + Notifies schools + Reviews journal
58	Death threat Damage to neighbor's car	Physical harm	For safety	+ Notifies police

Chapter	Red Flags--Missed/ Discounted	His Hurtful Behavior/Abuse	Her Fears	Her Actions (-Negative/ + Positive)
59	Witness a no show Stares at Dawn Taylor's song	Intimidation Abandonment	For safety	+ Documents in binder + Taylor deals with abandonment
61				+ Dawn/Joey fix swamp cooler
62	Comes into yard Animals die	Harm to property Harm to pets		+ Wrote letter to dispute lies— saved money + Home blessed + Family song/ family night + Neighbors support
63	Changes insurance w/o notice Lies about support—lowered	Control Abandonment		+ Insures children on own + Prays; God protects
64	Cockfight	Harm to animals		+ End of most yard visits + Wrote closure letters - Davey overhears conversation with detective
65				+ Disneyland; friends
66				+ Surrogate grandparents + Joey becomes very skilled + Children happy, confident + Financial blessings + Respect from children
67				+ Blessings from God/Peace

As you reviewed the chapters and the chart, were you able to put into context the information from the chart back into Dawn's life? Did you find any additional emotional abuse and other abuse left off the chart? More importantly, I hope it assisted you in your review of your own life and circumstances. Each of us can always benefit from reviewing our previous goals and dreams and seeing how they fit into our current situation. It helps us to reset and get our life back on track or moving again in a positive direction.

SELF-EVALUATION INVENTORY

The Self-Evaluation Inventory which follows is meant to help you continue to assess your current circumstances. As you check the items in the inventory, please be honest. If you only mark a few, review those items and make a decision to talk to someone about the items you marked and what those items represent to you. Regardless of how many you mark, remember that marking one of the items may be as critical as marking multiple items.

Only you can decide whom to talk to, when and how. Take your own safety and that of your children into consideration. At the end of this information, you will find a phone number for the National Domestic Violence Hotline. No matter what state you live in or how serious your situation, they can direct you to the individuals and services in your local area. Even if you are just beginning to notice changes in your partner that concern you, the hotline can direct you to someone to consult with and answer your questions.

No matter whom you decide to talk with, remember that healthy individuals talk out and share their concerns. Healthy couples talk and honor each other's opinion and concerns. They are not threatened or worried if partners are talking with others in order to help themselves feel comfortable in the relationship or to find ways to improve and better the relationship. The key is to begin talking and continue to talk.

Remember, this tool is not meant to replace the counsel of professionals or your own good judgment. It is not meant to judge or condemn but to help you make an accurate and honest appraisal of your own personal relationship.

Has your partner ever done any of the following? (Check those which apply.)

EMOTIONAL HURT:

- ☐ Abandoned you
- ☐ Accused you of being a whore
- ☐ Accused you of being unfaithful
- ☐ Behaved rudely to you in front of others
- ☐ Blamed you for many things
- ☐ Blamed you for promises not kept
- ☐ Blamed you in front of others
- ☑ Called you names: "bitch, whore, etc."
- ☐ Criticized you
- ☐ Criticized your sexual performance
- ☑ Degraded you openly in front of others
- ☑ Embarrassed you in front of others
- ☐ Forbid you to make decisions
- ☑ Forbid you to work, handle own money
- ☐ Forced you to sign over property/possessions
- ☑ Forced you to watch pornography
- ☐ Had an affair
- ☐ Humiliated you
- ☐ Humiliated you sexually
- ☐ Hurt you with objects
- ☐ Ignored your feelings or ideas
- ☐ Insulted you
- ☐ Intimidated you
- ☐ Made jokes that demean you financially
- ☐ Made you dependent
- ☑ Made you feel inadequate or worthless
- ☐ Manipulated you with lies
- ☑ Minimized your feelings about sex
- ☐ Prevented you from sleeping
- ☑ Punished the children to hurt you
- ☑ Put you down
- ☐ Refused to work or provide for family
- ☑ Ridiculed your most valued beliefs
- ☐ Sexually acted out with others in your presence
- ☑ Talked sexually about other women
- ☑ Threatened to take children
- ☑ Threatened you, your family or friends
- ☑ Threatened suicide, emotional blackmail
- ☑ Told you he can't make it without you
- ☑ Told you to leave or locked you out
- ☐ Treated you like a sex object
- ☑ Undermined your power and confidence

HURT TO THE BODY OR BELONGINGS:

- ☐ Bit you
- ☐ Broken furniture
- ☐ Broken mirrors
- ☑ Broken windows
- ☐ Burned you
- ☐ Caused broken bones
- ☑ Caused bruises
- ☑ Choked you
- ☑ Created extreme pain during sex
- ☑ Cut you out of pictures
- ☑ Deprived you of food, sleep, basic needs
- ☐ Deprived you of medical care/ medicine
- ☐ Destroyed your property
- ☑ Disabled phone
- ☑ Forced you off road
- ☑ Forced you to strip
- ☑ Forced you to have sex with others
- ☑ Forced unwanted sexual acts on you
- ☑ Hit you

- ☑ Humiliated you sexually
- ☐ Hurt you with objects
- ☑ Kicked you
- ☑ Neglected you when ill
- ☑ Neglected you when pregnant
- ☑ Pinched you
- ☑ Pulled your hair
- ☑ Punched holes in doors, walls
- ☑ Raped you
- ☑ Restrained you
- ☐ Ruined family pictures
- ☐ Scratched you
- ☑ Shook you
- ☑ Shoved you
- ☑ Slashed tires
- ☑ Spit on you
- ☐ Tampered with gas tank
- ☑ Threatened your pets
- ☑ Threatened you with object
- ☑ Threatened with weapon
- ☐ Thrown away clothes
- ☑ Thrown you down stairs
- ☐ Tortured pets
- ☑ Violent when having sex

POTENTIAL BATTERING PERSONALITY INVENTORY

You have just evaluated your experiences. Now evaluate your partner. Try and make a non-judgmental, accurate and honest appraisal:

☐ Alcohol and/or drug use
☐ Anger at parents; i.e., father for abusing and mother for not protecting
☐ Batters to prove masculinity
☐ Black-and-white thinking; i.e., either happy or angry
☐ Blames others
☐ Cruelty to animals
☐ Destroys property of others, selfish with own possessions
☐ Extreme jealousy; keeps victim totally isolated
☐ Hypersensitive
☐ Impulsive: acts without thinking about consequences
☐ Initially and with others demonstrates good qualities: charming, charismatic and lovable

☐ Irrational beliefs; i.e., "If she/he really loved me, she/he would know what I want."
☐ Lack of awareness of other's feelings
☐ Easily frustrated
☐ Need for total control
☐ Poor self-image, including doubts about masculinity
☐ Preoccupation with weapons
☐ Unemployment or high turn-over and job-dissatisfaction
☐ Use of violence and fear as problem solving
☐ Violent temper, sparked by insignificant things

SIXTEEN CHARACTERISTICS OF BATTERERS

The more the following signs a person has, the more likely the person is a batterer. If a person has three or more behaviors, they may have a strong potential for physical violence. The last four signs listed are almost always predictive of a batterer. Some may only have a couple of the behaviors but can become extremely violent over those character traits, i.e., jealousy.

☐ 1. **Jealousy**. It is never a sign of love. It is a thought, which can drive an action, but it is always based on insecurities and control issues. It may begin with wanting to know where she is going and questioning why she was gone so long. It soon becomes multiple checkups on her throughout the day, requests for her not to socialize, checking car mileage, questioning loyalty, accusations, open mistrust, and threats for unseen strangers and her.

☐ 2. **Controlling Behavior**. At first, the batterer might say that this behavior is because he's concerned for her. Protecting her from harm is how he shows affection. His need to control soon leads him to make all the decisions. The woman loses her partner status, and if his need to control continues, she will soon be treated and perceived as his property. This ownership level of control isolates her and the children and moves her to a sense of fear. She can be limited to asking permission for everything, just like a child to a parent, even for leaving his sight.

☐ 3. **Hurried Involvement**. Many battered women dated or knew their abuser for less than six months before they began living together or were married. He might claim, "love at first sight;" "you're the only person I could ever talk to;" or "I've never felt loved like this before." This quickness is often due to his insecurities, jealousy and need to control. He's like an empty bucket that is dry and longing desperately to be filled. Many women can't see past the shining, glimmering outside to the multiple holes in the bottom on the inside. The pressure to hurry comes from wanting to move from a relationship of two individuals to a union of one. The Bible says that the marriage of a man and woman is to unite two as one, but not "one" meaning him and only him; I believe the Bible referred to being equal and one in focus, ideas and love.

☐ 4. **Unrealistic Expectations**. He may be very dependent on the woman for all of his needs. He might expect perfection from her as his lover and mother of his children. He may say things like, "If you love me, I'm all you need." Soon he will expect her to fulfill and be responsible for all of his needs. Imagine having to have food hot and ready for him no matter what time he decides to come home and without any notification. She is supposed to take care of everything for him emotionally and in the home.

☐ 5. **Isolation**. The man might try to cut the woman off from all resources. Her past friends become interfering troublemakers. He sees her family as people who want to take what's his and change her back into an individual. He thinks her male associates are after her, even religious clergy and affiliations. To him, male or female friends have sexual impropriety as their sole purpose. He may want to live in an isolated area, like the country. His control over the phone and car keep her limited and afraid to ask.

☐ 6. **Blames Others for His Problems**. If he is often out of work, it is somehow her fault. He misses opportunities because she trapped him and is holding him back. He makes mistakes and then blames his spouse for upsetting him and keeping him from doing his job. He tells the woman it is her fault for everything and anything that goes wrong.

☐ 7. **Blames Others for His Feelings**. He might tell the woman, "You make me mad; it's your fault I'm angry, because you didn't do what I asked." They are his thoughts, feelings and actions, and he is in full control of them. He uses blame and ownership to displace his responsibility onto her and to manipulate her. He makes her accountable for his feelings, thoughts and actions as if she were in control; but does so in order to manifest and sustain and tighten his control over her.

☐ 8. **Hypersensitive**: He sees the slightest setbacks as personal attacks. He complains about the injustice of everything, while being completely unjust in his dominion over his partner and the children.

In order to have his control continue to grow, he finds less and less to be happy or content with and more and more to be dissatisfied, miserable and angry about. Simple things, like being asked to help with the household chores while his wife is sick, are seen as a huge sacrifice and something to be enraged over.

☐ 9. **Cruelty to Animals or Children**. This is a man who may punish animals brutally or is insensitive to their pain. He may even use treatment or threats against pets to manipulate his partner and children. Often he has unrealistic expectations for his children, like expecting a two-or-three-year-old to talk and act like an adult. He might even tease the children until they cry and blame his wife for their crying. Half of all men who beat their wives also beat their children. As his ownership and control become complete, he may even use the children to gratify his sexual needs and tell them it is their mother's fault.

☐ 10. **"Playful" Use of Force in Sex**. This man may like to throw his wife to the ground and forcibly hold her down during sex. His fantasies during sex may include his partner acting as if he were raping her. Her not wanting sex may excite him, and he might be highly stimulated by manifesting his control through force. Her compliance and sexual responses are reached through fear and not pleasure. Sex is demanded and taken, even if his wife is tired, sleeping or ill.

☐ 11. **Verbal Abuse**. The man might say things that are meant to be degrading, cruel and hurtful to the woman. Hurtful language such as "you're stupid, worthless and incompetent" is commonly used. Often her name has been changed to "loser, bitch, whore," etc. He says she is nothing and unable to function without him. He uses abusive language to promote his non-traditional abusive male role. He expects and demands her to come when she is called. She gets called like a dog but is treated worse.

☐ 12. **Dr. Jeckyll and Mr. Hyde**. Many women are confused by their abuser's sudden change in mood—they will describe him as nice one minute and evil and exploding the next minute. This does not indicate some special "mental problem" or that he's "crazy." Explosiveness and mood swings are typical of men who beat their partners. It is common for the batterer to beat his spouse so that he can make up—a cycle that he controls. Some women, when they know the abuse is coming, will even play into it and bring it on, in order to alleviate the stressful anticipation of the abuse and to look forward to the make-up time. These women have given up their sense of self-preservation for a few non-abusive moments.

☐ 13. **Past Battering**. A man who has hit a prior partner is more likely to abuse his next partner. If he tells you he has hit women in the past, but they made him do it, be careful. Listen to relatives or ex-spouses. If they report he is abusive, he may very well be. Unless treated, a past batterer will continue to batter. Situational circumstances do not make a person an abusive personality.

☐ 14. **Threats of Violence**. This would include any threat of physical force meant to control the woman. Most men do not threaten their partners, but a batterer would have his spouse believe that "everybody talks like that," in order to excuse his threats. Remember that each threat adds to the likelihood that he may act on those threats, especially if he feels his threats are being challenged; and he needs to ensure immediate obedience from all his possessions, including his partner and his children.

☐ 15. **Breaking or Striking Objects**. This behavior is used as a punishment, i.e., tearing up pictures of better times and breaking loved possessions. As women become desensitized to fear and verbal and even physical abuse, the batterer will intensify his abuse to terrorize his spouse and children into submission. The man may beat on tables with his fist and throw things toward his partner and children. If a batterer has not yet openly hit his spouse, this may be the step before it happens. Remember, however, that any time a person is enraged, regardless of the reason, he can and will do horrible things that even he didn't think he was capable of. Only very immature or enraged people, who are not thinking clearly, break or strike objects in the presence of other people in order to threaten them.

☐ 16. **Any Force During an Argument**. This may involve a man holding a woman down and physically restraining her to "get her to listen" to him or "for her own good." Far too many women put up with bruising and bleeding from pushing, shoving, sexual torture and being restrained against their will and continue to stay, reporting as their reason, *He Never Hit Me*.

If you have found that your partner shares several or even a few of these characteristics, please evaluate you own situation and circumstances and determine to start talking. Whom you talk to will be up to you; reach deep inside yourself to the intuition and value God created you with. It may be necessary for some to leave and start talking outside of their house. (It stopped being a home when he started being a batterer.) It may be that a third party will be enough to talk with. Please review the tools you have just completed and share your findings with someone.

Think back over your relationship. Have you and the children been conditioned by fear to keep the family secret, that your partner and their dad is a batterer? Remember a secret is not a part of a healthy relationship. Don't confuse secrets with surprises. When a surprise is found out everyone experiences joy and happiness; when a secret is discovered the result is resentment, disappointment, fear and anger.

WHY WOMEN STAY, 3 FACTORS: ECONOMIC, SOCIAL AND EMOTIONAL

Listed below are the three most common reasons women stay in and return to battered relationships. Notice none of them have to do with love or respect or honoring the innate value that is in you and that you should be bringing out in the children.

Economic Factors include: Economic dependence and perceived lack of support from the criminal justice system. Fear of involvement in the court process. Lack of alternative housing. Lack of job skills. Fear of losing custody of children.

Social Factors include: Social isolation resulting in lack of support from family or friends and lack of information regarding alternatives. Cultural and religious constraints and shunning.

Emotional Factors include: Fear of loneliness. Insecurity about potential independence. Lack of emotional support. Guilt and shame about self and marriage. Fear that the partner is unable to survive alone. Belief that the partner will change. Uncertainty and fear about making formidable life-changes. Fear of emotional damage to children. Fear of religious leader and God's disapproval. Fear of retaliation and greater physical danger to themselves and their children if they leave.

These factors should clearly point out that fear is the main part of each reason women stay or return to a battered relationship. If you or someone you care about is thinking of returning or has returned to a relationship based on these common reasons, please realize that they are based on fear and that fear is not part of a healthy relationship. You don't get married to have a relationship of fear, so why return to a relationship because of fear?

Regardless of your shame or guilt for what you have allowed in your relationship, you have a choice. *Today, right now*! You can allow your shame and guilt, that mostly has been assigned to you, to continue to blacken your future with degradation and fear; or you can begin talking and acting in such a way as to create an opportunity for a brighter, out-in-the-sun future. A future where you can expect respect for yourself and children and help yourself and them learn how to reject disrespect. A future where love can finally replace fear.

May God grant you the ability to want to change the things you can—you and your thoughts, feelings and beliefs—and to not take on responsibility for those things you cannot change, i.e. his or their thoughts, feelings and actions. May you have the insight and self-sight to see and know the difference. Once again, stop and look at the choices you are making or help a friend to do the same. Are they returning and staying in a battering relationship to fill his needs? If so, you or they are returning to continue on as his victim. Who are you really returning to, the person you were in love with or the batterer? It is rarely possible to return to a battering relationship as a real partner without getting help first.

HEALTHY VS. ABUSIVE RELATIONSHIPS

In healthy relationships, couples set up household tasks and assignments agreed on by both partners and then the children as they increase in age. These assignments relate to the individual strengths of each and are acknowledged as gifts or personal contributions, not demands or expectations. Couples are grateful for the help and service the other is able to provide each day, and each understands and is flexible when "life happens." Both partners are willing to help and be responsive to each other as complications arise.

In healthy relationships, both partners are just that—equal partners. They both have the right to and are encouraged to voice their opinion about family and financial issues. They let their partner know what their plans are and discuss their plans out of respect and love, not out of duty or fear. They are not asking permission; they are free to choose for themselves. They are each encouraged to pursue their own interests. Their individuality and personal growth is viewed as adding great interest to the relationship and value to the family as a whole. This kind of relationship models the unique value and worth of both genders to the children and helps both male and female children honor their gender as well as that of the opposite gender.

In healthy relationships, no double standards exist. Each couple not only pursues individual strengths and interests, they also foster positive relationships and spend time with friends and extended family members independent of their partner and without judgment or jealousy.

In healthy relationships, his happiness or sadness or anger is his. She can do everything and anything to provide him with opportunities to experience joy and receive the love she is offering; but he is the only one responsible for what he does receive and the meaning he takes and adds to life based on his feelings, thoughts and actions.

In abusive relationships, the tasks and roles of the relationship are usually determined by and under the control of the male. If "life happens," the wife is still expected to meet the demands and time frame of her partner, regardless of personal sickness or circumstances. Out of this lack of respect and these unrealistic expectations springs blame. Blame is projected for what is done and not done. Soon the blame is not only heaped upon the battered woman for what she should do and control but begins to include those things which are not even under her control. Finally, the man begins to blame his wife for how he feels, thinks and acts and for the behavior of everyone around him. This blame is a total displacement of the man's responsibility onto his partner.

In abusive relationships, ownership replaces individual worth and value. Webster defines ownership as: to have or hold as property; possess, to have power over, control. Ownership tells her that she is only as valuable or worthwhile as *he* says she is. She is no longer seen as a person but more as a possession or piece of property belonging to him. Sometimes this serves as justification for unrealistic expectations and blaming. Other times it is a part of family beliefs and concepts which allow and support the expectations and blame. If she has become nothing more than his property, without opinion, and he holds control over her, she is already no longer his partner. She has accepted a position less than his equal and most often less than the position he saves for his offspring. She has become the scapegoat for his and his children's failings and has become his servant, maid and prostitute; giving up the right that most teenagers have—to determine what job they will do and whether they are willing to accept the wage offered.

In abusive relationships, ownership fosters a set of double standards. He can do things independent of her, hang out with friends, go to the bar or hunting and spend money as he wishes. However, she may not even think of doing something without him. If she has to ask her partner's permission to do anything, he has taken possession over her and they are no longer partners. His controlling ownership can create a great sense of suspicion and mistrust and fear of loss for him. He may begin to count mileage, time and money to exacting degrees, until he forbids his partner to go anywhere unnecessary or to even talk to others on the phone. His suspicions can take control of him and make him think that if he can't control what he sees as his possession then no one else can either. Women who are raped are often considered as someone who sadly and tragically had their rights and freedom over their bodies criminally and unjustly taken away by the rapist. Yet millions of women exist in relationships where not only their rights and freedom over their bodies have been stripped away from them, but their rights to their own thoughts and feelings have been ravaged as well.

EXPECT RESPECT; REJECT DISRESPECT

A world religious leader recently referred to disrespect as the number one cause of divorce. He indicated that disrespect manifests itself in criticism, abuse and abandonment.

Learning to stop being someone else's property or possession is tough to do and can be very dangerous. Please be careful. This great country of ours, whose constitution protects the rights and liberty of all men and women, declares that all are created equal. A civil war was fought because some did not want to give up the slaves they counted as their personal property. You have to reach deep down inside of yourself and find the value and worth that was in you all the time. You must realize that being responsible and accountable for your own thoughts, feelings and actions is a full-time job. In healthy relationships, you rightfully refuse to accept the displacement of your partner's or anyone else's responsibility or their attempts to blame you for things beyond your control—especially their thoughts, feelings and actions. Give and do because it's your choice, as a gift, and not because you're expected to. Accept the little things done for you each day as wonderful gifts.

Each of us has the right to exist in relationships where our value, worth, opinions and feelings are honored. Accepting disrespect places you on a path in which unrealistic expectations, blame and ownership can thrive and destroy relationships and individuals in a descending, plunging spiral. Always expect respect. Accept nothing less. Reject any and all disrespect.

*Note: There was no real abuse on Jace's part until the day he was married to Dawn. Note, also, the increase in positive actions and consequences for Dawn when she decided to leave the relationship.

RELATIONSHIPS SIMPLIFIED

All the charts, inventories, and evaluations we've looked at, while providing needed specifics and a deeper self-examination, might also be somewhat overwhelming. Let's try and look at relationships in a simple way.

Whenever you want to re-evaluate your relationship (which we all need to do), picture where you are on these life scales. You may be doing well and should reward yourself and your partner, or your relationship may require some adjustment. Talk to someone about where you find yourself, then set up a plan to stay on track or to get back to where *you* want to be.

Individuality <———————————————> No Identity

When we begin dating we are two individuals who have individual interests, hobbies, likes and dislikes. This is what makes us interesting and exciting to our partners. We can give ourselves 100% to the relationship without giving up 100% of ourselves. When all we are is what our partner wants and expects us to be, we lose our identity. In addition, parents who lose their sense of identity have a difficult time helping their children find theirs.

Partnership <———————————————> Property

Most of us when dating look forward to and expect to enter a relationship as a full partner. With an equal voice, both partner's opinions are encouraged, honored and respected. As you move towards Property and away from Partnership, one voice begins to discourage, discount, and demean the other. The further you move, the more possessive your partner becomes, until everything becomes his and what he says goes. As your relationship deteriorates, your partner begins to tell you what you can or can't do or say with others; even what you do with your hair and your own body has to be authorized by him. You have become nothing more than another one of his possessions, his Property.

May God bless you in your relationships to always be accountable for knowing where you are on these life scales and for taking the responsibility to think, feel and act in such a way that you truly maintain a full and equal partnership. Be sure to maintain and develop those interests and hobbies which excite and move you towards being a better you.

WE BELIEVE IN YOU

You are special, unique and worthwhile: special, because God encoded *your* DNA with greatness; unique, because no one else is exactly like you or has the gifts that were given to you and only you to share with the world; worthwhile, because God knows you and your infinite worth.

If you are among the more than 21 million women affected by emotional abuse, please begin talking to someone. There are always caring, understanding and concerned individuals available day or night.

RESOURCES

If you feel you are in immediate danger, call **911** to physically protect you and your children.

If you have any questions or concerns about abuse in your relationship, call the **National Domestic Violence Hotline: 1-800-799-SAFE (7233)**. They are willing to listen to you and recommend shelters and programs in your area for all types of abuse, whether you're just beginning to experience difficulties or you've lived in fear for many years.

211 is a National non-profit service available in most calling areas. Its purpose is to be an information resource for abused and battered women. They can help you find and make contact with a variety of local shelters, support groups, food kitchens, government assistance and Human Service Programs.

The most important place to start is to begin talking; whether it is with your partner, parents, siblings, relatives, clergy, counselor, therapist or national or local help line may depend on your relationship. You are the expert in your life. Don't let anyone talk you into doing something that is not right for you or keep you from doing what is right for you and your children. Contrary to the stigma that help professionals and government agencies may have, they are there to listen and help in any way you indicate they can. Calls are always confidential, and no call is considered insignificant or a waste of time, if it is a heart-felt concern or question about you, your family or your relationships. Local Community Action agencies and police can also direct you to local services.

There are more than 40 national and 30 regional websites and resources for women and children of emotional abuse and domestic violence, along with many state and local services. Here are a few:

a) Endabuse.org. The Family Violence Prevention Fund (FVPF) believes violence comes in many forms, is learned and can be unlearned. Abuse can happen to anyone in any walk of life, economic status, and culture. The FVPF fund works to protect all battered women, including immigrant women, http://endabuse.org/links.

b) Victory (VAWO). An independent office on Violence Against Women, within the Department of Justice, www.ojp.usdoj.gov/vawo.

c) The Violence Against Women Act of 2000 (VAWA), www.ojp. usdoj.gov/vawo/regulation.htm.

d) The Oprah Winfrey Show and "O" Magazine, which continue to take a lead in exposing the enormity of this hidden abuse taking place in America, involving over 21 million women and their children, www.oprah.com.

e) The United Nations Convention on the Elimination of All forms of Discrimination Against Women (CEDAW) at 1-212-687-8633 or www.un.org/womenwatch/daw/cedaw.

f) heneverhitme.com. This website has information on e-zines, e-books, tele-seminars and live conferences. Go to: www.heneverhitme.com, or email: janebryant@heneverhitme.com.

g) From "Abuse to Abundance." A non-profit organization endowing a perpetual education fund for seminars and training to provide battered women and their children hope for an emotionally, socially, spiritually and financially abundant life; www.abusetoabundance.com.

SAFETY PLAN

If you are experiencing an increase in abuse and are considering leaving, most experts and agencies recommend a safety plan such as the following:

• Pack a suitcase with toiletries, extra house and car keys, a change of clothing for both you and your children. Store it with a friend or a neighbor.

• Have the following items in an easy-to-locate place: medicine, I.D., money, checkbook and savings book, birth certificates, social security numbers, address book, protective orders and other legal papers.

• Know exactly where you will go: family, friend, police or shelter.

• If you don't have time to gather these items because you are going to be hurt, call 911 and get out. Shelters have emergency provisions.

NON-PROFIT ORGANIZATION

At some point, as your individual situation allows, the authors would like to hear from you and learn how you are doing. You can contact us at janebryant@heneverhitme.com or joel@heneverhitme.com. You can access additional information and comments from us through the He Never Hit Me website, www.heneverhitme.com. We will be posting a personal e-zine or letter, based on questions and concerns received from individuals like you. We will also be providing e-books, tele-seminars and seminars for groups and individuals to help continue bringing answers and light to this epidemic, demeaning, and degrading secret.

You may also seek out help and information though the Abuse to Abundance non-profit organization. It is the goal of this organization to provide services not covered by other organizations and individuals, as well as assist them in their endeavors, by providing a perpetual training fund and other services for abused women and their children.

The Abuse to Abundance organization is an enlightened non-profit group focused on helping abused women and their children by developing and providing educational seminars, workshops and programs that meet their physical, mental, emotional, financial, and social needs, through empowering self-help techniques, life-skill training and mentoring. You may donate or access information at: www.abusetoabundance.com.

If you have the means, please donate. It is only though working together and combining our efforts that we have a hope in addressing this scourge and building a better tomorrow, with hope and opportunity and choice for women and their children.

ACKNOWLEDGEMENTS

The author would like to acknowledge the Utah Domestic Violence Council and Your Community Connection of Ogden/Northern Utah, for providing materials and understanding from which some of the information and inventories in this section were adapted.

Special thanks to the members of Enlightened Pursuit; Annette, Myron, Tammie, Jason, Charlotte, Scott, Joshua, and Jakob, for their love, assistance and support on this project.

With deep gratitude to Imal Wagner and the members of Mark Victor Hansen's and Robert G. Allen's original Inner Circle family for their encouragement, enlightenment, caring, and insight.

BONUS SECTION AUTHOR BIO

Joel P. Brandley is a nationally licensed therapist. Mr. Brandley has a Bachelors Degree in Child and Family Studies with an emphasis in Counseling from Weber State University; a Masters Degree in Family and Human Development with an emphasis in Marital and Family therapy from Utah State University; and a Masters Degree in Counseling-Mental Health Counseling from the University of Phoenix. His education has been built around better understanding and working with children and families. He has spent the last two decades in a variety of counseling and therapeutic positions in which he has witnessed and worked first hand with abused and battered women and children. Joel and his wife of twenty-five years are the proud parents of nine confident, competent children.

CPSIA information can be obtained at www.ICGtesting.com
Printed in the USA
LVOW10s1821130414

381514LV00023B/1252/P